Reshaping City Governance

India's cities are in the midst of an unprecedented urban expansion. While India is acknowledged as a rising power, poised to emerge into the front rank of global economies, the pace and scale of its urbanisation calls for more effective metropolitan management if that growth is not to be constrained by gathering urban crisis.

This book addresses some key issues of governance and management for India's principal urban areas of Mumbai, Kolkata and Hyderabad. As three of the greatest Indian cities, they have evolved in recent decades into large metropolitan regions with complex, overlapping and often haphazard governance arrangements. All three cities exemplify the challenges of urbanisation and serve here as case studies to explore the five dimensions of urban governance in terms of devolution, planning, structures of delivery, urban leadership and civic participation. London, with its recent establishment of a directly elected mayor, provides a reference point for this analysis, and signifies the extent to which urban leadership has moved to the top of the urban governance agenda. In arguing the case for reform of metropolitan governance, the book demonstrates that it would be too simplistic to imagine that London's institutional structure can be readily transposed on to the very different political and cultural fabric of India's urban life.

Confronting India's urban crisis with a comparative analysis that identifies the limits of policy transfer, the book will be particularly valuable to students and scholars of Politics, Governance and Urban Studies.

Nirmala Rao is Professor of Politics and Pro-Director at SOAS, University of London, UK. She has published extensively in the field of urban governance and her other publications include *Cities in Transition: Growth and Change in Six Metropolitan Areas* (Routledge) and *Governing London* (with Ben Pimlott).

Routledge Contemporary South Asia Series

1 **Pakistan**
Social and cultural transformations in a Muslim nation
Mohammad A. Qadeer

2 **Labor, Democratization and Development in India and Pakistan**
Christopher Candland

3 **China–India Relations**
Contemporary dynamics
Amardeep Athwal

4 **Madrasas in South Asia**
Teaching terror?
Jamal Malik

5 **Labor, Globalization and the State**
Workers, women and migrants confront neoliberalism
Edited by Debdas Banerjee and Michael Goldfield

6 **Indian Literature and Popular Cinema**
Recasting classics
Edited by Heidi R.M. Pauwels

7 **Islamist Militancy in Bangladesh**
A complex web
Ali Riaz

8 **Regionalism in South Asia**
Negotiating cooperation, institutional structures
Kishore C. Dash

9 **Federalism, Nationalism and Development**
India and the Punjab economy
Pritam Singh

10 **Human Development and Social Power**
Perspectives from South Asia
Ananya Mukherjee Reed

11 **The South Asian Diaspora**
Transnational networks and changing identities
Edited by Rajesh Rai and Peter Reeves

12 **Pakistan–Japan Relations**
Continuity and change in economic relations and security interests
Ahmad Rashid Malik

13 **Himalayan Frontiers of India**
Historical, geo-political and strategic perspectives
K. Warikoo

14 **India's Open-Economy Policy**
Globalism, rivalry, continuity
Jalal Alamgir

15 **The Separatist Conflict in Sri Lanka**
Terrorism, ethnicity, political economy
Asoka Bandarage

16 **India's Energy Security**
Edited by Ligia Noronha and Anant Sudarshan

17 **Globalization and the Middle Classes in India**
The social and cultural impact of neoliberal reforms
Ruchira Ganguly-Scrase and Timothy J. Scrase

18 **Water Policy Processes in India**
Discourses of power and resistance
Vandana Asthana

19 **Minority Governments in India**
The puzzle of elusive majorities
Csaba Nikolenyi

20 **The Maoist Insurgency in Nepal**
Revolution in the twenty-first century
Edited by Mahendra Lawoti and Anup K. Pahari

21 **Global Capital and Peripheral Labour**
The history and political economy of plantation workers in India
K. Ravi Raman

22 **Maoism in India**
Reincarnation of ultra-left wing extremism in the twenty-first century
Bidyut Chakrabarty and Rajat Kujur

23 **Economic and Human Development in Contemporary India**
Cronyism and fragility
Debdas Banerjee

24 **Culture and the Environment in the Himalaya**
Arjun Guneratne

25 **The Rise of Ethnic Politics in Nepal**
Democracy in the margins
Susan I. Hangen

26 **The Multiplex in India**
A cultural economy of urban leisure
Adrian Athique and Douglas Hill

27 **Tsunami Recovery in Sri Lanka**
Ethnic and regional dimensions
Dennis B. McGilvray and Michele R. Gamburd

28 **Development, Democracy and the State**
Critiquing the Kerala model of development
K. Ravi Raman

29 **Mohajir Militancy in Pakistan**
Violence and transformation in the Karachi conflict
Nichola Khan

30 **Nationbuilding, Gender and War Crimes in South Asia**
Bina D'Costa

31 **The State in India after Liberalization**
Interdisciplinary perspectives
Edited by Akhil Gupta and K. Sivaramakrishnan

32 **National Identities in Pakistan**
The 1971 war in contemporary Pakistani fiction
Cara Cilano

33 **Political Islam and Governance in Bangladesh**
Edited by Ali Riaz and C. Christine Fair

34 **Bengali Cinema**
'An other nation'
Sharmistha Gooptu

35 **NGOs in India**
The challenges of women's empowerment and accountability
Patrick Kilby

36 **The Labour Movement in the Global South**
Trade unions in Sri Lanka
S. Janaka Biyanwila

37 **Building Bangalore**
Architecture and urban transformation in India's Silicon Valley
John C. Stallmeyer

38 **Conflict and Peacebuilding in Sri Lanka**
Caught in the peace trap?
Edited by Jonathan Goodhand, Jonathan Spencer and Benedict Korf

39 **Microcredit and Women's Empowerment**
A case study of Bangladesh
Amunui Faraizi, Jim McAllister and Taskinur Rahman

40 **South Asia in the New World Order**
The role of regional cooperation
Shahid Javed Burki

41 **Explaining Pakistan's Foreign Policy**
Escaping India
Aparna Pande

42 **Development-induced Displacement, Rehabilitation and Resettlement in India**
Current issues and challenges
Edited by Sakarama Somayaji and Smrithi Talwar

43 **The Politics of Belonging in India**
Becoming Adivasi
Edited by Daniel J. Rycroft and Sangeeta Dasgupta

44 **Re-Orientalism and South Asian Identity Politics**
The oriental Other within
Edited by Lisa Lau and Ana Cristina Mendes

45 **Islamic Revival in Nepal**
Religion and a new nation
Megan Adamson Sijapati

46 **Education and Inequality in India**
A classroom view
Manabi Majumdar and Jos Mooij

47 **The Culturalization of Caste in India**
Identity and inequality in a multicultural age
Balmurli Natrajan

48 **Corporate Social Responsibility in India**
Bidyut Chakrabarty

49 **Pakistan's Stability Paradox**
Domestic, regional and international dimensions
Edited by Ashutosh Misra and Michael E. Clarke

50 **Transforming Urban Water Supplies in India**
The role of reform and partnerships in globalization
Govind Gopakumar

51 **South Asian Security**
Twenty-first century discourse
Sagarika Dutt and Alok Bansal

52 **Non-discrimination and Equality in India**
Contesting boundaries of social justice
Vidhu Verma

53 **Being Middle-class in India**
A way of life
Henrike Donner

54 **Kashmir's Right to Secede**
A critical examination of contemporary theories of secession
Matthew J. Webb

55 **Bollywood Travels**
Culture, diaspora and border crossings in popular Hindi cinema
Rajinder Dudrah

56 **Nation, Territory, and Globalization in Pakistan**
Traversing the margins
Chad Haines

57 **The Politics of Ethnicity in Pakistan**
The Baloch, Sindhi and Mohajir ethnic movements
Farhan Hanif Siddiqi

58 **Nationalism and Ethnic Conflict**
Identities and mobilization after 1990
Edited by Mahendra Lawoti and Susan Hangen

59 **Islam and Higher Education**
Concepts, challenges and opportunities
Marodsilton Muborakshoeva

60 **Religious Freedom in India**
Sovereignty and (anti) conversion
Goldie Osuri

61 **Everyday Ethnicity in Sri Lanka**
Up-country Tamil identity politics
Daniel Bass

62 **Ritual and Recovery in Post-Conflict Sri Lanka**
Eloquent bodies
Jane Derges

63 **Bollywood and Globalisation**
The global power of popular Hindi cinema
Edited by David J. Schaefer and Kavita Karan

64 Regional Economic Integration in South Asia
Trapped in conflict?
Amita Batra

65 Architecture and Nationalism in Sri Lanka
The trouser under the cloth
Anoma Pieris

66 Civil Society and Democratization in India
Institutions, ideologies and interests
Sarbeswar Sahoo

67 Contemporary Pakistani Fiction in English
Idea, nation, state
Cara N. Cilano

68 Transitional Justice in South Asia
A study of Afghanistan and Nepal
Tazreena Sajjad

69 Displacement and Resettlement in India
The human cost of development
Hari Mohan Mathur

70 Water, Democracy and Neoliberalism in India
The power to reform
Vicky Walters

71 Capitalist Development in India's Informal Economy
Elisabetta Basile

72 Nation, Constitutionalism and Buddhism in Sri Lanka
Roshan de Silva Wijeyeratne

73 Counterinsurgency, Democracy, and the Politics of Identity in India
From warfare to welfare?
Mona Bhan

74 Enterprise Culture in Neoliberal India
Studies in youth, class, work and media
Edited by Nandini Gooptu

75 The Politics of Economic Restructuring in India
Economic governance and state spatial rescaling
Loraine Kennedy

76 The Other in South Asian Religion, Literature and Film
Perspectives on Otherism and Otherness
Edited by Diana Dimitrova

77 Being Bengali
At home and in the world
Edited by Mridula Nath Chakraborty

78 The Political Economy of Ethnic Conflict in Sri Lanka
Nikolaos Biziouras

79 Indian Arranged Marriages
A social psychological perspective
Tulika Jaiswal

80 Writing the City in British Asian Diasporas
Edited by Seán McLoughlin, William Gould, Ananya Jahanara Kabir and Emma Tomalin

81 **Post-9/11 Espionage Fiction in the US and Pakistan**
Spies and 'terrorists'
Cara Cilano

82 **Left Radicalism in India**
Bidyut Chakrabarty

83 **"Nation-State" and Minority Rights in India**
Comparative perspectives on Muslim and Sikh identities
Tanweer Fazal

84 **Pakistan's Nuclear Policy**
A minimum credible deterrence
Zafar Khan

85 **Imagining Muslims in South Asia and the Diaspora**
Secularism, religion, representations
Claire Chambers and Caroline Herbert

86 **Indian Foreign Policy in Transition**
Relations with South Asia
Arijit Mazumdar

87 **Corporate Social Responsibility and Development in Pakistan**
Nadeem Malik

88 **Indian Capitalism in Development**
Barbara Harriss-White and Judith Heyer

89 **Bangladesh Cinema and National Identity**
In search of the modern?
Zakir Hossain Raju

90 **Suicide in Sri Lanka**
The anthropology of an epidemic
Tom Widger

91 **Epigraphy and Islamic Culture**
Arabic and Persian inscriptions of Bengal and their historical and cultural implications
Mohammad Yusuf Siddiq

92 **Reshaping City Governance**
London, Mumbai, Kolkata, Hyderabad
Nirmala Rao

93 **The Indian Partition in Literature and Films**
History, politics, and aesthetics
Rini Bhattacharya Mehta and Debali Mookerjea-Leonard

Reshaping City Governance
London, Mumbai, Kolkata, Hyderabad

Nirmala Rao

LONDON AND NEW YORK

First published 2015
by Routledge
2 Park Square, Milton Park, Abingdon, Oxon OX14 4RN

and by Routledge
711 Third Avenue, New York, NY 10017

First issued in paperback 2017

Routledge is an imprint of the Taylor & Francis Group, an informa business

© 2015 Nirmala Rao

The right of Nirmala Rao to be identified as author of this work has been asserted by her in accordance with sections 77 and 78 of the Copyright, Designs and Patents Act 1988.

All rights reserved. No part of this book may be reprinted or reproduced or utilised in any form or by any electronic, mechanical, or other means, now known or hereafter invented, including photocopying and recording, or in any information storage or retrieval system, without permission in writing from the publishers.

Trademark notice: Product or corporate names may be trademarks or registered trademarks, and are used only for identification and explanation without intent to infringe.

British Library Cataloguing in Publication Data
A catalogue record for this book is available from the British Library

Library of Congress Cataloguing in Publication data
Rao, Nirmala
 Reshaping city governance : London, Mumbai, Kolkata, Hyderabad / Nirmala Rao.
   pages cm. – (Routledge contemporary South Asia series ; 92)
 Includes bibliographical references and index.
 1. Municipal government–India–Case studies.
 2. Urbanization–India–Case studies. I. Title.
 JS7008.R348 2015
 352.3′672160954–dc23
 2014022359

ISBN 13: 978-1-138-49157-1 (pbk)
ISBN 13: 978-0-415-67209-2 (hbk)

Typeset in Times New Roman
by Out of House Publishing

In memory of Uday Marty

Contents

List of figures	xvi
List of tables	xvii
Acknowledgements	xviii
Abbreviations	xix

1   Urban governance in India 1

Understanding India's urbanisation 2
Patterns of urbanisation 4
Development of urban policy in India 6
The case for urban reform 10
   Infrastructure 11
   Governance 16
   Capacity 18
About the book 19
Why the three cities? 21

2   The conditions of effective metropolitan governance 27

Understanding governance 27
   Participatory governance 30
   Regime theory and coalition governance 33
   Metropolitan consolidation 35
The conditions of effective governance 38
   Effective devolution 39
   Consolidated governance 41
   Coordinated structures for service delivery 44
   Focused urban leadership 46
   An active metropolitan community 48

xiv *Contents*

3 London: a prototype for India?   52

Planning for a sustainable London 53
  A strategic authority for London 54
  The abolition of the Greater London Council 56
Rethinking London governance: post-GLC 57
  A new approach to planning 59
Enhanced powers for the mayor 60
  New developments in London's housing 62
  Traffic and transport in London 63
  Priority areas for transport improvement 64
Blurred accountabilities in the governance of London 66
Towards greater self-government for London 68
  The London City Charter 68
  The Congress of Leaders 69
Localism and the 'turn to community' 70
  The National Planning Policy Framework 72

4 Devolution of power to cities   78

Devolution: opportunities and challenges 79
The relationship with parastatal agencies 81
Financial autonomy of ULBs 85
  Municipal revenues 85
  Tax revenues 90
  Non-tax revenue 94
Financing urban services and infrastructure 95
  Power of ULBs to raise borrowings 98
Devolving human resource management 98
Digital governance 103

5 The reach of metropolitan power   106

Metropolitan growth and expansion 106
The planning process 109
Master-planning the cities 112
Implementing the master plan in Hyderabad 113
  City development strategy 116
Planning the Kolkata metropolitan region 117
  Managing Kolkata's peripheries 119
Mumbai's regional planning 121
The challenges of urban fringe and peri-urban areas 124
  Developmental opportunities 124
  Targeted development: the case of HITECH City 126
Stresses and strains: governing the peri-urban areas 128

6	**The structures of metropolitan authority**	**133**

Institutional arrangements 133
Planning for cities 136
Delivering services 140
   Housing 140
   Water supply and sewerage 143
   Traffic and transport 147
Modernising service delivery 154
Blurred accountabilities in governance 157

7	**Urban leadership and civic engagement**	**168**

The office of the mayor 169
   A directly elected mayor and council 172
   A directly elected mayor and commissioner 173
   An indirectly elected mayor and council 173
   The role of municipal commissioner in urban management 176
Engaging the public in policy making 178
   Ward committees 179
   Area sabhas 181
New accountabilities 183
   Integrating information and communication technologies 184
   Accountability through financial reporting, disclosure and audits 185
Inclusive urban management 186
   Localism in Mumbai 189
   Engaging communities in Kolkata and Hyderabad 190

8	**The future of India's urban governance**	**195**

How distinctive is London? 196
Strategic authorities for India's cities 200
Greater devolution: lessons from London 204
Enhancing accountabilities in India's governance 207
Focused leadership for urban management 209
Prospects for the future 213

References	215
Index	227

Figures

1.1	Financing of urban expenditure	15
3.1	Map of Greater London	56
5.1	Map of Hyderabad Metropolitan Area	115
5.2	Map of Kolkata Metropolitan Area	120
5.3	Map of Mumbai Metropolitan Region	123
6.1	Institutional framework for better governance for service delivery	136
6.2	The institutional framework for Kolkata	139
6.3	The current performance of India's cities	141
7.1	Patterns of political systems	170
7.2	Ward committees and area sabhas	182
8.1	A mixed model of governance at the metropolitan and local level	211

Tables

4.1	Parastatal agencies in Mumbai, Kolkata and Hyderabad	82
4.2	Spread of functions across the municipal corporations of Mumbai, Kolkata and Hyderabad	85
4.3	The constitution of State Finance Commissions: Maharashtra, West Bengal and Andhra Pradesh	89
4.4	Tax regimes in Mumbai, Kolkata and Hyderabad	91
4.5	International experience on property tax collections	92
4.6	Key recommendations: SARC, HPEC and the Working Group on Capacity Building for Twelfth Five Year Plan	99
4.7	Key capacity building initiatives in India	101
6.1	Projections for housing stock, households and housing shortage (2010–2025)	143
6.2	The state of water supply and waste water treatment in selected cities in India	144
6.3	Water management in selected Indian cities	145
6.4	Number of vehicles and share of public transport in selected Indian cities	148
6.5	Projected passenger volume for public transport in Kolkata Metropolitan Area	151
6.6	Main agencies for transport in Kolkata Metropolitan Area	152
6.7	Institutional arrangements for governance, infrastructure and services in Kolkata Metropolitan Area	158
6.8	Multi-level (central and state) agencies functioning in Mumbai Metropolitan Region	161
6.9	Multiplicity of institutions in Hyderabad Metropolitan Region	164
7.1	Mode of election of municipal chairperson and terms of office	172

Acknowledgements

In writing this book I have drawn on conversations and correspondence with several serving officials and city planners to whom I owe debts of great magnitude. I am particularly grateful to Dr V. Bhaskar and Mr Sanjay Kaul, both formerly officers of the Indian Administrative Service, without whose help I could not have gained access to key contacts in Hyderabad and Mumbai. My special thanks to Dr Partha Mukhopadhyay, Centre for Policy Research, New Delhi, for giving access to data, and to Dr Yezdi Karai and Ajay Singh for hosting my visit to Kolkata and for introducing me to the mayor and city officials. I benefited enormously from my exchanges with Dr Mitra, former Director General of Planning, whose encyclopaedic knowledge of Kolkata was a much tapped source.

I wish to acknowledge many colleagues who helped me with research for this manuscript. Aparna Mukerjee, Chandana Dey, Rekha Batura, Sharmila Ray, Charlotte Barrow and SOAS students – Reza Gholani and Matthew Philips – who assisted in collecting material with great diligence. I would like to thank all my colleagues in the Directorate, in particular, James Yabut, for his help with accessing figures and tables. I am grateful to Prachi Sinha for sharing her knowledge of cities to my great profit, and to Michele Acuto for his invaluable advice. John Riley's pedantic reading of the chapters helped me progress at a considerable pace and saved me from errors of both facts and judgement. I would like to express my deep appreciation to CVS Ramany, Fiona and Suzanne for their support and encouragement. Only they will know how much I owe them for keeping my flagging spirits up. To them, my warmest thanks.

I am deeply grateful to my family for their unfailing love and support. In more ways than they are aware, this book could not have been completed without them. My special thanks to my son, Prashant, who sustained me through the most testing times; his secret plan for my 'great escape' to the Chilterns enabled the final push to complete the manuscript on time. Finally, to our granddaughter, Lara, whose arrival brought joy I never knew before.

This book is dedicated to my beloved nephew, Uday Marty, whose untimely passing leaves a void hard to fill. Through his extraordinary intellect, wit and courage he inspired many and enriched the lives of all who knew him. Uday, you are always in my heart.

Abbreviations

ABS	Area Based System
ACCGS	Asian Centre for Corporate Governance and Sustainability
AGNI	Action for Good Governance Network of India
ALG	Association of London Government
ALM	Advanced Locality Management
AMDA	Association of Municipalities and Development Authorities
APIIC	Andhra Pradesh Industrial Infrastructure Corporation
APSRTC	Andhra Pradesh State Road Transport Corporation
AP TRANSCO	Andhra Pradesh Transmission Corporation
ARV	Annual Rental Value
AUWSP	Accelerated Urban Water Supply Programme
BATF	Bangalore Agenda Task Force
BEST	Brihanmumbai Electric Supply and Transport
BF	Bombay First
BMA	Bangkok Metropolitan Administration
BMTPC	Building Material Technology Promotion Council
BRT	Bus Rapid Transit
BRTS	Bus Rapid Transit System
BSUP	Basic Services for the Urban Poor
CAA	Constitutional Amendment Act
CAG	Citizens' Action Group
CAP	City Assistance Programme
CAPEX	Capital Expenditure
CBD	Central Business District
CBO	Community Based Organisation
CBULB	Capacity Building for Urban Local Bodies
CDA	Cyberabad Development Area
CDP	City Development Plan
CID	Community Improvement Districts
CIDCO	City and Industrial Development Corporation
CIT	Calcutta Improvement Trust
CIWTC	Central Inland Water Transport Corporation
CLG	Communities and Local Government

CLIFF	Community Led Infrastructure Finance Facility
CMC	Chandannagar Municipal Corporation
CMP	Comprehensive Mobility Plan
CoE	Centres of Excellence
COVA	Confederation of Voluntary Associations
CPDCL	Central Power Distribution Company Limited
CTC	Calcutta Tramway Company
DCMS	Department of Culture, Media and Sport
DfID	Department for International Development
DLR	Docklands Light Railway
DMAUD	Department of Municipal Administration and Urban Development
DP	Development Plans
DPC	District Planning Committee
DPD	Development Plan Document
DPR	Detailed Project Report
DTI	Department of Trade and Industry
EDS	Economic Development Strategy
EKWMA	East Kolkata Wetland Management Authority
FIRE-D	Financial Institutions Reform and Expansion – Debt
FSI	Floor Space Index
GDP	Gross Domestic Product
GHMC	Greater Hyderabad Metropolitan Corporation
GIS	Geographical Information Systems
GLA	Greater London Authority
GLAA	Greater London Authority Act
GLC	Greater London Council
GLDP	Greater London Development Plan
GoI	Government of India
GOL	Government Office for London
GoWB	Government of West Bengal
GSS	Global Shelter Strategy
GST	Goods and Service Tax
HADA	Hyderabad Airport Development Authority
HCA	Homes and Communities Agency
HDFC	Housing Development Finance Corporation
HGCL	Hyderabad Growth Corporation Limited
HITECH	Hyderabad Information Technology Engineering Consultancy City
HMC	Hyderabad Municipal Corporation
HMDA	Hyderabad Metropolitan Development Authority
HMR	Hyderabad Metropolitan Region
HMWSSB	Hyderabad Metropolitan Water Supply and Sewerage Board
HPEC	High Powered Expert Committee on Indian Urban Infrastructure and Services

Abbreviations xxi

HRBC	Hooghly River Bridge Commissioners
HUDA	Hyderabad Urban Development Authority
HUDCO	Housing and Urban Development Corporation
HUMTA	Hyderabad Unified Metropolitan Transport Authority
IALA	Industrial Area Local Authorities
IAS	Indian Administrative Service
ICT	Information and Communication Technology
IDFC	Infrastructure Development Finance Company
IDSMT	Integrated Development of Small and Medium Towns
IIA	Integrated Impact Assessment
IIFCL	India Infrastructure Finance Company Limited
ILCSP	Integrated Low Cost Sanitation
IMC	Indian Merchants' Chamber
IMF	International Monetary Fund
IRR	Inner Ring Road
IT	Information Technology
ITES	IT-enabled Services
JICA	Japanese International Cooperation Agency
JNNURM	Jawaharlal Nehru Urban Renewal Mission
KEIP	Kolkata Environment Improvement Project
KIT	Kolkata Improvement Trust
KMA	Kolkata Metropolitan Area
KMC	Kolkata Municipal Corporation
KMD	Kolkata Metropolitan District
KMDA	Kolkata Metropolitan Development Authority
KMPC	Kolkata Metropolitan Planning Committee
KMRCL	Kolkata Metro Rail Corporation Limited
KMWSA	Kolkata Metropolitan Water Supply Authority
KUA	Kolkata Urban Agglomeration
KUSP	Kolkata Urban Services for the Poor
LCC	London County Council
LCCI	London Chamber of Commerce and Industry
LDA	London Development Agency
LDS	Local Development Schemes
LFEPA	London Fire and Emergency Planning Authority
LIP2	Local Implementation Plans
LPAC	London Planning Advisory Committee
LSC	Learning and Skills Council
LTGDC	London Thames Gateway Development Corporation
LUDCP	Land-Use and Development Control Plan
LUMR	Land-Use Maps and Registers
MAPP	Municipal Action Plan for the Poor
MCGM	Municipal Corporation of Greater Mumbai
MCH	Municipal Corporation of Hyderabad
MHADA	Maharashtra Housing and Area Development Authority

MIDC	Maharashtra Industrial Development Corporation
MJP	Maharashtra Jeevan Pradhikaran
MMC	Mumbai Municipal Corporation
MML	Model Municipal Law
MMR	Mumbai Metropolitan Region
MMRDA	Mumbai Metropolitan Region Development Authority
MMTS	Multi Modal Transport System
MOPC	Mayor's Office for Policing and Crime
MOU	Memorandum of Understanding
MoUD	Ministry of Urban Development
MPA	Metropolitan Police Authority
MPC	Metropolitan Planning Committee
MRTA	Metropolitan Rapid Transit Authority
MRTS	Mass Rapid Transit System
MRVC	Mumbai Railway Vikas Corporation
MSRDC	Maharashtra State Road Development Corporation
MTS	Mayor's Transport Strategy
MTS2	Mayor's Transport Strategy
MTSU	Mumbai Transformation Support Unit
MUDP	Mumbai Urban Development Project
MUTP	Mumbai Urban Transport Project
NBO	National Building Organisation
NERUDP	North Eastern Region Urban Development Programme
NGO	Non Governmental Organization
NHAI	National Highway Authority of India
NHB	National Housing Bank
NHDP	National Highways Development Program
NHP	National Housing Policy
NIUA	National Institute of Urban Affairs
NPPF	National Planning Policy Framework
NPM	New Public Management
NSDP	National Slum Development Programme
NTDA	New Town Development Authority
NUIS	National Urban Information System
NUTP	National Urban Transport Policy
O&M	Operations & Maintenance
OAPF	Opportunity Area Planning Frameworks
OMA	Outer Metropolitan Area
ORR	Outer Ring Road
PDL	Public Disclosure Law
PHE	Public Health Engineering
PPPs	Public–Private Partnerships
PUCAAR	People's Union for Civic Action and Rights
PUI	Peri-Urban Interface
RPMC	Reform and Performance Management Cell

RRR	Regional Ring Road
SARC	Second Administrative Reforms Commission
SDS	Spatial Development Strategy
SERPLAN	South East Regional Planning Conference
SFC	State Finance Commissions
SHMA	Strategic Housing Market Assessment
SJSRY	Swarna Jayanti Sahari Rozgar Yojana
SMS	Street Mukti Sangathana
SOI	Strategic Outcome Indicators
SPV	Special Purpose Vehicle
SSK	Sishu Siksha Kendra
TAG	Transparent Accountable Governance
TCPA	Town and Country Planning Act
TfL	Transport for London
TLRN	Transport for London Roads Network
TP&TED	Transportation Planning and Traffic Engineering Directorate
TTWA	Travel To Work Areas
UBSP	Urban Basic Services for the Poor
UDA	Urban Development Authority
UDP	Unitary Development Plans
UIG	Urban Infrastructure and Governance
ULB	Urban Local Bodies
UMTA	Unified Metropolitan Transport Authority
UPA	United Progressive Alliance
URIF	Urban Reform Incentive Fund
UWSS	Urban Water Supply and Sanitation
VAMBAY	Valimiki Ambedkar Awas Yojana
VGF	Viability Gap Funding
WBBB	West Bengal Biodiversity Board
WBHIDCO	West Bengal Housing Infrastructure Development Corporation
WBIDC	West Bengal Industrial Development Corporation
WBIWTC	West Bengal Inland Water Transport Corporation
WBPCB	West Bengal Pollution Control Board
WBSCZMA	West Bengal State Coastal Zone Management Authority
WBTIDC	West Bengal Transport Infrastructure Development Corporation
WGCB	Working Group on Capacity Building for the Twelfth Plan
WRAP	Waste and Resources Action Programme
ZDP	Zonal Development Plans

1 Urban governance in India

> The speed of urbanisation [in India] poses an unprecedented managerial and policy challenge ... Surging growth and employment in cites will prove to be a powerful magnet ... Yet India has barely engaged in a national discussion about how to handle this seismic shift in the makeup of the nation. Indeed, India is still debating whether urbanisation is positive or negative and whether the future lies in its villages or cities.
>
> (McKinsey, 2010: 13)

'Cities are fundamentally ungovernable', observed Yates in the 1960s, implying that urban policy making was incapable of producing coherent decisions, developing effective policies or implementing state programmes. The implications of this assertion, while serious, are as pertinent today as they were then, reflected in the growing volume of work on ungovernable cities and fragmented metropolises. Whatever the shortcomings of previous urban solutions, the problems that they addressed still persist. Urban issues have the distinctive characteristic of being tenacious, conventional and seemingly intractable.

Cities remain central to the policy agenda for nations across the world. The expanding body of urban literature is increasingly incorporating the importance of international networks, leadership styles, good governance and participatory initiatives. Yet despite this increased academic focus, the integrated metropolitan area has often been overlooked, under-resourced or contested as a place in which effective governance can and should take place. There remains a gap in understanding how cities in the global North and South can be constructively compared and related in terms of policy improvement, a vacuum that is only just beginning to be addressed.

As centres of innovation and creativity, cities are drivers of national growth and development. In India the major metropolises play a hugely important role in the country's drive for development, and in its connections with the wider global economy. Indeed, the three Indian cities examined in this book are amongst the most globally connected and expanding metropolises in the world. Yet millions of urban residents live in poverty, with insufficient resources and lack of access to basic public services. India's cities face unique developmental challenges, while exhibiting some similarities with other large metropolitan areas around the world.

In most countries, economic growth and industrialisation have been accompanied by steadily rising urbanisation. India's urbanisation trajectory appears to be lower than the majority of industrialised countries, although in more recent years the country has witnessed phenomenal transformation both in terms of population and areal spread. An estimated seven to eight million people are being added to India's cities every year, and the rate of urbanisation is set to rise (Planning Commission, 2000: 7). It is predicted that by 2030, around 40 per cent of the country's population will be housed in urban areas and 70 per cent of all jobs will be created in cities (McKinsey, 2010: 14). More people are likely to live in urban than in rural areas, at least in the five large states of Punjab, Gujarat, Maharashtra, Tamil Nadu and Karnataka (McKinsey, 2010). Cities in India have been growing laterally too, absorbing villages and smaller towns in the surrounding area to create continuous urban spread, known as urban agglomeration. In the four largest metropolitan cities in the country the urban agglomeration has been growing faster than the main city.

These transformations pose a number of challenges for city governance, including the growing disparity in service provision between urban and rural areas (Mohan and Dasgupta, 2004). The demographic surge has out-performed the speed with which urban management has been able to respond, with the service gap greatest in the case of the urban poor and slum dwellers, who constitute about 75 per cent of city populations (McKinsey, 2010: 40). It is widely acknowledged that cities in India have failed to deliver equitable and quality services to the urban population and there is a significant deficit in technical, human and financial capabilities at all levels of governance (McKinsey, 2010; Nallathiga, 2005). Local governance, especially in the urban sector, continues to be fraught with ambiguities in terms of its function, capability, authority and autonomy.

This chapter contextualises urban management in India, drawing upon its history, social and political legacy. It reviews the trends and patterns in India's urbanisation and the wider implications of growth and expansion, set to continue for the next 20 years. The key challenges of urbanisation are identified for policy makers and planners in their efforts to create sustainable cities, issues that are the subject of detailed discussion in subsequent chapters.

Understanding India's urbanisation

Urban population globally is currently growing at three times the rate of the rural population. In 1950, 17 per cent of the population in developing countries was urban; in 2020 this is expected to grow to 54 per cent (Mohan, 2005: 215). It is estimated that by 2030, Asia alone will have 2.7 billion urban people, accounting for over 50 per cent of its total population. All other regions of the world combined will have an urban population of about 2.3 billion. Of the 21 cities expected to reach ten million by 2015, 17 will be in developing countries. Of these 17 cities, 11 are expected to be in Asia and will include Dhaka, Mumbai, Delhi, Kolkata, Jakarta, Shanghai, Beijing, Metro Manila, Tianjin, Karachi and Istanbul (Mohan, 2005).

The scale of Indian urbanisation in its current recorded form is large in absolute terms, at around 32 per cent. However, according to a World Bank study, this figure is an underestimation and does not capture the full extent of the urban revolution in progress. India's stringent definitions of 'urban' – not updated in 50 years – create a statistical artefact. The globally used agglomeration index – a comparable measure of urbanisation using population density (150 people per square kilometre), the minimum size of a large urban centre (50,000 inhabitants), and travel time to that urban centre (60 minutes) – shows India to be 52 per cent urbanised; a much larger proportion than India's official figures suggest (World Bank, 2013: 14). There is also an absence of criteria to determine areas with significant urban characteristics such as temple towns, pilgrimages and tourist centres. These, and the rapidly urbanising industrial areas, military stations and small towns are covered under the discretionary status of 'urban settlements' (Datta, 1999: 90).

Despite the complexity of tracking India's urbanisation, the latest census shows 90 million people to have been added to India's urban areas since the previous census in 2001 (World Bank, 2013: 15). According to the 2011 census, decadal urban growth was modest, increasing from 31.2 per cent in 1991–2001 to 31.8 per cent in 2001–2011. This was in parallel with a steep decline in the growth rate of the rural population, which reached an all-time low of 12.1 per cent during the same period (Shaw, 2012: 44). India's urbanisation nevertheless is still significant: currently 340 million people are estimated to be living in cities and this figure is expected to rise to 590 million by 2030. Sixty-eight cities will have populations of more than one million by this time, 13 cities with more than four million and six megacities with a population of ten million or more. Mumbai and Delhi are predicted to be among the five largest cities in the world. According to the 2011 census, India now has 53 cities with over a million inhabitants – in absolute terms no country in the world, with the exception of China, has experienced such a pace of urbanisation (McKinsey, 2010).

Although the country has enjoyed an impressive growth over the past two decades, economic growth has not been matched by a commensurate pace of urbanisation, with the urban share of national net domestic product at around 52 per cent, compared with 75 per cent for the most advanced economies. Currently at an annual GDP growth of around 7.5, the economy has not been able to produce adequate jobs for all new entrants, even in these urban centres. India's urbanisation trajectory appears to be lower than in other developing economies (World Bank, 2013: 23).

Problems of governance, planning, traffic and congestion, pollution, poverty and slums pose major constraints for policy makers. Concerns have focused largely on ensuring adequate provision of basic services for a rapidly growing urban population. The migration of large populations towards cities has continued unabated and metropolitan management has been unable to keep pace with the rate of urbanisation. Although space and land-use patterns have called for policies to control migration and the creation of new centres of economic growth (with appropriate incentives for businesses and industry to relocate to medium-sized cities), urban management in India is still viewed as ad hoc and disorganised. There exists a policy vacuum that risks rapid urban decay. It is a telling fact that currently 75 per cent of urban citizens belong to the bottom income segment, with an average income of less than £1 a day (McKinsey, 2010; Shaw, 2012: 46).

Despite the many problems, some would, however, argue that issues of urbanisation in India have been relatively well addressed and have led to an overall increase in standards of living and the quality of life of its people. Improvements in access to water and sanitation facilities, transport, housing and infrastructure are discernible (Mohan, 2005: 218). New and emerging cities in India are fast becoming centres of excellence in terms of education, research and development and as locations for high-tech industries and service activities. In this respect, cities are indeed magnets of growth and attractive to people from the countryside, smaller towns and generally the less dynamic regions (McKinsey, 2010: 18; Shaw, 2012: 45).

Patterns of urbanisation

By 2030, India is set to become the third largest economy in the world, with a dramatic rise in per capita income (CEBR, 2013). Urban economy will provide for 85 per cent of the country's total tax revenue, contributing significantly to the nation's development (McKinsey, 2010: 13). States with high GDP such as Gujarat, Maharashtra, Tamil Nadu and Karnataka are much more urbanised than the less economically productive Uttar Pradesh, Orissa and Bihar (Planning Commission, 2012a). The next 20 years will see an increase in the number of urban states and the concurrent rise of a large number of cities, some of which will be counted amongst the largest cities in the world, not merely for size, but economic output as well.

In 2001, the industrial and service sectors accounted for about 80 per cent of India's GDP growth. Services employ only 22 per cent of the Indian workforce but account for more than 50 per cent of value added. India's manufacturing sector has grown equally fast, contributing to growth in employment opportunities, especially in the chemicals and pharmaceuticals industry: the share of these products in exports more than doubled from around 25 per cent in 1993 to 54 per cent in 2010 (Veermani, 2012: 101–102). One of the consequences of the increasing dominance of industrial and services-based jobs has been the emergence and rapid expansion of peri-urban areas, as they provide locational advantage for these industries. Land values are cheap and these areas deliver economies of agglomeration and specialisation. It has resulted in a readjustment between city cores and their suburbs, especially in the high-tech and fast growing export manufacturing industries, the cores witnessing a drop in high-tech industries, with suburbs experiencing a parallel rise (Veermani, 2012). More recently, the development of a knowledge-based economy has become a key determinant of the competitiveness of cities and their subsequent growth. In the Information Technology (IT) sector, the country has emerged as a leader among developing countries in providing cross-border IT services. The IT sector contributes an estimated 7 per cent to India's GDP and about 20 per cent to exports, while employing less than 2 per cent of the total workforce (Chandrashekar, 2010). The southern cities of Bangalore, Hyderabad, Chennai, Mumbai and Pune are competitive IT hubs, contributing to economic growth, both in their own right and as a complement for other activities. India's strength in IT is proving useful in manufacturing and other industries, helping it to produce high value added products.

The pattern and growth of India's economy has not been uniform, with the fastest growth rates concentrated in the southern states of Maharashtra, Tamil Nadu, Kerala, Andhra Pradesh and Karnataka. At the city level, larger cities in these states have grown rapidly – Chennai in Tamil Nadu due to its robust manufacturing and services sector; Bangalore in Karnataka owing to its high-tech industries, services and IT; Hyderabad in Andhra Pradesh with its strong IT sector; and Pune in Maharashtra through the strength of its manufacturing and services sector. Among these, the IT cities of Hyderabad and Bangalore account for a large share of urban growth in the states of Andhra Pradesh and Karnataka (Shaw, 2012).

While opportunities in the industrial and service sectors have undeniably led to urban growth, the poor performance of the agricultural sector has led to migration in search of employment and relocation to cities. In this respect, India stands in contrast to other developed nations where urbanisation has primarily been a product of industrial pull from the main urban cities. Between 2001 and 2011, rural to urban migration increased from 42 per cent to 56 per cent. The 2011 census revealed the emergence of a large number of new towns, increasing from 5,161 in 2001 to 7,935 in 2011, with the states of Kerala, Andhra Pradesh, West Bengal and Gujarat experiencing the largest number of new towns (Bhagat, 2011: 12).

These forms of urban explosion have consequences as they expose the vulnerabilities and capabilities of cities (UNDP, 2011). McKinsey's report on *India's Urban Awakening* estimated that each year the economy would require between 700 million and 900 million square metres of residential and commercial space and 350 to 400 kilometres of metros and subways, both of which account for more than 20 times the capacity built over the last decade. In addition, 19,000 and 25,000 kilometres of road lanes would be required, which equates to the length constructed over the last decade (McKinsey, 2010: 18).

Development of urban policy in India

While the urgency of rapidly growing urban needs makes it imperative for large-scale infrastructure developments within short timescales, the challenge to execute such projects remains huge. This is not entirely a matter of capacity and capability. It calls into question the appropriateness of the nature of urban management and policy focus that are crucial in facilitating the execution of extensive projects. Cities develop over a period of time and require long-term vision, planning and implementation. Strategic integration of land-use planning, transportation and housing, close working between administrative departments, and coordination among various agencies and organisations are key to well-rounded urban management and policy planning (McKinsey, 2010: 84). Charting the development and evolution of urban policy in India helps put the current state of resource capabilities, challenges and milestones in perspective.

In the wake of the large-scale rural to urban migration outlined in the previous section, substantial overseas development aid was made available for urban poverty alleviation programmes to mitigate the risks associated with migration and shortage of housing. Post-1991 liberalisation saw an increase in private sector participation and the emphasis by central government on the management of cities as a stand-alone activity. This was manifested in a range of new procedures and regulations that brought distinct changes in policy making and implementation, both striking and significant (Shaw, 2012: 46). The focus of some of the reforms between 1991 and 2001 was on financial and industrial deregulation and the growing acceptance of New Public Management (NPM) tools as an efficient approach to delivering public services (Shaw, 2012). In many cities, new urban development authorities were created and urban land ceiling legislation and regulations enacted. By 1999 the Urban Land (Ceiling and Regulation) Act was discarded as the Central Act and private players were allowed to transact large plots of land for development. The centre also passed regulations such as the Municipal Solid Waste (Management and Handling) Rules, 2000; Urban Transport Policy, 2006; National Urban Housing and Habitat Policy, 2007; and the National Urban Sanitation Policy, 2008. There was also a growing dependence on parastatal agencies for service delivery across these sectors.

At the same time, the 1990s experienced a revival of interest and strengthening of local governments and governance, with various programmes launched by the central government to strengthen Urban Local Bodies (ULBs). Foremost among them was the enactment of the 74th constitutional amendment in 1992, which granted constitutional status to local institutions, with a view to making local government more responsive to the needs of urban citizens. The aim was to achieve better representation and efficiency through decentralisation and greater administrative autonomy (Datta, 1999; Nallathiga, 2005: 2).

These developments represented a significant change in direction. For several years following India's independence, the positive aspects of cities as 'engines of economic growth' in the context of national economic policies were not adequately acknowledged (Datta, 1999). The problems of urban areas were treated as welfare problems and urbanisation was considered a sector of residual investment rather than an area of national economic importance. In part, this was an extension of the political legacy vis-à-vis urban governance of India; local government suffered a 'total eclipse' while national politics and federalism dominated (Datta, 1999: 87).

This was reflected in the priorities that were accorded to urban affairs in the Five Year Plans initiated by India's first prime minister, Pandit Jawaharlal Nehru. Between 1950 and 1990, urban policies were based on central directives and within state jurisdictions. The urban management system was highly centralised, with local administrations closely aligned to the central and state governments through field administration (Datta, 1999: 88). In the First Five Year Plan (1951–1956), the needs of housing and rehabilitation of refugees from the partition were prioritised. Emphasis was on building institutions and constructing houses and a sizeable part of the plan's outlay was spent on the rehabilitation of refugees from Pakistan. The Ministry of Works and Housing, the National Building Organisation (NBO) and the Town and Country Planning Organisation were set up. The Second (1956–1961) and Third (1961–1966) Five Year Plans continued to accord greater priority to weaker sectors, introducing new schemes for rural housing and slum clearance. Town and country planning legislations were enacted in many states and several agencies were established to prepare master plans for new towns. A scheme was introduced in 1959 for the distribution of loans to state governments from the centre to enable them to acquire and develop land to make sufficient building sites available to people. The emphasis of the subsequent Five Year Plans was to achieve balanced urban growth and create smaller town in an effort to contain population growth in large cities. The Housing and Urban Development Corporation (HUDCO) was established to fund development programmes. Schemes for the improvement of the environment and urban slums were also introduced to provide a minimum level of services such as water supply, sewerage, drainage and street pavements in cities with a population of 800,000 and above.

Policies to promote smaller towns in new urban centres, to ease the increasing urbanisation pressure, were reiterated in the Fifth Five Year Plan (1974–1979). For the first time, a comprehensive and regional approach to addressing the problems in metropolitan cities was adopted. To this end, a task force was set up to develop small and medium towns, together with a comprehensive programme for the Integrated Development of Small and Medium Towns (IDSMT). At the same time the Urban Land (Ceiling & Regulation) Act was enacted to ensure the availability of land for the construction of houses for middle and low income groups. The Sixth Five Year Plan (1980–1985) progressed from dealing with issues of urban housing and town and city planning to civic services for towns with population under 100,000. Positive incentives were given to promote the establishment of new industries and commercial and professional centres in small, medium and intermediate towns.

A key development during the Seventh Five Year Plan (1985–1990) was the enhanced role of the public sector in housing. The National Housing Bank (NHB) was set up to expand the base of housing finance, provide for subsidised housing and the development of land. There was a revival of the activities and functions of the NBO, originally constituted in 1954. During this planning period, a new organisation, the Building Material Technology Promotion Council (BMTPC), was set up to promote commercial production of innovative building materials. The objective of these initiatives was to address the problems of the urban poor and alleviate poverty through schemes such as the Urban Basic Services for the Poor (UBSP). These were supplemented with other housing promotion plans and programmes supported by the central government. The Global Shelter Strategy (GSS) and National Housing Policy (NHP) were announced in 1988 with the long-term goals to eradicate homelessness, improve housing conditions for the poor and provide a minimum level of basic services.

By this time, the growing intensity of urbanisation had begun to exert considerable pressure on housing, city infrastructure and basic services. Employment growth in urban areas was now around 3.8 per cent per annum compared with only 1.6 per cent growth in rural areas, but policies and investment in services had failed to address the difference. Despite the importance given to urban housing and basic services in the Five Year Plans, the implementation was far from effective. The report of the National Commission on Urbanisation highlighted several weaknesses and outlined the impact of poor governance on income and productivity levels of enterprises. Against the backdrop of the report's recommendations, the Eighth Five Year Plan (1992–1997) reiterated the importance of the urban sector for the national economy and the need for efficient management. The plan identified a number of key issues such as the widening gap between demand and supply of infrastructure services, proliferation of slums and the progressive decay in city environment.

For the most part, the inability to address urbanisation challenges was attributed to stringent regulations and controls by central and state governments (Shaw, 2012). The 73rd and 74th constitutional amendments, introduced in parliament in 1992, proved significant landmarks. While the former aimed at giving greater autonomy to rural local governments through the panchayat raj (a decentralised form of government where each village is responsible for its own affairs), the latter targeted urban and municipal governments. The 74th Constitutional Amendment Act (CAA) highlighted the weak and ineffective nature of ULBs and the inadequate devolution of powers and functions. Designed to bring about greater effectiveness in self-administration, the 74th amendment ensured a five-year term for urban governments, made elections the norm and reserved seats for members from minority groups to achieve better representation (Shaw, 2012: 46). The act heralded several positive changes and paved the way for many others. By bringing urban affairs closer to the people through local governance mechanisms, it encouraged citizen participation and a voice in the management and design of urban services. Political accountability was built in through the election of municipal bodies. More importantly, the amendment enabled cities to make prudent decisions autonomously and invest finances to provide for better services.

Despite several shortcomings in its implementation, as will be seen in subsequent chapters, the 74th amendment remains an important step in initiating the process of decentralisation. The Ministry of Urban Development (MoUD) and various states promoted key projects in respect of municipal accounting, resource planning and other innovative financing mechanisms to facilitate urban infrastructure development and municipal service management. The Model Municipal Law (MML), passed in 2003, provided a legislative framework to take forward the government's agenda, its provisions focusing on five-year terms for mayors and chairmen, guidance for the management of wards and ward committees, and the preparation of municipal accounting manuals by state governments and annual balance sheets by municipalities. Amongst its other proposals are regular assessments of property tax, participation of the private sector and NGOs in the delivery of services, representation of municipalities on district and metropolitan planning committees and the implementation of development plans by municipalities (Government of India, 2003).

To take forward the programme of urban reform, the government launched other initiatives aimed at enhancing the efficiency of ULBs. Foremost among them was the establishment of an urban reform incentive fund in 2003, which incentivised state governments to improve local governance and undertake reforms. To manage better the incentive fund programme and to create economically productive and efficient cities, the central government, under the United Progressive Alliance (UPA) coalition, launched the Jawaharlal Nehru Urban Renewal Mission (JNNURM) in 2005 with built-in accountabilities and incentives for urban reforms (Datta, 1999; Nallathiga, 2005; Shaw, 2012). JNNURM incorporated two major priority areas – Urban Infrastructure and Governance (UIG) and Basic Services for the Urban Poor (BSUP) and covered 65 cities with a government allocated budget of over £20 billion until 2012. The UIG scheme for small and medium towns aimed at improving the urban infrastructure of towns and cities in a planned manner and enhancing Public–Private Partnerships (PPPs), while BSUP focused on improving slums through integrated access to shelter, basic services and other related civic amenities. The objective was to encourage reforms and fast-track planned development of identified cities to improve efficiencies in urban infrastructure and service delivery mechanisms. Other measures comprised community participation, preparation of city development plans (CDPs) and enhancing accountabilities of ULBs and parastatal agencies. State governments were given the power to designate existing institutions as nodal agencies for implementation of the scheme (JNNURM, 2009).

During the 1990s, the private sector also gained momentum, with enhanced policy support from central government in the form of outsourcing and building PPPs in a range of industries from IT to construction. In this respect, city governance was beginning to change character, with the emergence of the new network system of governance aided further by the increasing influence of non-governmental organisations and other voluntary agencies. This in turn shaped ongoing debates about better governance and management of cities.

The case for urban reform

Notwithstanding the new opportunities that came to be unlocked by India's policy decisions, numerous problems in urban management persist. The 'new urban revolution' in India posed considerable challenges, with cities and towns under pressure to address key issues of access to employment, land and basic amenities to the local population. Rather than being looked upon as 'generators of opportunity', urban areas came to be considered 'unruly, chaotic and problematic', epitomising environmental degradation, generation of slums, urban poverty, unemployment and chaotic traffic (Mohan, 2005: 217). Recent studies have shown the failure of cities to improve their modes of governance or implement governance structures capable of safeguarding and delivering current and predicted urban requirements.

The sustainability of cities depends on robust urban infrastructure, good governance and effective participatory approaches for multi-stakeholder involvement (TERI, 2011). The report of the 13th Finance Commission, while highlighting the need for providing adequate financing for urban infrastructure, emphasised its importance for overall inclusive growth, arguing that while

> India's recent economic growth performance has, indeed, been creditable ... such growth must make a demonstrable difference to the lives of the poorest and most vulnerable citizens ... India has the potential and the means to secure such a future for its citizens ... inclusive growth means that such growth [is] accompanied by a concerted effort, by all levels of government, to invest in the delivery of public services ... To achieve this potential, it is necessary that resources be mobilised and deployed in such a manner that the recent high rates of growth are maintained and even increased.
>
> (Government of India, 2009: 22)

The complexities involved in governing large cities make appropriate administrative structures and processes essential, yet India suffers from weak urban management and continues to rely on 'outdated leadership and delivery choices' (McKinsey, 2010: 84).

States and municipal bodies are deeply resistant to adopting new practices. The response of states to the CAA, which devolved power and responsibility from the state government to cities, has been slow and limited despite the clear governance and accountability mechanisms set out by the act for both state and city governments for the implementation of the defined mandates. The problem is exacerbated by the state control of municipalities through parallel legislations or executive decisions to operate in similar areas, causing confusion and duplication. The common practice is for states to retain the development component while delegating the tasks of maintenance and operation to municipal bodies (Datta, 1999: 94). Even in the case of targeted local government programmes, such as the JNNURM, there has been a failure to engage with city governments. Most reform programmes under the JNNURM are state government owned and their corresponding funding sought directly by the state government, bypassing city governments in the process (Shaw, 2012: 48).

JNNURM is one of the few public sector programmes that enjoys high visibility in both state and national level urban policy discussions and has attracted substantial investment from the central government. For the most part, however, the urban sector continues to suffer from under-investment while policy and resources are directed mainly towards the rural sector. This neglect has created a huge infrastructure challenge of having to meet the needs of the new population while addressing the problems associated with past backlogs. Attempts to involve the private sector have often failed due to the low viability of many projects such as those relating to water supply, sewerage and public transport (Ministry of Urban Development, 2012).

The management of urban planning in India needs radical transformation. As cities grow, planners will be increasingly required to make informed judgements about investments in infrastructure and on the use of resources such as land and finance. Urban systems will need to ensure that supporting mechanisms and infrastructure are in place to provide an environment where people can live and work (McKinsey, 2010: 22). The growing urban population will make new demands on the public sector and will call for innovative ways of collaborating in service delivery (Nallathiga, 2005). Currently there remains substantial deficit in all respects of infrastructure, governance and resource capacity.

Infrastructure

As India implements its Twelfth Five Year Plan (2012–2017), the urban transition is acknowledged to be a major challenge and one that requires massive expansion in urban infrastructure and services. The country faces an enormous task in terms of urban management, building infrastructure and providing adequate housing and basic services, as its cities fall well short of providing a basic quality of life. The report by the Sub Committee on Financing Infrastructure for the Twelfth Five Year Plan stated that only 71.2

per cent of the urban population had access to within-premises drinking water, while 20.7 per cent had access to near-premises drinking water and none had access to a 24/7 supply. Further, only 32.7 per cent had access to piped sewer systems and 12.6 per cent still defecated in the open. On average in most cities and towns, only 20 per cent of the sewerage generated was treated before disposal. Similarly in the case of waste disposal, landfill sites were commonly used as dumping grounds. Transport and housing shared a similar dismal state of affairs, with public transport accounting for only 22 per cent of total transport services availed and almost 21 per cent of the urban population living in squatter settlements (Planning Commission, 2012a: 10–11).

One of the major consequences of urbanisation without adequate infrastructure and employment opportunities is the widespread prevalence of slums. The city of Mumbai is illustrative:

> As the leading edge of the urban economic future, [the city] is well represented in a highly developed financial services sector and a globalizing film industry. The new middle class is carving out a consumptive niche in the urban landscape but is doing so in competition with about 6 million slum dwellers for whom a living space is a matter of survival, not luxury ... Mumbai is two cities, one deemed modern and desirable, and the other city of the slums, unintended and undesirable. The two cities are economically connected and in some ways they exist by virtue of each other, as in a symbiotic relationship.
>
> (Nijman, 2010: 15–16)

According to the 2001 census, 640 cities and towns in 26 state and union territories reported slum populations. Of the total slum population of the country (around 25 million), 11.2 million is in Maharashtra followed by Andhra Pradesh with 5.2 million, Uttar Pradesh with 4.4 million and West Bengal with 4.1 million (FICCI, 2011: 3). McKinsey estimates that the number of households that cannot afford a house could rise by additional 13 million to reach a total of 38 million by 2030 (McKinsey, 2010: 121).

Despite substantial increases in expenditure on poverty and slum alleviation programmes, the demands have been growing at a faster rate than can be delivered, which, in turn, has placed considerable constraints on both the city and city dwellers. There is a huge mismatch between supply and demand of basic services. While this gap is only likely to grow, McKinsey predicts that the demand for every key service will increase five to sevenfold across cities within the next two decades. If India continues to invest in urban infrastructure at its current rate, which is subpar by international standards, urban infrastructure will fall significantly below the level required to sustain prosperous cities:

> the quality of life will fall further, with water supply dropping from 105 litres a day to 65 litres a day for an average citizen, while large sections

will have no water access at all. Almost 70–80 per cent of the sewage will go untreated.

(McKinsey, 2010: 18)

Compared with international rates, India's current rate of investment to sustain the expected urban growth potential is strikingly low. In terms of infrastructure spending and investment, India lags far behind China whose per capita spend stands at $116 compared to a $17 per capita infrastructure spend by India (McKinsey, 2010: 19). Between 2002 and 2007 India invested around 6 per cent of its annual total GDP in infrastructure; China within this same period invested 9.3 per cent. To sustain urban growth at its expected rate, it is estimated that India needs to invest around Rs 53 lakh crore ($1.2 trillion) in urban infrastructure capital over the next 20 years, an increase from Rs 765 per capita ($17) to Rs 6,030 per capita ($134) per year, almost eight times the current per capita spend. Another $1 trillion will have to be kept aside for operating expenditures (McKinsey, 2010: 23). More than half the capital investment is essential to address the country's infrastructure backlog and the rest to fund cities' future needs. While this seems daunting, it is achievable, a fact testified by examples of countries that have turned around their urban infrastructure and management within a decade. Citing the case of other cities, McKinsey recommends that India should capitalise much more on the existing sources of funding including monetisation of land assets, collection of higher property taxes, user charges and debt, PPPs and formula-based government funding (McKinsey, 2010: 23).

Financing basic amenities in India has largely been the responsibility of the public sector. In broad terms, cities in developed countries tend to rely on user charges and municipal taxes in addition to state and central government tax sharing, grant and debt to fund urban services. By contrast, cities in developing countries, with limited ability to raise user charges and property tax revenue, have tended to tap other sources including the monetisation of land and raising loans from banks. Of the $82 billion spent on urban services in New York in 2006, almost 62 per cent was financed through New York's own taxes and user charges. Property tax collections in New York are buoyant at 2–3 per cent of property values. The UK is unique in that central government funds most urban services – almost 70 per cent of the £38 billion spent in 2007 by local governments came from direct grants from central governments (McKinsey, 2010: 70–71). India has not yet used monetisation of land assets to any great degree, while revenues from property taxes have not been forthcoming due to poor assessment methods and non-compliance. Local government bears much of the burden of urban expenditure with very little support from state and central governments (see Figure 1.1). As the High Powered Expert Committee on Indian Urban Infrastructure and Services (HPEC) noted:

Urban local governments in India are among the weakest in the world both in terms of capacity to raise resources and financial autonomy.

While transfers from state governments and the Government of India have increased in recent years, the tax bases of ULBs are narrow and inflexible and lack buoyancy, and they have also not been able to levy rational user charges for the services they deliver.

(HPEC, 2011: XXVI)

The fiscal devolution mandated by the constitution was aimed at achieving robustness, but according to the State Finance Commissions (SFCs), states have failed to transfer functions and schemes to ULBs as dictated by the constitutional amendments (Ministry of Housing and Urban Poverty Alleviation, 2012). Several states, however, have given rural local governments a share in state taxes such as land revenue, land-cess, royalties in mines and minerals and forest revenues, and empowered ULBs to levy taxes including the professional, property and entertainment taxes. However, these are less buoyant than the taxes and cess levied by the state such as sales tax and excise duties, which have been kept outside the jurisdiction of local governments (Ministry of Environment and Forests, 2000). It is recommended that larger cities with stronger economies should allow ULBs to retain 18 to 20 per cent of revenue from the Goods and Service Tax (GST). Since GST is a consumption-based tax, revenues generated by it could potentially incentivise local growth (McKinsey, 2010: 23). Yet, at this critical juncture of urban growth when local governments need to be fiscally strengthened, the movement appears to be in the opposite direction. The state government of Maharashtra, for instance, took control of the collection of the octroi transport tax, which had been a source of good revenues for urban bodies for a long period. In lieu of this, ULBs were given a static annual payment, which did not measure up to octroi collections (Rao and Bird, 2010: 7).

The resource-capability of local bodies in its current state is, therefore, weak, which reduces both financial and political autonomy either to spend on infrastructure or plan necessary investments. Resources collected by municipal authorities barely account for 0.6 per cent of the national GDP (Rao and Bird, 2010: 7). There are large variations in the level of municipal revenues across states, ranging from Rs 2,600 (£26.36) in Maharashtra to Rs 38 (£0.39) in Orissa. In all but the two states of Maharashtra and Punjab, the municipalities' own revenues are insufficient to meet revenue expenditure. The problem is acute in the low-income states of Bihar, Madhya Pradesh, Orissa and Uttar Pradesh, where the ULBs' own sources are able to recover only one-fifth of the revenue expenditure. It is estimated that, with some changes to the mode of operation and revenue collection, the largest Indian cities will be capable of generating 80 to 85 per cent of the revenues they require from internal sources (McKinsey, 2010: 23).

Other attempts by central government to strengthen the financial condition of ULBs have included increased budgetary allocations for the issue of municipal tax-free bonds, raising the total annual cap on municipal borrowings and fixed ceiling on states' overall borrowings. Specific central grants

Urban governance in India 15

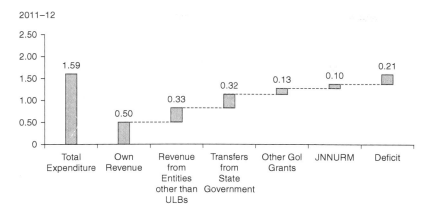

Figure 1.1 Financing of urban expenditure (percentage of GDP)
Source: HPEC (2011: xxvii).

have also been initiated for selected infrastructure projects like the Integrated Development of Small and Medium Towns (IDSMT) with an annual support of about Rs 100 crore (£10.14 million), the Mega City Scheme for big cities, the Accelerated Urban Water Supply Programme (AUWSP) and the JNNURM (Datta Dey *et al.*, 2006). In addition to direct central government grants there has been a growing recognition of the need for private financing of infrastructure projects. The Eleventh Five Year Plan called for 30 per cent of the overall investment target to be obtained from the private sector and actually achieved 38 per cent, while the draft Twelfth Five Year Plan aims for 48 per cent of the planned investment to come from private sources (Government of India, 2012). There are several private partnership models already in operation across electricity, transportation and construction, although the low visibility of services such as waste collection, water distribution and sewerage systems do not make them sufficiently attractive. In view of the importance of urban infrastructure for economic growth and inclusion, HPEC came to the view that the Government of India and state governments will have to intervene, both by providing substantial funds and by facilitating the use of additional mechanisms for funding, which will require the strengthening of the finances of ULBs (HPEC, 2011: XXVI).

The involvement of several external agencies for infrastructure improvement has been on the rise. For water supply, sanitation and slum improvements, long-term loans have been received from external agencies like the World Bank, Asian Development Bank, Department for International Development UK, Japan Bank for International Cooperation, USAID and French International Development Agency. The Community Led Infrastructure Finance Facility (CLIFF) is another example where venture capital was made available from the Department for International Development (DfID) and Homeless International for community-driven housing and related infrastructure for the urban poor (Datta, 1999: 27).

Such investments and programmes take on a different character from one city to the next and there are wide variations in the quantity, nature and type of infrastructure investments. The high investment corridors in the country include the Ahmedabad–Mumbai–Pune corridor in West India, Delhi–Gurgaon–Faridabad–Gaziabad in North India, and Chennai–Bangalore–Hyderabad in South India. These stand out in striking contrast to other cities as economically dynamic regions, due in large part to the phenomenal growth of services, manufacturing and IT led industries in these regions. Investment in cities that are not economically dynamic is significantly lower, as is the case of Kolkata even though it is one of the largest urban agglomerations in the country. There are also variations in the proportion of public to private investment in different cities. Sixty per cent of the total public sector spend is invested in Delhi, while private investment from domestic sources is much higher in Kolkata, Hyderabad and Ahmedabad (Shaw, 2012: 49–51). These factors contribute to the different stages of infrastructural development within states and to the nature of development.

Governance

Investments determine to a large extent the availability, quality and operation of urban infrastructure, but strong governance is essential to attract the right investments from the right sources (Rao and Bird, 2010: 3). Urban governance does not rely solely on municipal management but on the interconnections between different stakeholders that exert influence – the bureaucracy, civil society, state and national government, and parastatal agencies (Mukhopadhyay, 1999: 109). As was highlighted by the United Nations (UN), 'effective governance within the available frame of power and resources appears to be the only solution to minimizing the managerial stress and maintaining an adequate level of urban services and facilities' (UN Habitat, 2003). The UN defines good and effective governance as the condition necessary for the improvement of the human condition and lists accountability, transparency, participation and rule of law as mandatory administrative functions (Nallathiga, 2005). Indeed, streamlined and accountable governance structures provide for both transparency and responsiveness, which are key to good urban management.

Within India's governance and political tradition, considerable attention has been paid to national and state level governments as key players in facilitating good governance. The emphasis on clearly defined and autonomous local government is relatively new. Until the 1990s, local governments were neither clearly defined nor integral to policy focus as they were under the mandate of the district administration and state government. Municipalities were created to take responsibility for city development and ensure an efficient delivery of basic infrastructure services, their activities controlled by state governments. Over a period of time, through the process of agglomeration, they effectively gained responsibility for urban areas that were actually beyond their jurisdiction.

An important factor that has impeded the smooth functioning of municipal bodies has been the proliferation of agencies tasked with similar responsibilities as those held by municipal authorities. This has led to jurisdictional overlaps and ambiguities between agencies, parastatals, municipal corporations, civil societies and state government mandates. Decisions on local matters of infrastructure, for example, are state decisions, while guidelines regarding land valuation are handled by national, state and district level governments concurrently, sometimes completely bypassing municipal authorities. State interference in matters within a ULB's mandate is also evident through the functioning of parallel agencies set up by states themselves such as urban development authorities (UDAs). Created in the 1980s, UDAs functioned as Special Purpose Vehicles (SPVs) for urban development, but with a governance structure entirely different from a municipal body with which it shared little in common. A lack of clarity and insufficient autonomy compromise the ability of ULBs to pursue their goals and policies in line with their cities' needs (Nallathiga, 2005).

Good governance requires strong political leadership. Its relative absence in India's cities has created a vacuum that has come to be occupied by a proliferation of groups, networks and independent institutions. They are generally governed by bureaucrats with short, fixed-term tenures; this contrasts with large cities elsewhere, which often have powerful mayors with long tenures and clear accountabilities for the city's performance (Bhattacharya, 1978: 40). Most cities follow a structure that features a weak mayor and council coupled with a strong commissioner, who leads the administration. The mayor has little role in shaping city development, planning and operations. The commissioner – a civil servant appointed by the state government – wields greater power and control over the city's planning, resources and development. The powers and monopoly role of commissioners have raised important issues of accountability and transparency and shaped the debate about the need to widen city governance through greater public participation. Kolkata's modified mayor-commissioner model provides an exception and possibly an example for taking forward the reform of municipal structures in other cities.

Another governance issue relates to the growing number of urban agglomerations and their fragmented jurisdictions. The Kolkata Municipal Corporation (KMC) oversees just 31 per cent of the population in the overall urban agglomeration, and the Mumbai Municipal Corporation (MMC) covers 68 per cent of its urban agglomeration. The peri-urban areas most in need of infrastructure and service improvements are often under separate administrative arrangements from the core city and overarching planning bodies such as metropolitan development authorities. In order to address this, the JNNURM programme embarked on reforms that aim to separate the roles of policy makers, regulators and service providers, and enhance local autonomy, while attempting to solve the problem of the fragmentation of authority and accountability to citizens. Most importantly, the aim of the reform programme has been to bring about a process of change at the state and city level designed to channel central resources in a way that creates incentives for improved service delivery at the local level. The success of this new initiative is, however, contingent on the collective effort of the states, ULBs and national government to bring about greater coordination in service delivery. All these issues are brought to sharper focus in the following chapters which present evidence from the three cities under study.

Capacity

It is estimated that city capacity will need to grow nearly 400 per cent in less than 50 years (FICCI, 2011: 3). The conventional Indian method of dealing with urban issues, with responsibility residing with planners and administrators, is increasingly perceived as outmoded and ineffective. A growing recognition that urban issues are better tackled through appropriate governance structures and institutional processes at the local level led to the constitutional reforms highlighted above. While the 74th amendment was a landmark ruling in favour of local governments, these bodies still lack the necessary power, authority, resources and training to manage new responsibilities effectively.

Urban Local Bodies lack the independence to revalue property tax, and have narrow jurisdictions over financing or executing major investments in transport, water supply or sanitation (World Bank, 2010). Even where JNNURM has enhanced capacity for ULBs, it has not been without its limitations, as the report on the urban infrastructure commented:

> While the conception and implementation of projects under JNNURM has led to significant capacity augmentation and efficiency gains particularly in respect of urban transport, the JNNURM project has highlighted several issues and challenges. These range from capacity building at the ULB level to the need for ULBs to become financially self-sustaining – it is a moot point whether the huge dollops of credit under JNNURM enhance the financial status of the tier II and III ULBs or create a dependence syndrome.
>
> (FICCI, 2011: 5)

The large municipal corporations do enjoy reasonable influence in local governance and are assigned significant functions with respect to education, healthcare, industry regulation and the provision of intra-city and inter-city transportation services. More generally, however, ULBs work on an ad hoc basis, often without strong and sustained backing from the state (World Bank, 2010). Local administrations have been universally criticised for not having the necessary capacity to carry out their statutory responsibilities, and progress in urban management has fallen seriously short of expectations (UNDP, 2005). Their experience is confined to works contracts and managing contractors and sub-contractors and they lack the technical capability to develop and implement, in particular, PPP projects, which generate substantial revenue streams (FICCI, 2011: 12). It is an institutional reality of local governments in India that needs to be addressed if they are to realize fully the role and responsibilities accorded to them. Most cities in the world have established systems to build a pool of human talent, often developing a municipal cadre of qualified and experienced people capable of providing leadership and training new entrants (McKinsey, 2010: 25). Such an approach is necessary for India's cities to be able to bridge the gap between supply and demand of qualified public sector professionals. In this respect, the capacity building scheme developed by the MoUD, aimed at improving overall governance and financial management, has to some extent addressed this gap, having instituted wide ranging activities for capacity building, including setting up centres of excellence, implementating property tax reforms and e-governance initiatives. It is also backed by strong financial support and appropriate mechanisms for monitoring and evaluation.

About the book

This book addresses some key issues of governance and management for India's principal urban regions. It reviews the planning and urban policy challenges facing India's major cities and argues the case for reform of metropolitan governance. The focus is on three capital cities that have evolved in recent decades into large metropolitan regions with complex, overlapping and often haphazard governance arrangements. All experience to varying degrees what might be termed a 'governance deficit', reflecting an absence of clear and accountable institutional arrangements for the planning of urban development and the coordination of urban services, including urban infrastructure.

Chapter 2 discusses the premise that we cannot appreciate the failures of urban problem solving without a clear understanding of what constitutes good governance and the prerequisites necessary for effective management. While it is essential to fit governance structures to the particularities of each metropolitan context, all governance structures must share a number of imperatives. Drawing upon experiences from various metropolitan cities worldwide, this chapter sets out to explore the key prerequisites for effective urban governance as they relate to devolution and decentralisation, the structures of service delivery, issues of governance within and beyond the formal metropolitan areas, and urban leadership and civic engagement. These issues are analysed in-depth in the subsequent chapters as they arise in the cities of Mumbai, Hyderabad and Kolkata.

Chapter 3 explores the themes of metropolitan governance and planning in the context of London's governance, and examines the proposition that

London provides a prototype for India. While it is possible for an urbanising economy such as India's to replicate the experiences of developed economies like London, no assumptions are made that London's government should be judged a success story. Rather the capital city's experience is used as a reference point against which the politics of urban problems and policy making in India's cities is examined. The chapter discusses the problems raised by the relentless growth of metropolitan London as they relate to physical planning and governmental organisation. It offers a brief history of London's evolving governmental structures, including the new arrangements for the government of London set up in 2000. The success of any system of metropolitan government lies in its ability to manage a complex network of relationships; this chapter assesses how such networks work out in practice and the role of the London mayor in promoting the interests of the capital city against the backdrop of central government's continuing control of key London issues and the localisation of power in London boroughs.

Turning to the Indian cities that provide the core of the book, Chapter 4 deals with the first theme, the extent to which decision-making power is devolved from the national and state governments to the urban level. While urban development programmes such as urban renewal missions and urban infrastructure development schemes aim to empower municipalities to become viable units of governance, they have yet to make a visible impact on capacity building and accountability. This chapter examines, in particular, the significance of the 73rd and 74th constitutional amendments, which called for greater devolution to ULBs and the extent to which they have led to greater, more effective service delivery.

Chapter 5 focuses on the relationship between metropolitan structures and local community government, within and beyond the formal metropolitan area. As populations expand and metropolitan borders push farther out into surrounding rural areas, issues of governance, administration and infrastructure facilities have implications for territorial management. This chapter examines metropolitan growth and expansion and shows how the three Indian cities of Hyderabad, Kolkata and Mumbai are finding ways of planning and managing growth while coping with the strains on the infrastructure and public services.

Chapter 6 explores the organisational structures and processes for tackling urban problems and delivering services. Urban services such as housing and water supply continue to pose considerable challenges, as do environment, planning and transport. The chapter highlights the problems of the multiplicity of institutions involved in service delivery and argues for a more streamlined and accountable system with greater coordination between agencies to meet the growing challenge of urban governance.

Strong governance is not simply a matter of structures and processes but also requires effective participation by citizens and their representatives. Concepts such as participation, engagement and inclusion have gained currency in city governance, and are recognised as key to good governance, but

Urban governance in India 21

the mechanisms, processes and institutions through which people and groups articulate their interests and express their rights have been subject to much debate and discussion. Chapter 7 examines the extent to which powers of metropolitan leadership are concentrated or dispersed and the degree of transparency, accountability and popular participation in decision making in the three cities.

Finally, Chapter 8 draws together conclusions from the thematic chapters and poses questions about the way forward for the governance of India's great cities.

Why the three cities?

These themes of governance and urban management are explored in Mumbai, Kolkata and Hyderabad, three of India's *Tier 1 Megacities*. India's economic future depends crucially upon the trajectory of these cities, which are home to concentrations of the most productive sectors: finance and banking, retailing, transport, communications and construction.

As India's largest city, *Mumbai*, formerly Bombay, located in the State of Maharashtra in western India, is a vibrant metropolis and the financial centre of India. The second largest city in the country, Mumbai ranks as one of the world's largest megacities. According to the latest data, the total metropolitan area population of Mumbai is over 20.5 million people with a density of 27,136.8 people per square kilometre. Mumbai faces the same challenges as any other city striving for sustainability, but on a much more complex scale. Urban sprawl, traffic congestion, poverty and inequality, slums, and environmental issues are some of its core challenges.

The Municipal Corporation of Greater Mumbai has responsibility for the civic and infrastructure services and is led by a mayor, who is indirectly elected from among the councillors. The municipal commissioner, a nationally appointed civil servant, is the chief executive officer and heads the executive arm of the corporation. An exception is the transportation and electricity supply agency which is run as an arm's-length agency through a general manager, appointed by the state government and answerable to a committee of the corporation. The Mumbai Metropolitan Region (MMR) comprises five municipal corporations (including Greater Mumbai), 22 urban bodies and almost a thousand villages. Planning responsibilities are shared between 40 different planning authorities at the local level. While MMR's total population continues to grow, Greater Mumbai's population of around 13 million is declining.

The MMR's districts contribute significantly to the GDP of the State of Maharashtra, accounting for 37 per cent in 2011. The region is dominated by the service sector, contributing to more than two-thirds of the region's GDP, followed by manufacturing at 23.6 per cent. IT and communications, biotechnology, media and entertainment, retail and the financial services, including banking and insurance, are some of the key economic activities driving the MMR's economy. The region accommodates about 23 per cent of Maharashtra's population, provides employment to 21 per cent of the state's overall workforce and 49 per cent of the state's urban workforce.

In the context of economic liberalisation policies, the region has a significant role to play not only in contributing to the national economy, but also in facilitating integration of the country's economy with the rest of the world. With its premier position as the country's financial capital, its leadership in the country's international trade, its strategic position in relation to global markets, Mumbai is emerging as a fast growing global city providing high quality office complexes, housing, telecommunications and transport infrastructure. Master planning of Mumbai is designed to maintain the city's vitality as the 'engine of economic growth'.

Kolkata, formerly Calcutta, is the capital of West Bengal and the eighth largest urban agglomeration in the world. Located in eastern India, Kolkata Metropolitan Area (KMA) had a population around 14 million in 2011, making it the third most populous city in the country. It is estimated that the population of the KMA is likely to increase to 19.9 million in 2021, and to 21 million in 2025. The metropolitan area is administered by 38 municipalities. The leadership structures of Kolkata provide a marked contrast to other Indian cities with an executive mayor working with a commissioner. The commissioner is directly accountable to the mayor, who is elected for a five-year term and has executive authority for the Municipal Corporation. The mayor appoints members from the municipal assembly to full-time posts as salaried heads of departments, and these comprise, in effect, a form of cabinet.

As the economic eastern hub of India, Kolkata is home to a large concentration of industry, financial services and commercial activities, much of which began with the East India Company. The metropolitan area occupies a primary position within the State of West Bengal, characterised by highly mono-centric urban hierarchical structure. Industrial development, especially the growth of engineering and jute industries along the banks of the River Hooghly, initiated the urban growth and the region continues to rely on the growing contribution from the secondary and tertiary sectors. About 80 per cent of the manufacturing industries of the state are based in the KMA, with its industrial profile dominated by basic metal and alloy industries, metal products, jute and cotton textiles and leather products. KMA accounts for around 27 per cent of West Bengal's total GDP, while accommodating only 17 per cent of the state's population. The tertiary sector has the largest share at 77 per cent, followed by the secondary sector at 19 per cent and primary sector constituting about 3 per cent. Manufacturing, while declining, continues to play an important role. The region has witnessed the growth of new industrial units following liberalisation in 2009. KMA provides employment to 32.2 per cent of the state's overall workforce and nearly 71 per cent of the urban workforce. A third of the metropolitan area's workforce is employed in the manufacturing sector and another third in trade, hotels, restaurants and transport.

Recently, Kolkata and KMA have become a preferred destination for IT and IT-enabled services (ITES) sectors. The region has witnessed a phenomenal growth in the number of operating companies in the software technology parks. Salt Lake is the fastest growing software technology park, with 185 IT companies employing more than 15,000 IT professionals. This has led to mounting pressure to provide the requisite infrastructure both for the industry and the migrating population. In order to accommodate this rapid expansion Kolkata Metropolitan Development Authority (KMDA) has developed an area of over 16 hectares into Sunrise City. The growing popularity of herbal drugs during the 1990s provided new opportunities for drugs and pharmaceuticals industry in the metropolis. The Haldia Petrochemicals Complex, south of KMA, has opened up growth prospects for both chemical and drugs and pharmaceuticals industries within the region. KMA functions as one of the most important regional, national and international routes for traffic and transport. Notwithstanding efforts to achieve a spatially balanced economic development across the state, KMA continues to dominate the economy of West Bengal. It is estimated that some additional six million people will reside in KMA by 2025.

Located in the State of Andhra Pradesh in southern India, *Hyderabad* is not just the administrative capital but also the economic and financial hub of a largely rural state. Hyderabad Metropolitan Region (HMR), with a population of 5.7 million, is managed by 11 municipal authorities spread over an area of 168 square kilometres. The core city, with a population of 3.4 million, is administered by the Greater Hyderabad Municipal Corporation (GHMC). A directly elected mayor heads the corporation, which is governed by an elected municipal council comprising 100 corporators. Administration is in the hands of a civil servant seconded to the city, as a municipal commissioner serving as a chief executive.

Hyderabad is the largest contributor to the state's GDP. Urban centres dominate the metropolitan region and the urban workforce constitutes 90 per cent of the total workforce. Since the early 1990s, the aim has been to make HMR a growth engine for the entire state. The city has attracted major private firms, both domestic and international, creating wealth and employment. A number of new buildings and infrastructure complexes have been undertaken by PPPs. After two decades of growth, the tertiary sector has emerged as the single largest source of employment, comprising more than 80 per cent of the city's total workforce, with major developments in IT, biotechnology and tourism. These service industries are expected to continue to be engines for future growth. Recognising the scale of other world-leading centres such as Silicon Valley and Malaysia's Multi-media Super Corridor, the state decided to create a thriving mega IT hub on land allocated at the edge of the city. Still under development, HITECH City already hosts a significant number of top-500 IT companies. Several hundred companies have registered with Software Technology Parks of India, an autonomous government agency based in HITECH City, which was set up with the aim of attracting enough international companies to create sufficient critical mass to allow Hyderabad to develop into a high-tech city.

The city is now emerging as one of the fastest growing IT cities in the country and is the fourth largest exporter of software products, achieving an annual growth rate of more than 80 per cent during the last decade. Having established HMR as a location for the development of world-class IT facilities, Andhra Pradesh has now set out to become a world leader in electronic government. The city has also recently been experiencing greater diversification into trade, commerce, industry, transport, communication and construction sectors. The manufacturing sector produces a range of pharmaceuticals, electronic goods and other industrial products. Pharma industry is a dominant player in the sector and is expected to play an increasing role in future in the exports of pharma products. Hyderabad is home to a large number of drug manufacturing units and is considered India's 'bulk drug' capital, accounting for about 30–35 per cent of the total drug production in the country.

In common with other cities, Hyderabad faces rapid and continuing population growth. In order to alleviate the problems of urban congestion, plans are under way to develop satellite towns with the provision of basic infrastructure and employment opportunities. Development of other major centres as counter-magnets is designed to avoid imbalance in the state's urban structure. A comprehensive urban development plan for the city covers provision for public services, investments in infrastructure, and institutional and financial arrangements for service provision and partnerships with the private sector. Public service reform is mandated constitutionally, through the CAA, which also provides for the institution of ward-level committees for public involvement. Governmental reform is intended to move municipalities towards greater self-sufficiency, with state control replaced by local management, vigorous public participation and public services provided through autonomous regulated corporations.

London exemplifies the issues that arise in all the major themes outlined above. A vast and disparate city, London's history has been in constant change. Developing over the years into a major centre of national government and international commerce, London has been an imperial capital, and a city embracing villages and towns during its period of growth. The city has been home to people from all walks of life, and from all parts of the world. Since the late 1980s, London's population has grown every year. According to the 2011 census, London's population was estimated to be 8.17 million. This compared with 7.17 million at the time of the census in 2001, showing an increase of 14 per cent over the ten-year period. During the same period, the population of England and Wales increased by 4.03 million (8 per cent). The population of inner London rose faster than outer areas. Inner London increased by 17 per cent to 3.23 million, whilst outer London rose by 12 per cent to 4.94 million. London's population has been changing in composition and diversity. It is estimated that the population of the capital city will continue to be younger than elsewhere in England and Wales – there will be more school-age Londoners in 2026 and 2031 and more aged 35–74. The number of people over 65 will increase, particularly significantly among the over-90s. Black, Asian and other minority ethnic communities are also expected to grow and, by 2031, an additional six London boroughs are likely to have a majority of their population from these groups.

London's workplace population increased by 18 per cent between 2001 and 2011, from 3.8 million to 4.5 million. Employment has grown fastest in central and inner areas of London due to the high concentration of financial business services in those areas, while sectors with lower levels of growth or declines have tended to be more dispersed. Wholesale and retail trade, and professional, scientific and technical activities are the two largest sources of employment in the capital accounting for 13.1 and 10.9 per cent respectively in terms of share of employment. The financial and insurance services sector accounted for 7.7 per cent of London's employed population. Overall, the professional occupations were the fastest growing occupational group between the 2001 and 2011 censuses, with an 82 per cent increase in the numbers employed in this group.

London has a two-tier system of local and regional government. The 32 boroughs and the City of London (often referred to as the 33rd borough) deliver most of the day-to-day services, while the Greater London Authority (GLA) plays a strategic role, setting out an overall vision on a range of issues including air quality, policing, development, transport and waste. Since its establishment in 2000, the GLA – with its directly elected mayor and assembly – has taken responsibility for a wide range of functions hitherto exercised by central government bodies. The GLA now functions as a metropolitan strategic authority across the defined metropolitan area. However, its relationships with local government units within its area are fluid and contested, while its metropolitan planning role is hampered by its lack of authority in the large outer metropolitan area. Furthermore, government ministries retain important powers despite subsequent waves of devolved powers. To that extent, the GLA experiences the classic metropolitan problem writ large.

The new system of London government was designed to provide a high degree of transparency and accountability to London's electors. Under both the first and second mayors, policy discussions have been open and participatory with a high degree of engagement from community groups and other interests. The mayor of London enjoys considerable concentration of powers within the GLA's areas of responsibility, as the legislation was framed to give the mayor a dominant role in relation to the elected assembly, though accountable to it. The establishment of arm's-length agencies for transport, fire and planning, policing and economic development created a symmetrical pattern of agencies accountable to, and under the influence of, both the mayor and assembly.

In all five of the themes, London's experience is used as a reference point against which to assess the achievements and direction of travel of India's cities in the face of the growing urban challenge. It would be wrong and simplistic, however, to judge the London experience as an unqualified success in its own terms, still less to imagine that its institutional structures can be readily transposed on to the very different political and cultural fabric of India's urban life. Each city must take its own course, but would be unwise not to learn from the experiences of others. The following chapter explores how improving urban governance is necessary to achieving sustainable development, and will examine the key conditions for effective urban governance.

2 The conditions of effective metropolitan governance

For more than two decades now, theories of urban governance have come to shape much of our understanding of inter-governmental relations, the ways in which cities function, and the values and strategies that give meaning to political processes. The growing interest in the concept of governance over the years has brought together a body of work, including regime theory, theories of the local state and urban political economy, and placed it into a broader analytical framework. Different theories manifest different views of local democracy, different styles of distributive policies and different conceptions of the role of the state in relationship to civil society.

Academic studies of governance lead eventually to new models and changing forms of governance that affect the fabric of civil society. To the person in the street – 'the governed' – with very little knowledge or understanding of the complexities of improving life in an urbanised society, and often rather sceptical about politicians and public administration, the word government means little more than the distant body that takes money in taxes and then spends as it sees fit. To the academic or practitioner – 'the governor' – government is a great deal more complicated, not just in terms of what actions governments take, but also the processes, motivations and multi-layered relationships, which include relationships with citizens. Even if viewed from different perspectives, both governors and governed are more than simply disconnected parts of the same system; they are in a symbiotic relationship, which, if it is to be mutually productive, relies on certain conditions of governance.

This chapter, then, explores some of the theoretical issues surrounding governance, not in an epistemological manner, but in recognition of the fact that some understanding of how governance works in theory is necessary in order to evaluate which aspects of city governance are effective in practice in the specific cities under scrutiny.

Understanding governance

The field of governance is cumulative and complex: cumulative because it inherits the knowledge of several theoretical developments that have taken place over a period of time; and complex because it has an applicability that cuts across several disciplines of economics, politics, sociology, anthropology, management and geography. The scale of interest is immense and contributions, intellectually stimulating. Broadly, governance has come to be seen as a product of the interaction of a multiplicity of actors – a network of public, private and voluntary actors participating in a particular policy area – 'a structure or an order which cannot be externally imposed' (Kooiman and Van Vliet, 1993: 64). Rhodes used the term to refer to a change in the meaning of government, 'to a new process of governing', identifying its several uses to refer to the minimal state, corporate governance and the new public management. Governance is 'self-organising, inter-organisational networks characterised by inter-dependence, resource exchange, rules of the game and significant autonomy from the state' (Rhodes, 1997: 15). In this respect, issues of trust, diplomacy and reciprocity dominated the analysis of innovative forms of local governance and relationships characterised by what came to be termed as the 'new public management'.

The discussion on governance as the new public management was extended to managerialism and new institutional economics. While the former focused on measures of standards in the conduct of public affairs, the latter introduced competition and choice to augment government functions. As these features became inherent in the idea of governance, further nuances were added, involving not just multiple interactions, but ideas about public management that emphasised a business-like approach to government focusing on performance management, de-regulation and privatisation. While aiming at a more efficient and customer oriented service delivery, the new public management gained a broader vision of a new community governance; one which redefined the role of government and stressed the emergence of governing coalitions based on public, private and voluntary actors (Stoker, 1999).

As an interactive process, governance takes various forms: principal–agent relations, inter-organisational negotiation and systemic coordination. The principal–agent form rests on one party hiring or contracting another to undertake a particular task, while the inter-organisational partnership involves organisations in negotiating joint projects. The systemic coordination form of partnership goes a step further by establishing a level of mutual understanding, a shared vision and capacity for joint working that leads to the establishment of a self-governing network (Stoker, 1998: 22). Stoker's analysis of the implications of the shift in governance for policy process is insightful: as networks compete with bureaucracy as key service delivery mechanisms, policy making is confronted with complexity, overlap, lack of transparency and reduced governmental capacity to steer. The value of the governance perspective rests in its capacity to provide a framework for understanding these changing processes of governing.

Stoker's analysis is simple but illuminating. He identifies several key propositions as constituting governance. Governance may refer to a set of institutions and actors that are drawn from within, but also beyond government; it identifies the blurring of boundaries and responsibilities for tackling social and economic issues; and locates the power dependence involved in the relationships between institutions involved in collective action. The concept of governance is also about autonomous self-governing networks of actors, and recognises a capacity to get things done that does not rest on the power of government to command or use its authority (Stoker, 1998: 18).

In a similar vein, the UN defines the concept of governance as:

> the process of decision-making and the process by which decisions are implemented, an analysis of governance focuses on the formal and informal actors, involved in decision-making and implementing the decisions made and the formal and informal structures that have been set in place to arrive at and implement the decision.
>
> (UNESCAP, 2006: 1)

There appears to be a consensus on the norms and principles of good governance put forward by the UN, which comprises eight major characteristics:

> It is participatory, consensus oriented, accountable, transparent, responsive, effective and efficient, equitable and inclusive and follows the rule of law. It assures that corruption is minimised, the views of minorities are taken into account and that the voices of the most vulnerable in society are heard in decision-making. It is also responsive to the present and future needs of society.
>
> (UNESCAP, 2006: 2)

As the following chapters show, all these attributes characterise much of urban governance both in India and in London. While they pose considerable challenges in providing for clear accountabilities, they also create opportunities for defining and redefining problems in novel ways. The presence of such an array of interactive relationships matters little if it is accepted that urban governance is multifaceted and that no single model can provide the solution. As Rhodes put it succinctly, 'the language of governance makes no apology for describing a complex world in all its complexity' arguing that 'it is the mix of steering strategies that matters; there is no simple solution based on either markets or hierarchies or networks' (cited in Stoker, 2000: xv).

In his elegant analysis of the political and institutional dimension of urban governance, Pierre offers yet another typology of models of urban governance, comprising managerial, corporatist, pro-growth and welfare. Similar to Stoker's analysis, Pierre offers a view of urban governance as a process that brings together public and private interests, working in collaboration to enhance collective goals. As urban governance is 'embedded in a myriad of economic, social, political, and historical factors', Pierre argues that different models of urban governance dictated by different systems of values, norms, beliefs and practices produce different urban policy choices and outcomes.

In Pierre's view, the significance of the national context within which urban governance is embedded should not be underestimated, as national politics and state traditions remain powerful factors in explaining the changing landscape of urban politics and urban political economy (Pierre, 1999: 375). The managerial governance focuses on costs, efficiency, demand and professional management, while according little role to elected officials. The emphasis is on professional performance over political involvement and it 'blurs the public-private distinction, not least on an ideological level, by portraying service producers and clients as actors in markets and by identifying market-based criteria as the main criteria for evaluation' (Pierre, 1999: 380).

On the other hand, participation is the defining characteristic of corporatist governance, which depicts local government as a democratic system that is all-encompassing of civic groups and organised interests in the urban political process. Its inclusive nature creates a high degree of civil society and, by virtue of involving key societal actors in the policy process, this model contributes to smoother implementation compared with other governance approaches. The third model of governance in Pierre's typology – pro-growth – is characterised by a shared relationship between bureaucrats and business elites in the interest of economic development. As the least participatory form of governance, pro-growth 'addresses one of the most salient sectors of current urban politics ... that of the politics of local economic restructuring', which enables it to lend itself most easily to comparative analysis (Pierre, 1999: 384). The fourth and final model of welfare governance emphasises the state as a provider and an enabler; purpose driven, with the focus on outcomes rather than processes. It refers to a form of governance in which cities have limited growth potential in the local economy and the main inflow of capital comes through the welfare system, making cities highly dependent on the state. Each of the four models displays its own organisational logic that dictates a city's capacity to act competently or otherwise. Local states are multidimensional, and different sectors of the state organisation lend themselves to different models as 'their different dimensions act upon different agendas, address different problems, respond to different pressures, and reflect different constituencies' (Pierre, 1999: 389).

Participatory governance

Participatory approaches to governance have emerged in a wide range of social and ecological contexts and have shaped local, regional and national policies. Although participation has the potential of making governments more accountable and transparent, these arrangements do not exist in isolation and must be seen in relation to political institutions in the broader context of governance. Elected leaders and representatives remain the central figures to be held responsible and accountable, and even where decision is delegated to community representatives, the setting of strategic direction and the actual enforcement of policies still come to depend on democratically accountable urban leaders. As Warren observed in his analysis of 'governance-driven democratisation':

> Elected governments have become increasingly aware that electoral legitimacy does not translate into policy-specific legitimacy. Initiated from within government and administration, new forms of democratic participation have emerged. These are not meant to replace other forms and spaces of democracy such as electoral democracy, social movements or deliberation through the media but might be supplementary to it.
> (Warren, 2009: 8)

Often, these new forms are democratic experiments engaging relatively few citizens, but with the potential to represent the wider population. Warren assesses the opportunities and dangers of governance-driven democratisation as measured by the democratic values of *inclusion of the affected*, *empowerment*, *representation* and *deliberation*.

Likewise, Smith's typology provides for a comparison of very different modes of citizen participation based on the 'manner and extent to which they realize desirable qualities or *goods* that we expect of democratic institutions' (Smith, 2009: 12). More specifically he compares participatory budgeting, deliberative citizen assemblies, direct legislation and e-democracy with regard to the 'democratic goods' of *inclusiveness*, *popular control*, *considered judgment* and *transparency*. Geissel, in turn, proposes to compare different forms of democratic innovations by their degree of inclusive *equal participation*, *perceived legitimacy* and *deliberative quality*, but also by their impact on the citizens' democratic skills (*civic education*) and on the actual achievement of collectively identified goals (*effectiveness*) (Geissel, 2012).

Participation is an important component of development programmes intended to facilitate greater control of the development process by local people. Some donors have sought to use participatory development projects and programmes to strengthen civic associations and create new mechanisms through which state institutions can be held responsible for their actions. In this context, the participation and governance debates have led donors to collaborate with non-governmental organisations and community based organisations to promote local solutions to sustainable development. By strengthening the process of local decision making, participatory approaches have enhanced local people's knowledge and capacities, given them more confidence and skills in negotiating with government and helped them to respond and resolve conflicts within their communities. In general, however, the role of participation has historically been ambivalent. Scholars like Arnstein maintain that the public does not have enough power, and measure the value of participation in terms of a ladder of citizen power (Arnstein, 1969). Another view advances the proposition that participation can cause delays and that public participation may result in bad decisions, as the general public may be out of touch with economic and political realities. More fundamentally, participation usually favours only a minority group whose narrow and deep interests always trump the broad interests of the citizens (Olson, 1965). Drawing on the experience in rural areas, another study shows how participation is likely to favour stronger groups in the community, especially when they can present their private interests as public concerns. As Mosse observes:

> far from providing a neutral vehicle for local knowledge, [participation] actually creates a context in which the selective presentation of opinion is likely to be exaggerated, and where minority or deviant views are likely to be suppressed ... the perspectives and interests of the most powerful sections in a community are likely to dominate, not through overt competition or confrontation, but through expression of consensus ... people in authority can 'officialize' private interests, by endorsing and putting on record dominant views.
>
> (Mosse, 1994: 508–509)

The powerful and the organised thus eclipse other voices and succeed in private deal-making processes. On the other hand, a more recent study examining participation in Delhi's unauthorised colonies concluded that a great many urban citizens engaging in participatory urban governance fit neither the 'elite' nor the poor, but comprise composite 'middle' spaces of urban participation. The authors argue for 'greater recognition in academic and policy debates of the nuances in everyday life that are not accurately captured by neat binaries' (Lemanski and Tawa Lama-Rewal, 2012: 102).

Regardless of these debates there is growing recognition of participation as central to the effective management of metropolitan governments, as decision makers increasingly seek public preferences to improve decisions by incorporating citizens' local knowledge into the calculus. Within this framework of urban governance, effective participation must involve collaboration, dialogue and interaction among the various stakeholders. It requires:

> a systems perspective that supports and builds on the interactions among public sector agencies, non-profits, business organisations, advocacy groups and foundations which make up the complex evolving reality of contemporary society.
>
> (Innes and Booher, 2004: 429)

Innes and Booher set out a new paradigm for participation in which, when the conditions for authentic dialogue are met:

> genuine learning takes place; trust and social capital can be built; the quality, understanding and acceptance of information can be increased; jointly developed objectives and solutions with join gain can emerge; and innovative approaches to seemingly intractable problems can be developed.
>
> (Innes and Booher, 2004: 429)

Collaborative participation as a form of governance appears the most representative, inclusive and best suited to help build civic capacity.

Regime theory and coalition governance

For several years, regime theory provided the dominant academic paradigm to explain urban governance. First introduced by Clarence Stone in his study of Atlanta, it maintains that, although politicians create electoral coalitions of voters and contributors to win elections, they establish a different coalition to actually govern. Regimes are 'informal arrangements by which public bodies and private interests function together in order to be able to make and carry out governing decisions' (Stone, 1989: 6). Extended most simplistically, regime theory modulates the importance of governmental structure and emphasises the importance of local leadership as the key factor in determining the quality of urban life. Regime theorists argue that a distinction must be made between holding political power and governing, and in order to be able to achieve anything, elected leaders need the support of other powerful interests, especially the business communities. They work through a system of civic cooperation. London's governance, following the abolition of the Greater London Council (GLC) in 1986, for example, was based on such partnerships. As will be seen in the following chapter, the emergence of new networks and the work of *London First* during the interregnum years (between 1986 and 2000) displayed some of the characteristics of growth coalition or business centred urban regimes, bringing together as it did banks, businesses, utilities and voluntary agencies in the governance of the metropolis.

This approach looks at not just the specifics of a certain partnership, but also at the nature of local politics and the way that a variety of interests coalesce to pursue joint goals:

> Urban regime analysis is about identifying the actors who have 'a capacity to act' in the locality and thereby bring about change; it also implies the forging of relatively stable and hegemonic links between actors and the development of a distinctive local leadership style.
>
> (Rydin, 1998:176)

At yet another level, some have attributed decision making to local politicians taking decisions on the basis of their relationships with voters, political activists, the demands of governmental policy, and the overall political culture of the area (Kraus, 2000; Simpson, 2001). Political leadership is crucial in bringing together the disparate elements of the local governance system. Some have gone further and shown how federal governments can shape metropolitan areas through public policies, both specifically directed at urban areas as well as indirect policies that can have significant impact on city regions. In their study of metro-politics for the twenty-first century, Drier *et al.* demonstrated just how the effect of federal policies in the areas of transportation, military spending, home ownership, tax deductions, housing, low-income subsidised housing policies and urban renewal have had the effect of promoting economic segregation and suburban sprawl (Dreier *et al.*, 2001). In these circumstances, local politicians have only modest control over policies and, in some instances, have no influence at all either in shaping or implementing policies. In the UK, the power of the central government is reflected in grants and loans to local authorities and in such initiatives as urban regeneration policies. Such policies are sometimes subject to relentless central management and control, forcing cities to compete with each other for a share of an ever-reducing resource pie. Indeed, some have argued that the new urban governance represents an attempt by central government to undermine the role of local authorities, to force them into new and dependent relations with the private sector (Rydin, 1998: 189).

Several theoretical and conceptual approaches have thus been brought to bear on the problems of new urban regimes. As the process of urbanisation unfolds, the institutional-territorial matrix for urban governance undergoes restructuring:

> bringing with it broader shifts in the geographies of state regulation both within and beyond the urban scale. In so far as the State's own spatial configuration impacts its capacity to confront place ... states are often pressured to reconfigure their internal territorial hierarchies and jurisdictional frameworks, not least within major urban regions ... during periods of sustained economic crisis, extant frameworks of urban governance may be viewed as ineffectual, and powerful social forces may promote the re organisation of inherited local and/or regional state structures. Under these conditions, new geographies of state organisation may be introduced, whether as a means to construct more viable industrial infrastructures, as a strategy to establish the extra-economic conditions for urban regeneration, or as a mechanism of crisis-management.
>
> (Brenner, 2004: 457)

On this view, urban governance is an important political-institutional arena in which the topographies of state activity are themselves continuously forged and reworked. Despite the various treatments of new urban governance, there is, however, a consensus that a fundamental framework is needed in which relevant actors can agree, negotiate, cooperate and establish trust. But for this to become possible:

> there has to be an opening up of politics so that actors have a chance of cooperating. Decision makers need to set up a dialogue with each other; the basis for the politics of process must be established. To overcome the difficulties of cooperation, regular contact and the involvement of actors in decisions are the bases for the trust needed when an actor fears that it

will lose out by making agreements. New networks are means by which better decisions are made.

(John and Cole, 2000: 85)

Such analytical models as described above help us understand the tensions in urban governance, ways in which city governments relate to their external and internal environments, and the circumstances that influence the adoption of strategies and policies. As Stoker observed, 'the governance perspective provides a simplifying lens to a complex reality. The issue is not that it has simplified matters, but whether that simplification has illuminated our understanding and enabled us to find an appropriate path or direction' (Stoker, 1998: 24). Analysed as above, the various components of governance are particularly relevant for understanding India's cities, which display deep political, social and organisational fragmentation, which poses fundamental challenges. The concept illuminates how local political collections of interacting agencies have emerged in a rapidly changing socio-economic environment of India's cities and directs our attention to the range of institutions involved in the local delivery of policies, strategies and services. Some argue that the traditional institutions are failing in the changing landscape and need to be replaced. For others, existing arrangements could be made to work through innovative strategies and with more streamlined, inclusive and transparent forms of governance.

Metropolitan consolidation

Rapid pressures of growth, along with the antiquated nature of local government forms resulting in fragmentation, have brought to the forefront a question that is a major political issue: whether existing systems of local government are capable of coping with metropolitan pressures resulting from the urbanisation of the areas beyond the political boundaries of central cities. In locating the problems of the great metropolises as arising from 'the unrestricted expansion of the principal city, the immense growth of suburbs and outlying townships and human settlements of one kind or another, and their gradual coalescence', Robson summarised the problems succinctly:

> Vast numbers of people work in the core city and reside in the surrounding areas, with a smaller movement in the opposite direction. An invading army enters the principal city on every working day for the purpose of enabling the people to earn their living and do their work. This invading army demands all kinds of costly and elaborate municipal services – water supply and sanitation, police and fire protection, highway services and so forth. At the end of the day, this army retreats to the places of residence, which are very often outside the city boundaries. One consequence of this characteristic movement is that the journey to work of this army

of commuters has become an ever larger feature of metropolitan life, and is growing more costly in time and money and nervous energy each year.
(Robson, 1966: 45)

In Robson's view, a single metropolitan-wide authority is needed for functions to be performed effectively, or in some instances, performed at all.

Many metropolitan reformers found the system of local government to be anachronistic and incapable of meeting the needs of vastly different economic, social and physical conditions. The fragmented governmental system has often been held responsible for conflicts of authority, the duplication of services, lack of area-wide planning and financial inequities. In order to strengthen the case for reform, of what was considered to be an immensely complex and irrational governmental system, the reformers continued to catalogue the multitude problems of metropolitan areas and advocated the use of structures, which they suggested would reap economies of scale (Barlow, 1991).

Prescriptions for consolidations varied from one area to another and included proposals that merged cities and counties to form new metropolitan governments, and created two-tiered governmental structures that enhanced the fiscal, management and service capacities of counties and districts. Governance approaches ranged from informal cooperation involving collaborative and reciprocal actions between special purpose bodies, to arrangements between two or more local governments to provide for joint planning, financing and delivery of services. In some areas, it involved the transfer of functions to another unit of government or the creation of special districts and authorities, usually area-wide governmental units providing single services such as water or sanitation, hospitals, mass transits or, in another model, multipurpose area-wide districts providing more than one type of service.

Broadly interpreted, metropolitan governance represents a system of governing in which inter-governmental relations play a major role. For any system of governance to be effective, reformers argued that these relations need to be such that they generate area-wide coordination, and are overseen by an umbrella body that has the capacity to view matters from a metropolitan perspective and so act in the interests of the whole area. In the absence of such a body, the separation of functions could potentially present problems, as individual special purpose bodies may not have the capacity to coordinate their activities with those of others. A number of important functions may also be too far removed from political accountability. Indeed, some took the view that analysis of urban governance must necessarily encompass the metropolitan scale, as the strong interdependencies of municipalities within city regions make more or less formalised forms of regional governance factually indispensable (Savitch and Vogel, 2000). Experiments in consolidation have shown significant benefits in relation to land-use planning and improving service efficiencies and, more significantly, in terms of containing the sprawl that has plagued metropolitan areas (Lewis, 1996). Regional approaches also came to be seen as providing the only solution to poverty and for achieving greater equity.

Yet opponents of consolidation objected to the creation of special districts on the grounds that they would further fragment the governmental system of a metropolis. Arguments were advanced that imposing limits on growth stifles economic development, that 'big government' adds to costs and has the potential to be dominated by suburban interests, at the expense of a deteriorating inner city. This group of urban political scientists focused on the intergovernmental nature of metropolitan politics and governance; on the way different governmental units interact with each other as they try to protect or promote the interests of their communities within the large urban complex. They studied the characteristics of suburbia and the political attitudes and preferences of suburban residents, which influenced their choice of maintaining the status quo over alternative modes of metropolitan governance. Amongst the reasons advanced were the fear of higher taxes, attachment to a small town and a desire to maintain distance from the social problems of the inner city.

The most influential, but also the most highly controversial challenge to proponents of regional government, came from a group of 'public choice' political economists, who not only explained, but also defended, political fragmentation as the best guarantor of local government efficiency and local democracy. They regarded the fragmentation of local government as a virtue: inter-local competition was perceived as resulting in better services that are more responsive to local needs (Keating, 1995; Tiebout, 1956). They argued that a 'highly unstructured metropolitan area possesses a very rich and intricate framework for negotiating, adjudicating, and deciding questions that affect ... diverse public interests' (Ostram *et al.*, 1961: 842). Proponents of public choice contended that metropolitan areas containing a large number of local government units allow individuals, households and businesses to shop around for the location that provides the combination of local services and local taxes that best suits their preferences. Such areas offer a large variety of locations for people to live and work and allows residents or firms that do not like a tax or service in any one area to 'vote with their feet' by moving to an area that offers a more acceptable mix. There was a growing awareness of the complexity of metropolitan problems and a questioning of the assumptions inherent in the case for consolidation of local governments.

Critics, however, pointed out that the theorists of public choice favoured a system that was ineffective at providing seamless services to a large settlement segmented by several municipal boundaries. They contested the large disparities in the wealth of different communities, in the services they offered and in the different quality of life of their residents. Historically, reformers have not been united on a given prescription for a given area. Different explanations have found favour at different periods in time and in different places. Some American writers attached greater importance to the federal government's role in metropolitan area governance, with state governments playing a minor, almost insignificant role. By contrast, those writers of metropolitan affairs in countries such as Canada accorded greater weight to provincial governments and their constitutional responsibility for municipal affairs. Several explanations have been advanced for the differences that dictated the approach of the day, including the different periods when suburbanisation took place in different countries.

This also helps explain the differences between the British and Americans in their approaches to reform. In the United States, the issue of metropolitan reorganisation has generally been decided by a public referendum. Under such circumstances, proponents of reform make every effort to enlist public support for their proposals so as to get a majority vote in the referendum. In London, the issue was ultimately the decision of a higher governmental authority – the central government. Even so, the reforms of London government have shown that metropolitan reform is not solely, or even primarily, an organisational issue; rather it is a political question that involves reconciliation of opposing interests, opinions and ideas. Several reformers have been increasingly seeking the middle road, concluding that governments of metropolises can be made functional without the need to create major disruptions either through consolidations, which tend to evoke negative reactions, or by creating other forms of new, untested, metropolitan structures.

The idea behind charting this middle road is to reduce or eliminate the most serious governmental deficiencies while maintaining a realistic balance between the interests of the metropolitan area and those of the individual units. At least, such is the mood of policy makers and practitioners involved in the governance of India's cities. Despite deep appreciation of the problems of integration in India's metropolitan governance and the conflicts between central cities and their expanding suburbs, no single solution has yet been put forward either for the improvement of existing metropolitan structures or advocating a wholesale consolidation. In the case of London, the consensus in the 1990s was that it was not possible to solve area-wide problems without a fundamental reorganisation of London's government. Yet in the preceding years when London did not have a metropolitan government, the consensus was that the system functioned well through joint action and pooling of resources to provide services on an area-wide basis. Hence when considering the future of metropolises, it perhaps matters little whether one chooses a fragmented system or a consolidated one as long as the basic conditions for effective governance are satisfactorily met.

The conditions of effective governance

What, then, are the basic conditions for effective metropolitan governance? Metropolitan regions pose unprecedented governance challenges given their size, continued growth, social diversity, spatial heterogeneity, economic status and institutional dimensions. The challenges are based on the need to provide public services across a multitude of local jurisdictions, while delivering effective governance through strong leadership and efficient and robust delivery structures. In the context of the rapid change, growing uncertainty and the diverse and conflicting policy preferences, it is all the more important to focus our understanding of governance on what actually works in practice, on governance that is effective.

This is not to suggest that the study and development of theory should be ended or even lessened, and it is important that the many new ideas flowing from such academic work are tried out in real life. Without such theoretical work and the implementation of fresh approaches, stagnation would set in and our ability to cope with the scale and pace of change would be severely hampered. This, of course, is precisely what has happened in the governance of some cities, in which the conditions of governance may have been suitable when first implemented, but are no longer effective in current circumstances and unlikely to enable cities to develop sustainably into the future.

Unlike academics, politicians, managers and administrators have to translate theory into practice. Debating how better to implement reform in policy making, the Institute for Government noted that:

> earlier reform attempts delivered only limited improvements because they failed to take account of the real world of policy making: the pressures and incentives experienced by various players, including ministers. Moreover, many existing models of policy making are increasingly inappropriate in a world of decentralised services and complex policy problems.
> (Halsworth and Rutter, 2011: 8)

The important issue here is the need to be pragmatic and flexible, and so theories should be tested and evaluated before being implemented on a large scale or put into operation elsewhere. Sometimes an idea works well; at other times a model has to be adapted to suit the specific situation; and in other instances the finest theory simply does not work in practice.

The same is true for models of governance: it is neither sensible to take a successful governance model and attempt to translocate it piecemeal on the assumption that what is effective in one place will automatically be so in another, nor to attempt to implement a demonstrably flawed theory on the grounds that it is theoretically sound and so might possibly work in a different location. The principles of evidence-based policy making should be applied as much to the policies of governance as to the policies developed by governments. Accordingly, the next section of this exploration into the governance of cities examines the particular conditions of governance that have been widely studied in both theory and practice, and shown to contribute significantly to effectiveness.

Effective devolution

Cities throughout North America and Europe have a wide degree of autonomy in service provision, while cities and regional governments in France, Germany and Spain enjoy high levels of fiscal autonomy (Marshall *et al.*,

2006). Although some have argued that such functions as water provision and waste management are better handled at the integrated metropolitan level, where unified infrastructure management and service provision can iron out inequalities, devolution is acknowledged to generate a range of other benefits involving citizen participation, enhanced efficiencies and improvements in service delivery across the metropolitan area. A growing base of research evidence suggests that strong city-regions are key to improving wider regional performance and driving national economic growth (Marshall *et al.*, 2006: 3). However, maintaining the right balance of functions between the various levels of government is paramount for effective devolution. As the subsequent chapters show, while India has made such provisions, the process of devolution has been far from effective.

Two forms of decentralisation are common across mega-urban regions in Asia. The first involves *delegation* of authority and responsibility for specific functions, from the central government to smaller, more localised units. For example, the governments of both Thailand and China retain supervisory powers over centrally-delegated governors, district officers and municipal mayors operating at the local level. Alternatively, decentralisation can mean *devolution*, as in the case of both India's Constitutional Amendment Act, 1992, and the Philippine's Local Government Code of 1991, which devolved a series of key functions from central to local government units. The latter has thus far achieved more practical success in devolving all functions including health, environmental protection, and public works and highways to local units (Laquian, 2005: 147). Within these two types of decentralisation, governments may provide functions in any of four ways: centrally, regionally (or metropolitan-wide), shared regionally and locally, or purely locally.

Some of the arguments rehearsed above in favour of metropolitan consolidation are echoed in more recent studies of mega-urban regions. In such studies pertaining to Asia, Laquian argued that allocating urban functions that are, of their very nature, area-wide adds to efficiency because they facilitate coordination. Such services should be vested in metropolitan or regional authorities to achieve economies of scale and management efficiency (Laquian, 2005: 147). While central governments are usually responsible for 'economic planning, construction, agriculture, transport, communication, regulation of commerce, manufacturing, and industry' and, in addition, set national policies and standards and allocate funds, regional structures may provide or share provision with local governments for a range of planning and management functions (Laquian, 2005: 120). Thus, higher-level functions are retained by central governments, while local governments focus on the need to coordinate local efforts and take advantage of economies of scale. This strategy has achieved success in some countries, but has proved less successful when devolution has led to inefficiencies and occasionally resulted in reversion to a more centralised system.

An example of ineffective devolution in a shared regional and local delivery context is what Gleeson *et al.* call a 'democratic deficit'. In the Australian governance systems for example, they refer to the disconnect between the general consensus of how to split state and metropolitan responsibilities, and the actual scenario *in situ*. In the latter, the appropriate divisions of responsibility are regularly reversed. Pressures arise from the focus on regulatory issues (at the expense of larger policy development tasks) by state planning agencies that should appropriately be the territory of local and regional authorities. The suggestion is that state planners responsible for setting higher-level policies should focus on state-wide urban development rather than control the lower-level decision making processes that 'guide infrastructure development and the delivery of urban services' (Gleeson *et al.*, 2010: 6).

Since the 1990s, countries such as the Philippines, Indonesia, Sri Lanka and Thailand have adopted strong measures of decentralisation. In the Philippines, legislation in 1991 redefined fiscal divisions, devolving taxation authority and other key governmental functions to local units, declaring that 'the State shall enjoy genuine and meaningful local autonomy ... provide for a more responsive and accountable local government structure instituted through a system of decentralization whereby local government units shall be given more powers, authority, responsibilities, and resources' (Laquian, 2005: 148–149). Yet, many local governments in the Philippines have not achieved full autonomy from the national government. In 1999, the Asia Foundation set up the Transparent Accountable Governance (TAG) Program to improve local governance by assisting municipal and village governments in the country to develop the necessary technical skills and civic and Public–Private Partnerships. The Foundation's assistance to local governments in the Philippines resulted in simplified business registration, a professionalized local bureaucracy, the efficient administration of property tax, enhanced efficiency of budget allocations and increased citizens' satisfaction with government services. Where there is political will and appropriate support for developing local governance, devolution can lead to practical improvements in people's lives.

Consolidated governance

According to McKinsey, India's 35 urban agglomerations, each with more than a million inhabitants, cross 20 municipal boundaries. Challenges such as mass-transit systems and affordable housing, widely seen to be within the remit of state-level governments, spill beyond the borders of individual municipal governments and require different solutions (McKinsey, 2010: 85). Even though resource management, job creation, provision of public transport and climate mitigation are, in many respects, regionally specific, responsibility in the Indian metropolises is diffused among many weak municipal-level bodies.

The large and growing population of India's cities, as well as the complexity of urban service requirements, is necessitating 'metropolitan-wide answers' as existing local governance structures are unable to meet the growing challenges (McKinsey, 2010: 85). Mumbai faces difficulty both from hyper-divided local administrative units (wards), which tend to focus only on local benefits, and larger units with autonomous but limited powers, leading to difficulties in coordination (Laquian, 2005: 114). In some cases, 'there is no single political or administrative authority, resulting in overlapping agencies' (Allen et al., 2006: 23). In France, the 1999 'Chevenement Law' sought to overcome a similarly high level of local fragmentation through strengthening the appeal of metropolitan governance by encouraging the integration of local (commune) and supra-communal levels of governance into cooperative bodies. These new local authorities receive financial incentives based on the number of integrated policies they accumulated from a portfolio of powers (Yaro and Ronderos, 2004: 5). Such a system of incentives might successfully encourage greater cooperation across Indian metropolises too, but the political realities of France and India are different. The federal structure of states and union territories in India is such that national initiatives are filtered through the state level of governance, and this often leads to nationally devised policies and procedures being diluted or even ignored.

Many cities, including Mumbai, Kolkata and Hyderabad, continue to spread geographically, transforming rural areas adjacent to the urban core. These peri-urban zones, containing characteristics of both urban and rural areas (such as their service structures and governance or resource accessibility), often experience higher population growth rates than the municipal region, and undergo rapid changes with regards to economic processes. These regions usually have mixed populations and their inhabitants have a diversity of incomes and livelihoods, and use resources in different ways than in the urban core. They comprised disproportionate numbers of poor households (Allen et al., 2006: 21). Despite rapid urbanisation and the rapid spread of border slums, there is an absence of effective area-wide planning to provide basic quality of life in these regions. In their study of water and sanitation services for the peri-urban poor in metropolitan areas, Allen et al. observe that:

> the problem of institutional fragmentation is particularly relevant in the metropolitan context, where often different administrative units are subjected to the policy decisions of a large number of public agencies. Weak links and limited municipal power in sectors such as transport, water, energy, solid and liquid waste management and land use planning often result in uncertainty as to which institution administers which specific area or activity. This has significant policy implications in the case of water supply and sanitation.
>
> (Allen et al., 2006: 22)

These Peri-Urban Interfaces (PUIs) are important because they often act both as resource providers and as waste sinks from the denser urban core which they support. However, despite the important role such regions play in the environmental functioning of the city, owing to their unplanned growth and development, PUIs are often outside the urban governance system. Centralised systems of management and service provision are not likely to work in these areas, and leave some of the poorest citizens without sufficient access to basic water and sanitation services. A high level of self-organisation often exists, which enables the needs of inhabitants to be met informally. Unified urban governance systems need to recognise and support local efforts to meet these needs, while reducing the fragmentation that prevents clear and well-resourced authority.

While decentralisation is seen as essential for effective service delivery and the economic growth of cities, this must be balanced against situations whereby municipal governments wield too much influence, undermining metropolitan planning, which can lead to poor governance, political fragmentation and a lack of social cohesion. Advocates for devolved city governance argue for a reduction in the significance of local boundaries, in order to establish a robust, regionally bounded metropolitan administration (Barlow, 1991). A strong and incentivised political executive at the metropolitan level must be given sufficient resources and decision-making ability to carry through a longer-term vision for urban development.

Bangkok is illustrative, where the formation of a strong unitary administration took roots in the 1970s with the creation of the Bangkok Metropolitan Administration (BMA). Facilitated by the traditional weakness of existing local government structures, the move to a unitary urban system was able to progress relatively rapidly, with a patchwork of districts and sub-districts being administered directly through an elected governor by the mid-1980s. The strength of this role was assisted by Bangkok's primacy as Thailand's capital and most populous city. Unlike, for example, the Philippines, local government in Bangkok is highly ordered through the office of the governor, enabling metropolitan regional planning to proceed relatively quickly and effectively (Webster, 2004: 93).

Rapid innovation in metropolitan consolidation also took place in Johannesburg, following the city's economic struggles in the late 1990s. Earlier in that decade, the city was made up of 13 local authorities and these were amalgamated in the mid-1990s into the Greater Johannesburg Metropolitan Area. Subsequently, Greater Johannesburg was consolidated into 'a governance structure of four autonomous or metropolitan local councils and a metropolitan council' (Smith, 2006: 7). Soon, the four operating councils and the metropolitan coordinating council faced various problems of confusion and duplication of roles between local councils and the metropolitan council, competition for resources between councils, and weak and complex institutional arrangements. In addition, problems of inadequate administration of the treasury resulting in deficits, the withdrawal of provincial funding for disadvantaged areas, and non-payment of rates and service charges exacerbated the problems. As part of its reforms, and as part of the structural adjustments aimed at overcoming the above challenges, Johannesburg created a strong and empowered political executive. The commonality of the experiences of Johannesburg and Bangkok is that the process of consolidation was eased by strong leadership.

London and Toronto are other examples of recent experiments in metropolitan government that have proved successful. Toronto sought a solution to the problem of over-complicated urban governance structures by merging the Regional Municipality of Metropolitan Toronto with six surrounding constituencies, creating the new City of Toronto. This reduced the number of elected officials in Metro Toronto, and streamlined senior administrative positions by 30 per cent. The reorganisation resulted in a standardisation and reduction in tax rates, common assessment and collection procedures, and reduced inequalities amongst tax-payers (Laquian, 2005: 126–127).

Coordinated structures for service delivery

India's cities lack consolidated structures for service delivery. The problem is compounded by the proliferation of state agencies and state departments working with city governments – organisational fragmentation that fails to map effectively on to urban problems. The web of arrangements lacks clarity of definition in tasks, goals and budgets. Devolution to smaller units of government runs parallel to transfer of authority to other non-governmental entities carried out through special franchises, or in the direct sale of public enterprises to private companies. This, in turn, is further complicated by the transfer of responsibility and authority to civil society groups, such as NGOs, which carry out research, training, information dissemination, community organisation, and other functions on behalf of the government (Laquian, 2005: 147). The role of the metropolitan government as 'enabler' is seen as central to the success of corporatised solutions, which ensures that accountability exists alongside effective coordination and delineation of functions between the various stakeholders.

Mumbai's transport system is illustrative of this fragmentation in service delivery, although the establishment of the Brihanmumbai Electric Supply and Transport (BEST) organisation, a quasi-autonomous entity supported by the government, has provided for greater coordination by bringing together transport and electricity services in the city. Formally, responsibility for coordinating transport in the region rests with the Mumbai Metropolitan Regional Development Authority (MMRDA), but it enjoys minimal influence on the planning and provision of the crucial service. The transport system is highly fragmented:

> Jurisdiction over the suburban rail service rests with India Railways, a specialized central government agency. Two zonal railway systems in the

Mumbai suburbs are also run by independent agencies that pursue their separate policies and activities without any significant efforts at service integration. The allocation of financial resources to support the building and operation of rail-based transport requires the approval of the Central Planning Commission. The planning and construction of roads and major trunk lines are vested in the Public Works Department of the State of Maharashtra. Maintenance of roads is the responsibility of the Municipal Corporation of Greater Mumbai as is the planning and implementation of traffic management.

(Cited in Laquian, 2005: 146)

As a result, the World Bank and a number of policy analysts have recommended 'closer integration and area-wide governance for the Mumbai city-region to rationally manage transport services'. The World Bank also recommended the 'strengthening of the MMRDA as a regional planning and coordinating authority that would manage the implementation of the Mumbai urban transport project' (Laquian, 2005: 146).

An effective model of transport policy has been demonstrated in Bangkok. Beginning in the late 1980s, the decision to embark on a number of mega-transit projects saw the involvement of private companies that were offered concessions for the construction of railway lines and expressways. The Metropolitan Rapid Transit Authority (MRTA) was set up to coordinate the projects. Overseeing a period of rapid economic growth, particularly during the 1990s, the BMA initially struggled to manage rising populations and resource allocation. Over time, however, its presence bolstered Bangkok's position as the country's most important industrial centre, and proved successful in establishing mechanisms for concentrating growth through the management of service provision. The creation of the mass transit system has been particularly successful in reducing congestion as urban dwellers moved on to the city's growing network of sky trains and underground systems. The system improved accessibility to central locations, and the benefits proved a powerful motivation for identifying ongoing development needs (Webster, 2004: 93).

Despite the complexity of the problems, metropolitan-level governance is a crucial platform from which both to take advantage of the economies of scale available to city-wide management in infrastructure and service provision, and to equalise the quality of this provision across city divisions in wealth and access. In Metro Manila, for example, the Metropolitan Waterworks and Sewerage System oversees water and sewerage services in the city-region, yet the

> actual production and distribution of potable water has been privatised to the Manila Water and Maynilad Water Company. Setting up area-wide agencies has been justified in terms of the need to coordinate local efforts and take advantage of economies of scale. When a metro-wide

department consolidates its purchases, it may be able to get lower prices and better terms than individual local government units.

(Laquian, 2005: 12)

Thus, as public services are in many cases best administered at the metropolitan level the advantage of a strong and unified system of governance is that power can then be devolved further, through what McKinsey has described as 'the creation of focused agencies with clear mandates, reliable budgets, and empowered CEOs' (McKinsey, 2010: 99). However, some have argued that the solution to India's organisational fragmentation might be found in giving a greater role to private agencies, which are capable of providing a more simplified, logical and efficient structure of authority for metropolitan areas.

Focused urban leadership

Studies of metropolitan regions have stressed the importance of focused urban leadership, with those at the top of the formal political institutions having 'influence over public resources and ... accountability and power relations with all the citizens within the area' (Greasley and Stoker, 2009). A capable leader is not a panacea, of course, for while leadership facilitates policy direction, maintains political support and represents the authority's goals in negotiations with other stakeholders, success in attaining a vision and goal will involve other factors, including the historical context, human and financial resources, and institutional structures. Leaders at the metropolitan level, however visionary and inspiring, administratively competent or powerful, cannot control the full range of activities that makes a city run effectively.

In their comparative study of 14 countries Mouritzen and Svara differentiated four ideal types of leadership forms. In *strong mayor* systems an elected mayor controls the majority of the city council and is responsible for all executive functions. In the *committee-leader* form the political leader is charged with some executive functions, but other functions are assigned to standing committees and to the top administrator such as a CEO, city manager or secrétaire générale. In the *collective* form there is one elected collegiate body responsible for all executive functions, where the mayor presides over the body. Finally, in the *council-manager* form all executive functions are in the hands of a city manager, appointed by the city council, and where the mayor has just the presiding role (Mouritzen and Svara, 2002). These forms are discussed and illustrated in-depth in a later chapter.

In contrast with North American and European cities, which are generally led by a strong political executive, usually in the form of an elected mayor, India's urban governance is largely provided by appointed 'career' officials. The role of mayors has not been sufficiently examined as pertaining to Indian urban governance. Thus, while elected urban leadership elsewhere provides for clear accountability and sufficient tenure in office to enable long-term planning and the implementation of change, most Indian cities lack this focus of responsibility. Kolkata provides a partial exception as it has a political executive leading the city for a five-year term, with a commissioner acting as chief administrator. While this system lacks some of the accountability of a directly elected mayor, it is seen as forming the first step in incremental change towards empowered leadership.

The need for strong local figureheads in maintaining all areas of urban governance is widely acknowledged. Dasgupta argues that a possible solution to India's serious deficiencies in its security infrastructure can be found in reinforcing city leadership rather than in looking for national solutions: 'If the people of Mumbai want a safer city, the city must be able to govern itself" (cited in Acuto, 2013: 484). ARUP, a corporate consulting body in London that provided work for the C40 Climate Leadership Group, has extensively documented policy capacity in a wide reach of mayoral powers across at least eight sectors of activity: transport, existing buildings, waste management, water, energy supply, outdoor lighting, planning and urban land use, and food and agriculture (Acuto, 2013: 494). Whichever the sector, visibly strong leadership makes a difference.

Some have argued that both flexibility and autonomy are essential in order to secure an empowered and effective mayoral system capable of offering strategic leadership. The system should be free from central government party politics, contribute to building an identity for the city and enable the development of strong partnerships both inside and external to the city. Ideally, the mayor should be elected with a strong executive power to give him or her the mandate to enact change in the city's interest (Warwick Commission, 2012: 8–11).

Although mayors should be held accountable for their actions, it is generally accepted that they must also have enough autonomy to administer the city in line with their personal vision and, in the case of direct election, the manifesto upon which their election was based. In Bogotá, for example, decades of poor governance, including deteriorating services, corruption among municipal officials, economic mismanagement and escalating crime rates began to improve once new laws enhanced the mayor's powers. The Organic Law, passed in 1993, sought to clarify the roles of both the city council and the mayor, by making the former responsible for legislation and overseeing the executive, and the latter for administering the city (Gilbert and Dávila, 2002: 44). For the subsequent two decades, Bogotans gave their mayors popular mandates by voting for independent candidates. This, combined with their new powers, gave the mayors confidence to appoint their own teams, and to work quickly to push through their programmes. Improved access to vital services, a reduction in corruption, and increased revenues have been seen as significant improvements by the urban population, 65 per cent of whom claimed the city was improving in 2005, compared with only 32 per cent in 1999 (Gilbert, 2006: 397).

In Europe, the adoption of powerful executive mayors, and a shift towards directly elected mayors during the 1990s was a means to provide 'better management of local affairs and more effective representation of the local community' (Fenwick and Elcock, 2005: 61). Reformers sought to promote and adopt stronger styles of urban leadership and strengthen the local executive function. As a result, directly-elected or appointed, yet powerful, mayors, now exist in Norway, Italy, Germany, France, Russia, Slovakia, Poland and the Czech Republic, among others. In Africa, meanwhile, Johannesburg made changes to its municipal structure, which resulted in an empowered political executive and an appointed manager acting as professional city administrator. Accountability was achieved through the use of memorandums of understanding (MOUs) signed by the mayor and agency chief executives. The chief executive's continued employment and compensation are determined by performance measured against the MOUs (McKinsey, 2010: 90).

China has powerful city mayors, appointed directly by central government, who are highly incentivised to perform well, being held accountable for important aspects of city reform (specifically, economic growth and improvements to quality of life) (McKinsey, 2010: 91). In recent years, the autonomy of Chinese city mayors has increased, for example in project spending decisions, where mayors can approve projects of up to $50 million without receiving central permission. While autonomy in decision making is important to successful implementation of projects and programmes, a crucial additional factor is their 'network of influence' within the central Beijing government:

> success in governance seems to be significantly correlated with a number of leadership factors such as strong linkages to the central government, metropolitan or regional scope of leadership, commitment of urban citizens to wider issues, and more generalized public support, often from civil society groups.
>
> (Laquian, 2005: 126)

Whatever the form, strong metropolitan leadership is necessary in order to achieve effective functioning of metropolitan service provision, as well as fiscal decision making. Strong leadership is a vital aspect of coordinating area-wide governance structures, which, if not managed properly, can lead to problems of fragmentation and failing governance.

An active metropolitan community

Community participation as the basis of strong metropolitan governance (as noted above) was most consequential within the field of urban planning, where several cities during the 1960s and 1970s introduced forms of public involvement, which then gradually expanded beyond spatial planning to include strategic planning and effective service provision. Systematic studies have shown how improvements to urban governance have been triggered by public demands for better services and accountability, and the ways in which cities in different institutional settings and with different political cultures combine urban leadership and community involvement to produce effective and legitimate outcomes (Heinelt *et al.*, 2006). Growing suspicion of elected representatives and political institutions, together with better educated, connected and informed citizens resulted in greater public involvement in political decision making, while political leaders, in turn, responded to popular pressures by cautiously reforming disproportional electoral systems, strengthening judicial and administrative review, decentralising the political system, and introducing various forms of citizen participation (Dalton, 1996). Enthusiasts of participatory democracy in countries as diverse as Brazil, the United States and Canada experimented with deliberative citizen assemblies, new forms of community planning and the use of new social media.

Except for isolated instances, however, Indian cities have not experienced strong and active citizen movements seeking better, more accountable government. The complexity of the social transformations affecting India's major cities demands devolved solutions that not only respond to local contexts, but are transparent and accountable to the communities for whom such governance exists. While rapidly rising populations provide new opportunities, integrating the urban population into a cohesive metropolitan community has substantial challenges. The institutional design of metropolitan governance often determines whether population groups across a metropolitan region will engage in collaborative action or whether some localities will suffer from conflicts and tensions caused by unilateral strategies pursued for and by other localities. As Young observed:

> Autonomous local jurisdictions exclude some people and activities through their use of zoning regulation; with their tax powers wealthy communities run high-quality schools and first-rate services while a neighbouring poorer municipality has a much lower tax base and need for more costly and complex service provision. The planning and development decisions of one jurisdictionally autonomous unit affect the investment patterns and atmosphere of many neighbouring communities who have no say in these decisions.
>
> (Young, 2000: 229)

In the short term, establishing social narratives of inclusion might be achieved through public relations activities or educational programmes aimed at informing local residents of the transformations, and at fostering a collective community identity. Yet, over time, mechanisms must be put in place that will provide practical channels for the growing metropolitan community to be actively involved in its own future.

Issues of participation, fairness, accountability, sustainability and transparency underpin good governance (Burris *et al.*, 2007: 155). A major problem of India's governance lies in dealing with issues of corruption and fairness. When public confidence and trust in governing institutions is reduced it tends to result in decreased engagement in public affairs. But any attempts to address corruption cannot succeed without governmental processes in place to ensure transparency and accountability. Some cities have addressed this successfully through laws, public education, closer monitoring of administrative procedures, or the creation of special anti-corruption agencies. For example, in 1974, Hong Kong set up the Independent Commission Against Corruption (ICAC) to reduce corruption within the city's police forces, using 'stop and search' interventions. This significantly reduced corrupt acts in subsequent years (Laquian, 2005: 157).

The need to ensure transparency should not, however, preclude metropolitan governments from receiving the necessary decision-making power and resources to achieve best outcomes. Indian urban administrations may fail to ensure accountability and delivery in part because they focus on processes, while only loosely tracking outcomes. As a result, goals are often difficult to gauge and outcomes cannot be clearly measured, resulting in weak accountability of government to its citizens. The solution requires a reversal of emphasis to a system 'which gives cities the freedom to make their own processes and decisions but holds them accountable for the outcomes' (McKinsey, 2010: 102). Two crucial components of ensuring accountability are the implementation of systems to ensure transparency and endowing metropolitan governments with the power to make decisions and experiment with processes.

The current conception of 'good governance' describes a networked system in which the widest range of stakeholders within the urban context can jointly determine the direction of development for their city. At its best, a good governance system offers a voice to the most under-privileged and under-represented groups, through the presence of participative processes and local organisations that are given a place within the governance system. Inequality, often most conspicuous in large cities, can serve to breed social fragmentation and political instability and so, in turn, affect economic competitiveness. Particularly for societies where institutions are built upon the premise of democratic citizenship, engagement with the needs of the whole of the urban community is vital, and makes the implementation of electoral politics particularly attractive. As mentioned earlier, mayoral elections can provide important spaces for civic engagement, and have in many cases helped to develop mechanisms of good governance for leaders whose principle focus has been on gaining support for re-election or on disassociating themselves from national politics. Elections alone, however, are not sufficient to ensure the transparency and accountability of governments, or to ensure inclusion and fair allocation of metropolitan resources. Participation must also be encouraged through other means.

The World Bank outlines a system to achieve this, known as Participatory Performance Monitoring. The system enables citizens, users of services and civil society organisations to participate in the 'monitoring and evaluation of service delivery and public works' through a series of tools, including Citizen Report Cards and Community Score Cards (World Bank, 2014). One of the most notable examples is in Latin America, where experiments with participatory budgets have done much to empower local communities in determining the focus of urban governance, as well as increasing accountability and transparency. Furthermore, 'over the last two decades, participatory budgeting – in which citizens take part in budget planning, overseeing public expenditures, and monitoring delivery of goods and services – has grown from a Brazilian experiment to an international model for socially accountable urban governance' (Burris *et al.*, 2007: 158).

India's urbanisation offers significant opportunities for improved levels of inclusion. Yet, the 'landscape of governance is littered with governance deficits, gaps between people's stake in governance and their access to governance institutions' (Acuto, 2013: 492). With changing conceptions of what governance includes, the opportunities arise for supporting citizen participation in developing urban leadership that meets their needs, improving the functionality and liveability of cities and, ultimately, improving India's wider sustainable development capability.

*****

Some forms of governance are more successful than others in meeting the needs of the various interests within expanding cities. Participatory systems in which the players can interact, negotiate and cooperate within a well-defined and transparent framework are more effective than those that are prescriptive and marginalise individuals and groups. Similarly, models of governance that have the in-built capacity to adapt to changes in urban issues are better placed to overcome problems and plan more effectively than models that are rigid and inflexible. When Pierre proposed his four models of governance he recognised the importance of different systems of values, norms, beliefs and practices in shaping city governance. Culture is important. As subsequent chapters show, all three cities of Mumbai, Kolkata and Hyderabad face common challenges of growth, governance, and the vertical distribution of competencies that are highly dependent on state traditions. These traditions do not vary greatly, nor do the socio-economic conditions that determine the pattern of investment and functional and financial devolution. If there is variation, it is best illustrated by Kolkata which, when compared with the other cities, exhibits a different pattern of separating the roles and powers of the most senior elected and appointed officials.

3 London

A prototype for India?

The research agenda for urbanisation that dominated the latter half of the twentieth century was driven by the need to identify common structures and processes that would transcend the idiosyncrasies of time and space and provide a value-free basis for a general theory of urbanisation. The consensus was soon reached that 'the phenomenon of urbanisation, universal in the contemporary world, is being generated by so many different factors, operating with different emphases in each separate country, that it would be impossible, as well as unwise, to try to summarise the process in any meaningful way' (Berry, 1976: 8). While the search for a universal commonality was deemed pointless on conceptual and socio-political grounds, more recent urban experiences have in fact demonstrated a variety of similar trends and common problems. Comparative interpretations, however, are not easy, as cities all over the world – and indeed even within a country – are at different stages of development, products of different historical experiences, and operate under very different geographic and institutional settings.

Nevertheless, it is possible to identify dominant themes that are common, and cities all over the world face the universal challenges of globalisation and its accompanying forces. Policy transfer in urban government is gathering pace, but sensitivity to the local political and constitutional setting is needed if such transfers are to be successful. With this caveat in mind, this chapter attempts to explore ways in which London's experience can contribute to a more informed discussion of the issues of urban governance and leadership that arise in the three Indian cities of Mumbai, Hyderabad and Kolkata.

It begins by examining London's planning and the twentieth-century's attempts at creating a metropolitan community. The rationale for the establishment of the Greater London Council (GLC) and its viability as a strategic authority is then examined, followed by an analysis of the new arrangements for London's governance that came into effect in 2000. The creation of the GLA in 2000 prompted a reconsideration of how service delivery should be consolidated and borough interests represented and protected. The concluding sections offer an assessment of how the mayor manages the melange of relationships within the limits of his own actual power, as defined by statute, and his de facto subservience to central government. London provides examples of structures and practices, which imperfect as they may be, could be used as the starting points for new thinking on how to improve city governance in India.

Planning for a sustainable London

Throughout the twentieth century, the question of London's governance was dealt with in isolation from that of the larger region within which it was located. As part of a larger metropolitan region, a region that contains vast number of urban settlements, London performs the functions characteristic of the central city. As the main generator of jobs as well as of culture, entertainment and shopping activities, it was always considered politically and administratively convenient to treat London as a separate entity defined by official boundaries, however artificial. However, this caused both a problem of regional coordination and an uneasy relationship between the governments of London and the surrounding counties. The pace and change of growth and emerging disparities and conflicts between the inner and outer areas exacerbated the problems. Despite recognition of these problems, it was not until the 1940s that the need to redevelop congested urban areas and diversify developments gained ascendancy. It was these needs that subsequently influenced much of London's post-war development.[1]

Land-use planning at both the regional and city level was primarily driven by three inter-related objectives: *urban containment*, to create self-contained and balanced communities and protect the countryside; *prevention of scattered development* by building up strong service centres; and *accessibility to urban services*, through promotion of high quality physical and social environments. The need to save good agricultural land from unplanned urban growth was considered important, and those concerned about the protection of the countryside and rural way of life were apprehensive of the expanding cities. For them, city and country were in conflict and the problem was the city, the growth of which had to be contained. The rural protectionist movement led to the setting up of the Council for the Prevention of Rural England in 1925 under the chairmanship of architect and city planner, Patrick Abercrombie.

Although the idea of containment greatly influenced the 1947 planning system, it was soon subject to pressures of population growth and expansion, the movement of people between home and workplace, and decentralisation of employment. The two notions of urban containment and rural preservation came together in the concept of the 'green belt' – an orbital parkway around the metropolis, with the objectives of preventing towns from growing larger, giving access to the countryside for recreation, and preserving agriculture and the rural way of life. New developments were to take place largely beyond the green belt in new towns rather than allowing London to continue to sprawl. The idea took hold, but not without a lingering fear that development might leapfrog the green belt, threatening even wider tracts of the countryside than before (Hall *et al.*, 1973: 49).

Another important characteristic underpinning planning was the creation of planned, new, self-contained and balanced communities variously termed 'garden cities', 'satellite towns' or 'new towns'.[2] Their rationale was set out in terms of easier access to the countryside, and cheaper public services and public transport. It was envisaged that a new town of 30,000 to 50,000 inhabitants would offer an appropriate balance in terms of age, sex, and social and educational backgrounds, and could provide a good range of services, jobs, entertainment and educational opportunities. In general, the theme of urban containment worked either to prevent low-density developments or isolated and smaller settlements widely distributed over the countryside (Frey, 2000).

The 1960s saw London changing under the pressure of rapid suburbanisation. It had an inner core and an outer ring with different problems and interests. The London County Council (LCC) reflected, to some extent, the realities of London's social structure, while Greater London was a constellation of competing communities, loosely tied to each other. The metropolis was seen as a 'vast sea of inchoate development' and a 'morass of dormitory suburbia surrounding the old economically active core' that could no longer be maintained (Westergaard, 1961: 93). By the end of the decade the need was felt for a machinery of government appropriate to planning and coordinating metropolitan development.

A strategic authority for London

The powerful LCC had exercised all the important local authority functions from the cultural and recreational to education, housing and health. It was said of the LCC during its heyday of 1929–1939 that it had become the 'greatest Local Health Authority in the Empire', while even its critics described the progress made in the development of the LCC hospital service as 'remarkable'. The council was able to make use of the General Powers Act, which meant it could propose extensions to its powers every year, and which sometimes succeeded. The largest and most ambitious of all municipal authorities, the LCC governed the capital for 76 years without challenge to its authority. However, with loss of population and industry to suburbs, and at a time when the future for metropolitan London seemed to promise only more growth and change, it soon became apparent that the LCC was increasingly becoming irrelevant to the metropolitan problem.

It was hoped that the abolition of LCC in 1965 and its replacement by the GLC would provide a new strategic direction for London, providing better coordination of the capital's services and a wider geographical locus. The GLC was seen as a genuine 'metropolitan' authority in that it appeared to cover a more appropriate area by incorporating the London suburbs. Its strategic functions included building the roads network, land-use planning and housing redistribution. The GLC included 'inner London', marked by the boundaries of the old LCC, and a ring of local authorities known as 'outer London', but several significant parts of the Outer Metropolitan Area

(OMA) still lay outside its jurisdiction, mainly due to resistance from local authorities against their incorporation into the new London-wide arrangements. In addition, the government plan for the metropolitan administration was significantly different to the original master plan in that it created new inner-city boroughs of almost twice the size of those proposed by the Herbert Commission in 1960. For what some critics termed the 'bricks and mortar' conurbation, the commission had recommended a metropolitan form of government with the establishment of a council for Greater London and 52 London boroughs.

The commission's idea was that the new council should be a new type of authority, focusing on metropolitan infrastructure and strategic planning and with area-wide responsibilities covering planning, traffic, refuse disposal, fire and ambulance services and general education policy. The council would also share with local boroughs some services relating to parks, open spaces, sewerage and land drainage, while the boroughs were to be the primary units of local government in charge of housing, health, welfare and children services, environmental health, roads and planning applications. The council's most important task was the preparation of a Greater London Development Plan (GLDP). In essence it was to function as a regional authority.

But the reality was different. The now powerful 32 London boroughs that comprised some of the largest and most affluent localities, together with the City of London, tended to resist any encroachment by the GLC, which rarely had the power to enforce its will. More crucially, the emerging disparities between inner-city boroughs and outer London boroughs led to political tensions within the GLC limits. The interests of the outer London boroughs, many of which had enjoyed the respect and cooperation of their former county councils (and some of which had previously enjoyed county borough status) were not at synergy with those of the GLC.

The conflicts did not arise as much from the strategic responsibilities of the GLC as from the concurrent powers that acknowledged both the boroughs and the GLC interests. The council found itself in the uncomfortable position of suffering from a lack of strategic and executive competencies to fulfil its planning and steering function – as originally envisaged by the London Government Act of 1965 – while at the same time being accused of being a monstrous bureaucratic apparatus. Important sources of conflict, for example, concerned decisions which had to be referred to the GLC for advice and which then became subject to GLC direction whenever boroughs proposed to grant planning permissions. Here, the GLC had to be notified by the boroughs of any planning applications and, although it could not directly intervene, it could request the minister to call in the application for his decision with the benefit of the GLC's advice (Self, 1971). Likewise, the GLC's rationale was the coordination of land-use planning and transport. Arguably, in order to perform that role effectively it needed the authority to override and give binding directions to the boroughs. In reality, even the limited powers the GLC possessed led it into corrosive disputes with the boroughs. There were,

56 London

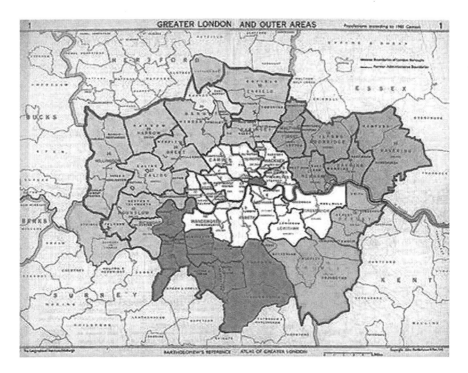

Figure 3.1 Map of Greater London
Source: HarperCollins.

therefore, several weaknesses that were not immediately apparent when the new council was established. First, 'functional London' extended far beyond the GLC area, so it made less sense in planning terms than it first appeared. Second, its vulnerability to electoral backlash led it often to shy away from conflict. Third, it failed to win confrontations with boroughs, especially over housing redistribution.

The abolition of the Greater London Council

All in all, these shortcomings of the GLC impacted upon its organisational effectiveness and political viability and in the long run it was not robust enough to stand the inherent tensions of its institutional architecture. In the words of an independent commentator, 'the GLC's failure can be summed up thus: it did the things it was supposed to do badly or not at all, and it tried to do too many things it should never have tried to do' (Hall, 1989: 170). In 1986, under the guise of 'streamlining the cities' the Thatcher government abolished the GLC, together with the other metropolitan authorities that had been set up in 1974 on a similar model.

The abolition of the GLC left London's future in the hands of central government, the 32 London boroughs and a web of joint arrangements. A number of city-wide operating single-purpose agencies as well as ad-hoc boards and committees completed the new landscape of London's government structure. These arrangements were firmly in place for the next 14 years, during which the role of the London Planning Advisory Committee (LPAC), responsible for the capital's planning, was paramount. Comprising chief executives, borough planners, engineers, surveyors and finance officers, LPAC's principal task and *raison d'être* was to make representations to the secretary of state on behalf of the London boroughs over the periodic strategic guidance that provided a framework of general policy within which boroughs prepared their own Unitary Development Plans (UDPs). Another major role of LPAC was to advise, on behalf of London boroughs, on major development proposals before local planning committees and be an important player within the London and South East Regional Planning Conference (SERPLAN). SERPLAN's main role was to offer strategic direction on major transport and planning issues facing the region, coordinating joint policies on waste disposal, regional shopping centres, maintenance of open land on the green belt, and the allocation of land for housing. A new organisation, London First, emerged to bring together London borough leaders, the voluntary sector and leading private sector interests. It took the lead role in shaping the debate on the future of London's government. London First launched the London Pride initiative to promote the locational advantages of London as a world city and business centre, demonstrating that the abolition of the GLC created new opportunities for business and the City of London to play a lead role.

Rethinking London governance: post-GLC

None of these developments and initiatives, however, solved 'the London problem'. During the 1990s, debate shifted towards the idea of a democratically elected strategic authority for London: 'in the long term establishing the strategic authority could offer scope for much larger savings on service delivery by major London-wide devolved services ... by allowing them to improve coordination, acquire facilities jointly, and share core administrative functions' (ALG, 1996: 12). The need to provide democratic leadership, promote London as a world city, and bridge the gap between community-led and national government resulted in new arrangements for London, which centred on a new elected body – the GLA – and the mayor. Elected in 2000, the relationship between the mayor and assembly was to be based on separation of powers, with the principal executive authority being vested in the mayor and the role of the assembly confined to securing the accountability of the mayor on behalf of Londoners. An elected mayor would negotiate with key players to provide vision and a direction for London's future, drive the development of the city and bring together the partnerships needed to make things happen. Diffusion, not concentration, of power was seen as the most appropriate approach to this new form of metropolitan governance. In part, this was to be achieved through checks and balances and an elaborate system of constraints to prevent an undue concentration of power in the mayor's office. The relationship between assembly and mayor was seen as the key to the success of the new system, and so division of power was essential to ensure that each had something with which to bargain.

Key metropolitan functions were separated from the GLA, but accountable to it through the mayor appointing their board members. Transport for London (TfL) absorbed London Transport and the functions of the highway agencies, and took overall responsibility for roads, buses, trains and the underground. The mayor, as chair of TfL, was responsible for drawing all these modes of transport together through the preparation of an integrated transport strategy for the capital. Likewise, the London Development Agency (LDA) became a major instrument of economic growth policies, taking over from central government funds for inward investment and regeneration, and land acquisition powers from English Partnerships (Pimlott and Rao, 2002: 64). Two other bodies – the Metropolitan Police Authority (MPA), which became the first locally accountable body, and the London Fire and Emergency Planning Authority (LFEPA) – were similarly structured. The mayor assumed significant planning powers over both overall strategy and development control, with responsibility for preparing a spatial development strategy for the improvement of London's physical fabric, housing, culture, economic regeneration and role as a world financial centre: in effect a *London plan*. Despite initial tensions and conflicts, the new arrangements for London, under Mayor Ken Livingstone, worked well to ensure that key infrastructure issues and problems of traffic and congestion, crime and policing were being addressed effectively. The new institution of the mayor as a single voice for London offered a new prospect of defining and speaking for the metropolitan community, even if the form in which Mayor Livingstone espoused this concept failed to command universal assent (Pimlott and Rao, 2002; Rao, 2002).

Among the important functions, those relating to planning, housing and waste proved the most contentious. Under the Greater London Authority Act 1999 (GLAA), the mayor was responsible for the overall planning framework while the boroughs were to operate development control. Approved by the secretary of state, the new Local Development Schemes (LDS), prepared by the boroughs, were required to be brought into conformity to the mayor's London Plan and would be subject to public inquiry.

Given the importance of affordable housing to the recruitment and retention of key workers in London's economy, Mayor Livingstone set a strategic target to increase the provision of affordable housing in the capital. His target was for 50 per cent of all new dwellings to be affordable and, within this, he sought to achieve 35 per cent social rented housing and 15 per cent intermediate housing. Some boroughs had already adopted the 50 per cent target; others wanted to see a greater increase in private housing or were more pragmatic. But the diffusion of responsibility was such that the mayor could only lead by persuasion. The GLA had no housing powers, and the mayor's targets relied for their achievement on developers proposing, and boroughs agreeing, affordable housing schemes. With no powers to provide or fund the provision of housing, which rested with the Housing Corporation, the mayor's only means of enforcing the affordability quota was to refuse consent for major development.

The organisation of waste was highly decentralised, with boroughs retaining primary responsibility for waste collection and waste planning. The City Corporation and 11 of the boroughs were individually responsible for waste disposal, while the remainder were organised into four statutory joint (sub-regional) waste disposal authorities acting on their behalf. The mayor had a statutory obligation to produce a regional framework for waste planning as part of the London Plan, but not accorded the powers to secure its implementation.

A new approach to planning

One of GLA's successes has been the new planning regime for London, encapsulated in the Spatial Development Strategy (SDS), which addressed the differences between inner and outer London and between east and west, and growth in the development corridors critical to London's economic regeneration and prosperity. For the first time, the heart of Greater London had achieved physical expression in the planning process. The GLA Act shifted the responsibility for strategic planning from the boroughs collectively, and from the secretary of state, to the mayor, who was empowered to monitor the implementation of the SDSs and of the boroughs' plans. Although, in one sense, the SDS fulfilled the functions of the earlier GLDP, it was not in itself a development plan and fell outside the mainstream of the statutory planning system. It was specifically intended that the SDS would not be a revival of the GLDP, but an entirely new kind of plan that set out the spatial implications of the other statutory strategies that the mayor needed to publish along with his other policies. Despite all the rhetoric of devolution and novelty, the SDS was in practice too closely controlled by the central government. The secretary of state retained the power to intervene if the SDS was found to depart from national or regional policies or was detrimental to the interests of an area outside Greater London. In formulating the SDS the mayor was required to have regard to a wide range of matters, some of which were matters of judgement by the secretary of state, who was also responsible for issuing regional planning guidance for London and adjoining areas.

Whereas overall responsibility for formulating the SDS rested with the mayor, that for economic development was located with the LDA. The mayor appointed the LDA's board and held it to account. The development agency declared a number of objectives as the basis for an agreed economic policy for London, central to which was the promotion of London as a

60 *London*

sustainable world city. It worked closely with private and public investors and the GLA on its spatial development proposals to empower London's communities. However, it was abolished in March 2012 and some of its functions transferred back to the GLA. Other residual tasks, particularly those relating to sites developed for the 2012 Olympic Games for which it acted as land assembly agency, were entrusted to the London Legacy Development Corporation.

In July 2011, Mayor Boris Johnson – elected in May 2008 – published a new London Plan, following his consultation on *Planning for a Better London*. The revised plan set out a fully integrated economic, environmental, transport and social framework for the development of London for the next 25 years. It forms part of the development plan for Greater London. As with its predecessor, its policies guide decisions on planning applications by councils, and the mayor and London boroughs' local plans had to be in general conformity with the London Plan. The plan forms an essential part of achieving sustainable development and a more inclusive society in London.

The mayor's vision for a polycentric enlargement across the megacity region involves the development of central London, London's town centres and towns in the wider region in a complementary manner. The expansion of Milton Keynes, Thames Gateway, London–Stansted–Cambridge–Peterborough and Ashford are major initiatives to ease pressure on land and complement the growth strategy for London. As the London Plan emphasised:

> London exerts a substantial effect over south-east England. It is inextricably linked with this wider region, whether looked at in terms of patterns of employment, skills and education, housing markets, town centres and planning for retail, airport policy, patterns of commuting, responding to environmental challenges like climate change, management of resources like water and energy, Green Belt, waterways and open spaces or the handling of waste.
>
> (Greater London Authority, 2002: 44)

The mayor's priority is to put in place appropriate arrangements for effective planning for London city region and to support cross-boundary work where appropriate.

Enhanced powers for the mayor

Since his first election, Mayor Livingstone had periodically sought to extend his remit, and in his second term proved in a stronger position to win increased powers from the government. A comprehensive package of proposals was put by the mayor's office to ministers. The government responded in 2005 with a consultation paper *The Greater London Authority: The Government's Proposals for Additional Powers and Responsibilities for the Mayor and Assembly*, declaring that:

The Mayor and Assembly have a pivotal role to play in ensuring London's continued success, and that it is crucial to have in place the right governance arrangements to meet the Capital's strategic challenges over the longer term. Additional powers and responsibilities for the GLA in key strategic services would help meet those challenges and underpin the Mayor's strategic leadership of London.

(ODPM, 2005: para. 2.21)

For the most part, the changes envisaged involved further delegation from central government in the fields of housing, planning, waste disposal and further education. Some of these proposals were supported, and some not, by the Commission on London Governance, a body made up of GLA members and representatives of the borough leaders (Commission on London Governance, 2006). In housing, the mayor was given the responsibility for developing the London Housing Strategy, to make recommendations to the national government on the distribution of housing capital allocations, and decide the allocation of affordable housing investment in London. The responsibility for the London Housing Board was also transferred from the Government Office for London (GOL) to the mayor. London's first statutory housing strategy was published in February 2010. In planning, the mayor was given considerable additional powers, enabling him to direct the boroughs to amend their local development schemes, direct their Development Plan Documents (DPDs) to ensure consistency with the London Plan, and become the development control authority for certain classes of applications in relation to defined strategic sites.

As regards waste management and waste planning, while the option to create a single waste authority for London accountable to the mayor was considered, other possibilities included an extension of joint arrangements to create a sub-regional pattern for waste disposal. Under the former, the mayor would be responsible for planning all waste streams in London, with powers to identify sites and compulsorily purchase land. Alternatively, a single borough-led waste authority would assume these powers.

Learning and skills issues cover post-16 education and much of 14–19 education. Responsibility rested traditionally with the Learning and Skills Council (LSC), which had an important role in funding further education colleges and sixth form provision. The LSC had five local centres in the geographical area of the GLA. The mayor's responsibility for the LDA, his concern for opportunity and London labour markets, and the fact that travel to work areas (TTWAs) do not map onto any local administrative boundary led him to bid for a merger of the five LSC centres into one regional organisation accountable to himself. The government incorporated the mayor's proposals in their consultation options, but with a strong steer towards a more limited change to strengthening the then existing LSC arrangements.

Many other detailed proposals for change were put out for consultation, including a broadening of the mayor's involvement in local and sub-regional issues and establishing clearer lines of responsibility for the GLA group of agencies. The most significant of these concerned responsibility for the police, for which the government proposed that the mayor should become chair of the MPA. The Association of London Government (ALG) – controlled by the Labour Party at the same time as the national government – supported much of the enhanced plan, with the exception of the planning proposals, although the views of individual boroughs differed widely. However, the 2006 local elections changed the balance of power on the ALG markedly, with the Conservatives controlling fourteen boroughs, Labour eight, and the Liberal Democrats three. The new political alignments would bear directly upon the mayor's ability to overcome borough resistance.

New developments in London's housing

In April 2012, the mayor gained responsibility for strategic housing, regeneration and economic development in the capital. The Localism Act, 2011, devolved the powers and responsibilities of the Homes and Communities Agency (HCA) to the mayor and removed all legal restrictions on expenditure housing by the mayor. These powers are now exercised within the GLA, directly under the mayor, rather than through an external body. The Localism Act also abolished the LDA, and its regeneration functions transferred to the GLA, together with the property, rights and liabilities of the London Thames Gateway Development Corporation (LTGDC). A new Housing and Land Directorate of the GLA brought together the former housing and land roles and responsibilities of the GLA, LDA, LTGDC and the HCA in London.

In November 2013 the mayor launched the consultation of his new, revised, draft London Housing Strategy, which aimed to build at least 42,000 new homes per annum for the next ten years, of which 15,000 would be affordable and 5,000 for long-term market rent. During the 2015–2018 investment period 40 per cent of affordable housing is to be designed for low-cost home ownership. The strategy sets out an ambitious new programme for London, based on a Strategic Housing Market Assessment (SHMA), which would address the shortfalls and provide for a better mix of housing. The housing strategy also calls for a relaxation of borrowing rules, to be accompanied in parallel by the devolution of property taxes to London government. The proposal enjoyed the support of the London Finance Commission, which examined the case in detail and called for the devolution of the full suite of London's property taxation, including council tax, business rates, annual tax on enveloped dwellings and capital gains property disposal tax. A devolved arrangement would include setting the tax rates and decisions over matters such as revaluation, banding and discounts. Such devolution would

> revolutionise the ability to address London's housing challenges, and to adjust property taxation to achieve a greater efficiency and fairness that reflects London's particular circumstances. It would represent a

significant ongoing income stream against which the Mayor and local boroughs could pump-prime infrastructure funding to unlock housing growth, invest in estate regeneration, and significantly expand the supply of homes of all tenures through grant, gap and equity funding. It would help to create greater confidence for developers to make long-term investments and get more complex and long-term schemes underway. This would have particular importance for bringing forward some of London's strategic sites within the Opportunity Areas that are fundamental to the delivery of additional homes in London, but where remediation, land assembly, infrastructure and other 'abnormal' costs demand a public-private partnership approach.

(Greater London Authority, 2013: 38)

The strategy identifies London's 33 Opportunity Areas as representing the greatest potential to build high-density housing on existing brownfield sites. These areas would provide 290,000 new homes, nearly 70 per cent of the 420,000 homes London needs over the coming decade (Greater London Authority, 2013: 42). A new board, Homes for London, which has an equal membership of mayoral appointees and borough representatives, is to oversee housing investment and delivery in the capital and contribute to the London Housing Strategy and the mayor's housing investment and business plan. Its other responsibilities include monitoring delivery of the housing programme, advising the mayor on risks relating to housing delivery, and providing guidance on decisions relating to GLA land and property holdings.

Traffic and transport in London

The problem of traffic and congestion on London roads is acute. Congestion on the main radial routes is heavy in peak hours, but some of the worst congestion is also experienced in and around suburban town centres. Although congestion charging has made a difference in central London, it is difficult to quantify by how much and for how long. The increase in congestion does not appear to be directly related to the volume of traffic, which, over London as a whole, remained fairly static throughout the 1990s. Although the total number of vehicles entering London has continued to increase, the rate of growth has slowed and while the number of vehicles entering inner London also increased, it has done so less sharply. Road management policies according greater priority to buses, cyclists and pedestrians, increases in road works brought about by the rise in the number of utility companies and by traffic enforcement practices that are not geared to facilitating traffic flow have been important contributory factors.

The growth in population and employment forecast in the mayor's London Plan is expected to lead to an increase in traffic. TfL has estimated that traffic volume will increase by 14 per cent by 2016. Boris Johnson's revised vision and strategy for transport (MTS) sets out London's projected growth beyond

2017, which is predicted to have an impact on the capacity of the transport system, road congestion and air quality (Greater London Authority, 2009: 4). The strategy takes into account the capital's success in being awarded the Olympic and Paralympic Games, parliament's approval of Crossrail, and the implementation of the PPP for the upgrade of the London Underground system (Greater London Authority, 2010).

The mayor's vision for London transport is unequivocal: it is for the city to excel on the world stage, expanding opportunities for all its people and enterprises, achieving the highest environmental standards and quality of life, and providing global leadership to tackle the urban challenges of the twenty-first century (Greater London Authority, 2010: 7). More specifically, his overarching vision aims to ensure that London is poised to meet the challenges of economic and population growth, and that the city remains internationally competitive and successful, with diverse, strong, secure and accessible neighbourhoods and access to jobs, opportunities and facilities.

Priority areas for transport improvement

The revised transport strategy places renewed emphasis on transforming the tube network to enable Londoners to enjoy 'thirty per cent more capacity, more stations with step-free access, a fleet of new air-conditioned trains and modern signalling systems' (Greater London Authority, 2010: 6). Major improvements in rail are also envisaged over a longer period, with the objective of reducing overcrowding, greater use of Crossrail and providing better north–south links across central London through substantial upgrades to Thameslink. London's cycling revolution was to be delivered mainly by improving infrastructure, which included providing more special cycle routes and secure cycle parks, and by the provision of better information and training (Greater London Authority, 2010: 7). The new 'cycle superhighways' are underway and the mayor is keen to encourage cycling in outer London through cycle hubs and by creating a local culture of cycling, which would see boroughs becoming 'Biking Boroughs'. With regard to London's bus service (described as the 'workhorse of London's transport system'), the main objective is to ensure that all buses entering service from 2012 have environmentally friendly engines. The mayor also proposed the introduction of a new bus based on the classic Routemaster, and to provide passengers with better information about services. These improvements were about making easy connections between railways, buses, underground, road and river services. It was deemed important to create better links between places in inner and outer London so that journeys could avoid congested central London areas.

One of the key aims of the MTS, published in May 2010, was to enhance expansion of rail services right across the region, an expansion designed to increase capacity, especially during the peak hours, by 30 per cent between 2006 and 2031. The bulk of this operation involves providing new trains, or lengthening existing ones, upgrading lines, adding new routes, and increasing frequency. Another objective is to improve transport connectivity through Crossrail, by increasing river crossings in east London and improving interchange between radial and orbital rail lines with a view to facilitating orbital travel. The largest civil engineering project in Europe, Crossrail is expected to launch in 2017 and increase capacity by a further 10 per cent. The Docklands Light Railway's (DLR) capacity is being increased by 50 per cent. The mayor is committed to achieving this despite the delays caused by difficulties with the contracts and with the private sector companies delivering them (Greater London Authority, 2010).

These strategies are to be implemented in conjunction with the London boroughs, taking into account local transport needs and aiming to 'enhance the vitality of Outer London' by improving links to and between metropolitan town centres (Greater London Authority, 2010: 17). Road congestion is estimated to cost £2 billion per year. The mayor's package of measures to tackle this problem includes improved traffic control, reducing the effects of road works, good maintenance of road network assets, and the development of the road network. The MTS proposes that, during the life of the strategy, the mayor may consider road user charging schemes if other measures prove to be inadequate or ineffective. The strategy supports 'the innovative remaking of London's streets through flagship schemes and good practice using "better streets" principles' (Greater London Authority, 2010: 18). Partnership is identified as key to ensuring that safety and security is maintained and improved. Improving connectivity, enhancing the urban realm and providing better accessibility are seen as ways to combat issues of deprivation, antisocial behaviour and fear of crime.

Securing the funding for the delivery of the transport strategy is predicated on a partnership between a wide range of stakeholders, including the boroughs, national government, Network Rail, the LDA, and various other bodies (Greater London Authority, 2010: 25). Over the years to 2018, funding committed to transport infrastructure stands at around £4.8 billion per year. Beyond and through to 2031, a further annual investment of between £3.5 billion to £4.5 billion is estimated (Greater London Authority, 2010: 315). TfL receives funding from a number of sources, including government grants, revenue from fares and other sources such as the congestion charge, secondary income from advertising and other activities, prudential borrowing against future revenue, private sector contributions, direct borough funding and other government funding sources such as allocations to support regeneration. The national government has committed to providing £39.2 billion of funding through to 2017/2018, although any funding is predicated on TfL maximising the benefits of already-secured schemes and investments and ensuring that it receives the best possible return from future investments. In this vein, sharing operational costs is a potentially attractive option.

The overall effectiveness of the MTL is monitored and reported annually through the 'Travel in London' report. Specifically, the outcomes are monitored through collecting and publishing strategic outcome indicators (SOIs).

66 *London*

Although the expected outcomes of the MTS are not statutory targets, the mayor may set certain statutory targets from time to time with respect to the delivery of the strategy, which might relate to mode share, carbon emissions, road safety, cycling, use of the River Thames, better streets, and air quality.

Blurred accountabilities in the governance of London

The creation of the GLA in 2000 marked the opening of a new era in the governance of metropolitan London. Drawing inspiration from the experiences of other great cities, the new authority replaced the plethora of bodies and joint arrangements that had characterised London governance for almost three decades. Foremost among the arguments for change was the need to provide clear mechanisms of accountability so that Londoners would understand the ways in which issues of concern to them were being addressed, and by whom, thus enabling them to hold the management of London to account. Although the relationships established by the GLA amount – at first sight – to a substantial streamlining of the government of London, a closer inspection reveals that the new system retains some of the diffused responsibilities and blurred accountabilities that have long characterised London governance.

Take, for example, the plethora of bodies concerned with the management of London's waste. The UK government has implemented European Commission Directives on landfill, recycling rates and producer responsibility, set regional targets for recycling, and established a Waste and Resources Action Programme (WRAP) to develop new markets for recycled products. London Remade plays a similar role to WRAP at the London level, while the London Community Recycling Network supports communities' engagement in waste and recycling, the LDA seeks to promote the 'green economy' and the Environment Agency monitors and regulates the whole. Lines of authority and accountability are complex. Within the context of these initiatives, the Mayor's Municipal Waste Strategy seeks to bring about more sustainable waste management in the capital. For their part, the London boroughs have statutory obligations to collect, manage and dispose of waste, for which purpose a number of inter-borough arrangements have been developed. The mayor has little direct power with respect to waste management at the borough level, while the boroughs themselves have different waste management processes, and relate to the central and regional funding streams in ways that express their own local priorities and preferences.

Likewise in London's transport, notwithstanding the mayor's formal powers, there is no discernible overall strategy for managing traffic and the road network in London and no single point of responsibility within this complex of TfL, boroughs, the Highways Agency, public utilities and enforcement agencies. The Highways Agency is responsible for motorways within London, while the mayor has responsibility for the Transport for London Roads Network (TLRN), the strategic network of 550 kilometres, representing just

5 per cent of the total network, but carrying a third of the traffic. The remaining 13,000 kilometres of roads are the responsibility of the boroughs, and the way that the boroughs manage them has a major impact on the performance of the strategic network and of the transport system as a whole.

Each borough's UDP, now replaced by a Local Development Strategy, defines priorities for roads, but problems arise where roads cross borough boundaries. Problems of accountability also arise when road works are carried out, whether instigated in order to repair roads, introduce new traffic management measures, repair or renew worn-out public utility pipes and cables, or make connections to premises. Londoners do not know to whom they should complain when such road works lead to perennial congestion. The boroughs maintain their own information systems for those road works that arise from their own activities, but they neither hold data from the utility companies nor promote coordination at the boundaries between boroughs.

The London media are quick to highlight the inconveniences caused by road works, whether by the lack of coordination between contractors leading to the same stretch of road being dug up many times, a lack of urgency in completing the work, or poor re-instatement requiring further work to make it good. Finally, problems also manifest themselves when attempting effective enforcement of traffic, loading and parking regulations in order to prevent infringements. The police traffic wardens enforce parking control on red routes, the busiest roads, and borough parking attendants on other routes. Bus lanes are enforced partly by cameras operated by the boroughs, partly by TfL, and partly by the police.

The mayor's determinations of planning matters are also subject to the overriding powers of the secretary of state to call in planning applications of national importance. Yet virtually any major development in the capital could be regarded as being of national importance, allowing the secretary of state to second-guess the mayor's judgement. Confusion in the planning system is compounded by English Heritage's right to press the secretary of state to call in any application to which it objects.

Likewise, much of the case for creating a mayor as a single focus for promotion – the 'voice for London' argument – rested on the assumption that the mayor alone would act as the beacon for attracting inward investment and enhancing London's competitiveness in the world markets. In reality, the mayor does not have sole responsibility for promoting London. That role is shared with other bodies, many of which are overseen by different Whitehall departments. They include the London Tourist Board with its Visit London campaign to attract tourists and business visitors, which comes under the purview of the Department of Culture, Media and Sport (DCMS), as does London International Sport, which aims to bring international events to London. The Department of Trade and Industry (DTI) has an important stake, expressed through two partnerships with predominantly private sector bodies: Trade Partners UK, with the London Chamber of Commerce and Industry (LCCI) for export promotion; and the London First Centre, which seeks inward investment. At the local level there are sub-regional partnerships; inescapably, the Government Office for London (GOL) attempts to take an overview of all these activities.

If the effectiveness of the new government of London is to be judged solely as a strategic authority providing public services, then it is apparent that the confusion, conflict and overlap that arise from multiple players impede transparency and accountability. More fundamentally, if the objective of the GLA Act was to create an authority for London with clearly focused and visible leadership, then the public must know who to hold accountable, and how, when things go wrong. This, however, is far from the case. The institutions of mayor and assembly and the dynamics of the relationship between them and other agencies has been in constant flux.

Towards greater self-government for London

New forms of governance and cooperation have continued to evolve since the establishment of the Greater London Authority in 2000. Greater coordination and sharing of complementary responsibilities is seen as central to resolving issues of crime reduction, the promotion of economic prosperity, widening access to culture and sport, and improving community safety.

The London City Charter

The London City Charter, the first statutory charter, was conceived by the mayor, the boroughs and the City of London Corporation in April 2009, and intended to give a more unified voice to elected leaders and authorities. It identified key priorities in terms of joint action by London's government and set out the possible future relationship between London's elected government and Whitehall. More specifically, the charter aimed to ensure open and transparent decision making and efficient public services. The charter 'is not a legal or quasi-statutory document' (London Councils, 2009: 3). Nor is it comprehensive – in the sense that it does not cover all the ways in which the mayor and boroughs interact. Rather, it is a work in progress that is intended to evolve with London. As such, it reflects current positions and legislation and describes devolution to local and regional government in London.

The main principle upon which the London charter was founded was that decisions affecting Londoners should be made at the most local level possible. As such, the mayor and leaders are committed to maximising the level of local and regional control. The role of the mayor and the GLA Group (the five organisations for which the mayor sets the budget) on the one hand, and the boroughs and City Corporation, on the other, varies depending on the nature of the issues. Issues where the mayor has a clear statutory role to which borough policies must conform include housing, transport and planning. Here, the boroughs can influence and shape delivery strategies. In respect of planning, strategic policy direction is set through the London Plan, while, in housing, the New Homes and Communities Agency London Board, chaired by the mayor, has strong London and local accountability, with three borough-elected members on the board. Boroughs have a statutory role in the delivery of education and social care and the role of the mayor is simply to complement or support local government. In the case of services delivered by national agencies or departments, such as the health service, the mayor and boroughs are required to act jointly to influence service delivery.

The Congress of Leaders

Chaired by the mayor and consisting of 34 members, including the mayor, deputy mayor and leaders of boroughs, the Congress of Leaders aims to promote the 'good governance of London' by identifying and discussing priority issues for Londoners such as economic recovery, healthcare, crime, effective policing and climate change. A key priority is providing effective transport for Londoners and the vision is to be achieved through a number of specific strategies. One of these involves the devolution of powers from TLRN to the boroughs themselves. The boroughs are also expected to have a greater degree of engagement in the revised mayor's transport strategy. Further options include boroughs attaining greater local influence and management of bus routes, as well as future strategies for door-to-door transport. Finally, local implementation plans, which allow local partners more flexibility, are to be revised, and cycling and walking are to be promoted.

The congress is driven by the need to achieve coordination of GLA and borough policies for the benefit of London as a whole, acknowledging that London's rapid and sustainable economic performance depends upon 'concerted and coordinated public intervention from national, regional and local government' (London Councils, 2009: 6). Joint action is proposed in a number of areas, the first of which is the promotion of positive procurement practices that maximise training and employment opportunities from large capital projects in London. The GLA Group, and local government, in particular, commit to delivering 5,000 apprenticeships over three years in cooperation with partners such as Crossrail. The relevant parties also commit to working towards achieving economic prosperity throughout London by increasing export, tourism and inward investment, as well as by supporting local economies and town centres.

While it is for the Congress of Leaders to agree policies, the Charter Board is tasked with the responsibility to deliver agreed actions. Comprising the chief officers of each authority, the aim of the board is to provide professional support to the Congress of Leaders, to help determine key issues and priorities, and to put in place policies and mechanisms to deliver the objectives of the congress. The membership of the board is wide ranging and comprises the chief executive of the GLA, representatives of the chief executives of the London boroughs and head of London councils, town clerk of the City of London Corporation, and commissioners of police, transport, fire, health and economic development. The board is tasked with coordinating advice, resources and actions effectively, with no legal delivery mandate of its own.

Looking to the future, while asserting that the directly elected mayor and assembly is an innovation which has improved strategic focus and leadership at the regional level, the London charter acknowledges the need for securing further devolution and self-governance. In support of this, it cites the Central-Local Concordat of 2007 which urges cooperation between central and local governments as a way to make public funding and spending more transparent and allowing councils greater flexibility and autonomy (London Councils, 2009: 12). Thus, Boris Johnson and Councillor Merrick Cockell, Chairman of London Councils, called upon central government to acknowledge that London's unique governance model is mature, efficient and accountable and so to 'devolve further powers, responsibilities and fiscal capacity to London's elected governments' (London Councils, 2009).

Localism and the 'turn to community'

Complementing the London charter is the Localism Act, 2011, representing yet another attempt to strengthening decision making at the local level. This features a range of reforms that give greater powers to councils and neighbourhoods over such matters as housing, planning, infrastructure, local service provision and local governance. Councils are given general power of competence, giving them more freedom to work together in creative and innovative ways, allowing them to choose to return to a committee system of governance and providing for referendums for elected mayors in certain authorities. Residents are given powers to instigate local referendums on local issues and to veto excessive council tax increases.

The Localism Act gave new housing and regeneration powers to the GLA, while abolishing the LDA. The planning and regeneration provisions called for abolishing Regional Spatial Strategies and the Infrastructure Planning Commission. Changes to the Community Infrastructure Levy are significant, allowing a proportion of the money raised by the levy to be passed to community groups to be spent in accordance with their local priorities. The intention was to put in place a more locally driven and democratically accountable system underpinned by financial incentives and revenue streams to deliver growth. To this end, government ministers are able to transfer local public functions from central government and remote quangos to local authorities, combined authorities and economic prosperity boards in order to improve local accountability or promote economic growth, although the secretary of state retains powers to take the final decision on major infrastructure proposals of national importance.

The government set out its vision of localism as 'one where power is decentralised to the lowest possible level'. For services that are used individually, this means putting power in the hands of individuals themselves. Where services are enjoyed collectively, they are to be delivered by responsible community groups or, where the scale is too large, by local authorities themselves, subject to democratic checks and balances. The reforms took effect in April 2012 and gave town and parish councils the opportunity to create plans with statutory weight. They empower groups to allow certain kinds of development without planning permission. It is the government's view that neighbourhoods will use their powers to shape the design and location of development. There are additional opportunities and freedoms for local groups to deliver local authority services or bid for community assets, including *Community Right to Challenge*, which would enable community groups to submit an 'expression of interest' to deliver local authority services; if accepted by the Council, this would trigger a procurement process whereby the challenger can bid for the contract. The *Community Right to Buy* would give local groups extra time to bid for and purchase such community assets as pubs, post offices, community halls or leisure centres. To strengthen further the role of local communities in planning, the act introduced a new requirement for developers to consult local communities before submitting planning applications for certain developments.

This drive to enhance local control of decisions is not new. For several decades now, successive governments have promised greater local accountability as an attempt to counter growing apathy and civic disengagement in politics and community life, each launching a wide range of consultation documents, pilots and initiatives to boost local participation in decision making. 'Power to the People' was the dominant theme in the politics of the late 1960s and early 1970s. In 1969, the Skeffington Report on *Participation in Planning* first established the right for the public to be consulted in development plans and promoted public engagement in planning. This was accompanied by a shift in the understanding of planning as essentially part of both representative and participatory forms of democracy, and the early 1970s saw increased mobilisation by community and tenant groups in local politics.

The need for positive engagement with the planning process became even more important following town and country reforms of the 1990s. The Town and Country Planning Act (TCPA), 1990, made it a requirement for planning applications to be determined in accordance with the Development Plan unless material considerations indicated otherwise. Development Plans encouraged local people to participate actively in the preparation of plans from the earliest stages so that they could be fully involved in decisions about the pattern of development in their area. The idea was that 'consultation with the general public, community groups, business, development and infrastructure interests would help local planning authorities secure a degree of consensus over the future development and use of land in their area' (PPG12). Following this, the Urban Task Force's report *Towards an Urban Renaissance* emphasised the need for public participation and involvement in the development of urban vision statements that underpinned the concept of sustainable communities (Urban Task Force, 1999).

In 2010, the Conservative Party's Green Paper on *Open Source Planning* reiterated the importance of civic engagement as the best way to balance growing the economy with sustainable development of places in which people wanted to live. It outlined policies such as the removal of regional bodies and regulations, proposed a new tranche of elected mayors, introduced police commissioners and required councils to pass powers down to local citizens. Communities should be given the greatest possible opportunity to have their say: 'If we enable communities to find their own ways of overcoming tensions between development and conservation, local people can become proponents rather than opponents of appropriate economic growth' (Conservative Party, 2010). The White Paper *Open Public Services*, published the following year, affirmed:

> We want control of public services to be as close to people as possible. Wherever possible we want to decentralise power to the individuals who use a service. But where a service is used by a community collectively, the control over services needs to be exercised by a representative body. In these circumstances ... the principle should be to decentralise power to the lowest appropriate level. For many services, this will mean the community groups and neighbourhood councils to whom power is decentralised, while for others it may be local authorities and other elected bodies such as a parish council taking responsibility.
> (HM Government, 2011: 8)

This commitment formed the basis of the coalition government's agenda for planning reform as expressed through the Localism Bill and the subsequent act of 2011.

The National Planning Policy Framework

The Localism Act was to be taken forward through detailed regulations and the National Planning Policy Framework (NPPF) that came into effect in 2012. At the heart of current national planning policy is the presumption in favour of sustainable development. It requires local planning authorities to prepare plans on the basis that objectively assessed development needs should be met, and with sufficient flexibility to respond to changes in demands, and to approve development proposals that comply with statutory plans without delay and grant permission where a plan is absent, silent, indeterminate or where relevant policies are out of date. The application of the presumption will have consequences for how communities engage in neighbourhood planning. The implication is that neighbourhoods should develop plans that support their strategic development needs, including policies for housing and economic development. A core principle is that the community should be in the driving seat of planning the future of their areas. A referendum at the end of the process ensures communities have the final say on whether a neighbourhood plan or development order or Community Right to Build order comes into force in their area.

Initial responses to the neighbourhood planning proposals from local authorities were mixed. Some planners took the view that these powers would hinder London's ability to grow, while others remained sceptical about the extent to which many of the proposals would actually work in practice. Evidence submitted in parliament to the Communities and Local Government Select Committee expressed several concerns, including communities' skills and capacities to shape plans effectively, the need to combine localism with sustainable development and the need for greater clarity in the scope and process of neighbourhood planning (Barclay, 2011). As the chief executive of the Town and Country Planning Association observed:

> Collaborative neighbourhood planning, so that more people can be involved in the process of shaping the places in which they live and work, is an opportunity to be grasped. However ... implementing such an ideal to be a meaningful choice will require communities to have intellectual as well as financial support.
> (TCPA, 2010)

Similarly, Planning Portal took the view that the bill was 'high on principle with neighbourhoods creating their own plans and granting development consents. It is unsurprisingly low on the detail of how this is to be achieved practically and fairly' (Milne, 2010).

However, the Centre for Cities, in a report on regeneration, illustrated just how neighbourhood plans might be used:

> Local and national politicians should accept that using regeneration plans to go for growth hasn't worked in every urban neighbourhood and can have negative as well as positive consequences on a city's economy and residents. A new way forward might mean building a park rather than a science park, or turning tiny terraces into larger homes, rather than knocking them down and building one-bed flats. Communities should be given the power to decide on plans, testing out the neighbourhood planning approach in the Localism Bill.
> (Centre for Cities, 2010)

The Manifesto for Londoners, published by the London Councils, proposed greater sensitivity in local provision: 'London boroughs [should] focus on joining up local public services through integrated commissioning that can respond more precisely to residents' needs and so deliver better outcomes ... giving people more power to shape decisions that affect them' (London Councils, 2009: 6–7). But as the Local Government Association observed:

> it has taken a long time for successive governments to give greater credence to the connection between people and place; the connection between how local perception and community spirit interacts with physical infrastructure like libraries, transport and superfast broadband access; the

connection between getting involved and making a difference, and standing back and having it done to you. There is something along the 'pride of place' theme that local regeneration programmes will need to tap into and make the most of. Whether such initiatives are called Big Society, community spirit and social bonds, or take place under a 'co-operative' umbrella, it all amounts to helping people to feel connected to their community and give them the opportunity to improve their quality of life.

(Howell, 2012)

Developing localism and engaging communities is particularly challenging in London. The presence of a strong regional tier, the 33 London boroughs, each acting as local planning authority for their administrative area, and the diversity of communities and neighbourhoods makes for a particularly complex landscape within which to implement the localism agenda. Even the perception of what constitutes a neighbourhood may vary across different communities and is something hard to prescribe. Importantly, in the absence of parish councils in London, there is no formal governance at sub-borough level. Neighbourhood planning would require the creation of neighbourhood forums to represent local people and these would have to be agreed by the borough, which in turn would need to ensure that they were in conformity with local and London plans. The individual needs and aspirations of local authorities are formulated into a Local Development Framework, which includes DPDs and these must be in 'general conformity' with the London Plan.

While some observers did not expect neighbourhood planning to change the planning process substantially, the proposals generated considerable public enthusiasm in localities across the capital. Bankside Residents Forum and Southwark Living Streets are good examples of groups actively promoting better streets and public spaces, while other campaigns have focused on issues such as improving the local high street or shopping parade. Some groups have sought to use neighbourhood plans to influence Opportunity Area Planning Frameworks (OAPFs), in which the mayor has a key role, while others have used them to raise issues such as litter collection or street cleaning, which are not currently covered in the existing planning framework.

Community involvement in London's neighbourhood planning has been greater than elsewhere. London boroughs have been a focus of major developments involving housing, commercial offices, arts and tourism, where residents and developers have engaged in both informal and formal collaborations for residential and retail developments and local business improvement districts. In the City of Westminster, a range of community-led neighbourhood groups have operated across the borough: the influence of the Queens Park Forum has been quite substantial in shaping local services, in providing a voice for the local community, and supporting and celebrating social, community and cultural life within its neighbourhoods. Other agencies and community groups active in the borough include housing tenant associations, registered landlords and voluntary organisations such as Voluntary Action Westminster. Likewise, in London's Covent Garden, community participation saved most of the fabric from becoming dual carriageways and office blocks: 'without community action, Tolmers Square, a socially and ethnically-mixed and much loved area, would have been a mono-functional office plaza' (London Assembly, 2011: 11).

Lambeth and Southwark Councils provide strong examples of the power of local residents to transform their neighbourhoods. Both boroughs have operated a wide range of regeneration projects, locally led, the outcomes of which have been greatly transformed urban landscapes. The More London Development, close to Tower Bridge, for example, has provided significant office and public space and itself benefited from the London Bridge Business Improvement District where local businesses contribute to a fund used for public events, projects and community services. In the same area, the Oxo Tower (originally a power station, now filled with shops, housing and restaurants) and the Coin Street neighbourhood projects, led by the Coin Street Community Builders group, have also had significant impact on the local landscape, shaping the development of the river walkway and the South Bank area. Bringing together the private sector and community groups, the South Bank not only transformed its image and architectural footprint but also serves as an example for well-integrated regeneration efforts carried out at the local level (Howell, 2012).

Despite these developments, a degree of cynicism continues to exist amongst planners and officials in local authorities about engaging the public in planning. The complexities are considerable, as are the public's own attitudes to involvement. While public participation is valued in its own right as a form of accountability, it is also accepted for the legitimacy it confers on decision making and the more efficacious policy outcomes that it can sometimes deliver. However, experiences of public participation – as reflected in the previous chapter – have demonstrated that the majority of the public do not participate. In matters of local government, they have identified lack of knowledge, interest, low levels of satisfaction and their inability to influence as key factors impeding participation (Fox, 2009; Stoker, 2000). A recent study examining the extent to which Community Improvement Districts (CIDs) engaged local people found a lack of citizen involvement and limited use of citizen knowledge in assessing local need and designing services. It identified factors such as overly bureaucratic processes that restrict local organisations such as co-operatives, social enterprises and local businesses from tendering for public services provided by the council (Travers, 2011).

In the wake of the Localism Act, several London councils established ward forums to provide opportunities for councillors and residents to work together to address issues in their areas. The mayor's question time has provided additional opportunities for the public to raise issues, while public involvement in the preparation of councils' development plan documents has raised greater awareness and knowledge among local residents. Local assemblies are gaining an increasingly important role and are used as a mechanism for democratic involvement, providing a platform to influence and learn about decisions made by the council, including issues relating to budgets and spending reductions. In operation for some three years now, local assemblies have engaged extensively with local businesses and statutory services to influence change. More recently Opportunity Areas, identified by the London Plan, are also being used as platforms for participation. Classified as the capital's major reservoir of brownfield land with significant capacity to accommodate new housing, commercial and other developments, they have proved particularly popular for urban regeneration. They are gaining popularity as important tools for soliciting public input on proposed environmental impact statements. Designed to promote civic participation, ownership and responsibility and to enable individuals, groups and communities to contribute to decision making at neighbourhood, borough and London-wide levels, the 33 opportunity areas identified in the mayor's London Plan are actively engaged in consulting with their communities. It is estimated that currently there are more than 200 neighbourhood projects, including those outside London, that are helping local communities and local authorities to start the process of planning in their areas.

Overall, the Localism Act seeks to take local participation to new heights, although it remains to be seen whether local communities will have the necessary drive, enthusiasm and momentum to see them through. Success will depend on a number of factors such as community mix, willingness to cooperate, political representation at local level and relationships between planning authorities and communities. In particular, it will call for closer working relationships between the GLA, London councils and neighbourhoods.

*****

Cities are essentially complex systems. In the case of London, the fundamental reform of its governance brought about by the new arrangements failed to remove all complexity. The range of activities requiring cooperation between different levels of elected bodies, agencies and private ventures still need to be managed and accountabilities ensured. The purpose of creating a powerful elected mayor was to make city management more effective and leadership more visionary. While still held to account both by an assembly and direct elections, the mayor was to have space to manoeuvre and the ability to set the political agenda with a distinct vision to create the sense of metropolitan community for London. As the above analysis shows, uncertainties remain and it remains unclear how these forces might combine in resolving London issues.

Whilst acknowledging that London is in a very different cultural setting and is, next to New York, more integrated with the global economy than any other city in the world, there are nevertheless interesting similarities and differences in governance with some of India's cities under study. The following chapters explore the governance of the chosen Indian cities in the context of the five conditions of governance discussed earlier. Of the differences, one of the most striking is the extent to which power is devolved to city governments in Hyderabad, Kolkata and Mumbai, which is the subject of the following chapter.

Notes

1 Three major master plans were produced for the county of London (Foreshaw and Abercrombie, 1943), for Greater London (Abercrombie, 1944) and for the City of London (Holden and Halford, 1951). Abercrombie's Greater London Plan, designed to restrict further population growth within the region and prevent new industrial development in London and the home counties, became the master plan and the key text for planning for the next three decades.
2 This concept, first developed by Ebenezer Howard in 1898, was a counterpart to the policies of urban containment and rural protection and later adopted by a number of writers in the 1920s and 1930s such as Raymond Unwin, Thomas Sharpe and F.J. Osborne.

4 Devolution of power to cities

Decentralisation has become an increasingly widespread and significant dimension of political and administrative reform. It takes many forms and its conceptualisation has raised several debates among scholars. The term 'decentralisation' implies that sub-national units of governments should have the autonomy and discretion to engage in effective decision making affecting their areas, but there is no clear conceptual definition of what the term actually denotes in practice. The lack of any concrete reference point when designing operational indicators of decentralisation has resulted in the emergence of a variety of proxy measures based on legal, functional and financial aspects. Of these, fiscal measures have proved perhaps the most satisfactory proxy, reflecting the principle that power lies with those who make the decisions about spending.

In the context of urban India, the CAA was a milestone as it gave constitutional validity to ULBs and defined their structures, functions and financial capacity. The act aimed at greater clarity between states and ULBs in terms of the devolution of powers, authorities and resources to enable the latter to function as vibrant institutions of local self-governance. Such devolution acknowledged urban diversity and encouraged bottom-up decision making and participatory urban governance. It transferred responsibility for a large number of urban functions to municipal corporations, provided for in the Twelfth Schedule of the Constitution, to be managed under locally elected leadership. Despite this, some of the functions continue to be managed by state governments through parastatal agencies, which often results in a fractured set of responsibilities for the ULBs.

In 2005, the JNNURM reinforced the commitment towards devolution of responsibilities to the local level. While earlier government schemes concentrated on a few select cities, this reform included 63 cities from all over the country, based on their populations and the amount of urban investment that was required. In order to access the central funds the cities and their respective state governments had to prepare CDPs and Detailed Project Reports (DPRs), with specific focus on the development reform measures. JNNURM designed the implementation of an integrated approach to all forms of decentralisation by attempting to devolve fiscal, political and administrative powers to the state and the local governments. The state governments were to have a higher share of the political decentralisation initiatives through legislations and reforms, while the city governments were entrusted with urban management and administrative issues. However, to some extent, the mission degenerated into a funding source for stand-alone urban infrastructure projects, often unrelated to reforms. The implementation status of key mandatory reforms across the states and identified cities has not been encouraging with only 11 out of 30 states and Union Territories, audited by the Comptroller and Auditor General, having transferred all functions in accordance with the CAA.

This chapter examines the extent of devolution from the states to Urban Local Bodies and the impact on city governance. It considers the opportunities and challenges facing devolution, the state of municipal finances, the relationships with parastatal agencies, and the policies and processes that empower local governments, including the transfer of functions under the twelfth schedule.

Devolution: opportunities and challenges

Post-independence India's commitment to industrialisation, economic growth and poverty reduction was strongly associated with decentralisation initiatives. Various commissions and committees, notably the Metha Commission of 1957, the Asoka Metha Commission of 1978, and the G.V.K. Rao Committee of 1985, were set up to investigate the functioning of local institutions and their weaknesses. They unanimously came to the view that the unwillingness of states to devolve power, combined with a resistant bureaucracy and the power of 'local élites' inhibited progress towards effective decentralisation. Concerns about the gradual weakening of ULBs over the years led to proposals for safeguarding their interests to include regular and fair conduct of elections and representation and placing the relationship between the state governments and ULBs on a firm footing with respect to their functions, taxation powers, revenue sharing, and the involvement of elected representatives at grassroots level in the planning process for districts and metropolitan areas. Following extensive deliberation, the 73rd and 74th constitutional amendments were introduced in parliament in 1991 and the resulting acts came into force in 1993. Urban policies, prior to the constitutional act, focused on town and land-use planning that were in accordance with the 'notions of hygiene, order and a sense of aesthetics' – policies that led to the control of urban land by the government (Shaw, 1996: 226). In the absence of elected city governments and a legitimate third tier of government, the powers and responsibility of urban governance and management remained with the state. The legitimacy and recognition given to city governments was seemingly symbolic (Indu, 2012: 12).

State intervention in urban planning led to the creation of institutions like HUDCO, the state housing boards and various parastatal agencies. However, state policies failed to increase the financial viability of urban areas, which resulted in inefficiencies and ineffectiveness of projects managed by ULBs and an increasing divide between the bigger and smaller urban areas. The absence of appropriate fiscal incentives and disincentives became one of the major factors inhibiting the effective implementation of urban policies (Ommen, 2010). During the late 1970s the focus was much more on achieving uniform, decentralised urban growth (Shaw, 1996). The Integrated Development of Small and Medium Towns (IDSMT) in 1979 was a step in this direction, with additional funding allocated to achieving balanced growth. The Seventh Five Year Plan called for greater devolution of finances and powers to urban entities and for greater private participation, while the establishment of the National Commission on Urbanisation in 1988 empowered it with powers to disburse funds to the respective states, based on the recommendations of the Central Finance Commissions.

The CAA, however, represented an important attempt at strengthening municipal governance (Mathur, 2007; Sivaramakrishnan, 2008). It recognised ULBs as 'vibrant units of democratic governance' – a legitimate third tier of the federal system. The legal status accorded to local governments enabled them such powers and authority as were deemed necessary to function as institutions of self-governance. Between them, the 73rd and 74th amendments identified different types of municipalities according to their size and area, including *Nagar Panchayat* for an area in transition from rural to urban; *Municipal Council* for a smaller urban area; and *Municipal Corporation* for a larger area. Other constitutional provisions included devolving greater functional and financial responsibilities to the municipal bodies, rules and regulations on municipal elections, coordination of the multiple agency functions through the Metropolitan Planning Committee (MPC) and District Planning Committees (DPCs), and defining the power of parastatal agencies vis-à-vis the ULBs.

The CAA was to enable ULBs to move away from their traditional role of executing projects directed by state governments to formulating and implementing their own programmes of economic development and resource allocation. In practice, the lack of functional autonomy for urban local organisations combined with tensions and conflicts over resources plagued urban governance for much of the period since the passing of the CAA (Indu, 2012; Shaw, 1996; Sivaramakrishnan, 2011). The Model Municipal Law 2003 was designed to provide a legislative framework for the government's urban sector reform agenda to enhance the capacity of ULBs to leverage public funds and improve service delivery, but this too had limited influence on city governance, with city level agencies contributing little to policy making. Instead, there was a renewed focus on initiatives by individual states to create democratic urban governance structures.

Urban Local Bodies have therefore been left with little discretion over local developmental expenditure priorities, which continue to be financed through tied grants from state governments. This is most pronounced in small towns, which also experience strong bureaucratic and political resistance to devolution. 'Para-statal and line departments convey their unwillingness to be a part of municipal governments, or to even have to collaborate with them. Influential people use political clout freely to get around rules and regulations while local municipalities watch helplessly' (PRIA, 2008: vii).

The system is too highly centralised and often results in:

> inefficient and poor quality of civic services, lack of accountability and lopsided and inadequate infrastructure development in suburbs and within the island city. Basic urban services such as sanitation, solid waste management, maintenance of roads and walkways are substandard leading to steep deterioration of quality of life in the city. Centralisation at the town hall level also keeps the top management in a fire-fighting mode without any time being assigned to strategic planning process. Thus one of the most prestigious urban bodies lacks vision, direction and strategic plan for the city.
>
> (MTSU, 2006: 6)

The lack of transparency and accountability in the planning and implementation of projects characterises municipalities in India. The ULBs perceive themselves as excluded in areas of city governance and have sometimes sought legal remedies to make their state governments comply with the provisions of national legislation.

The relationship with parastatal agencies

In many areas, ULBs perform minimal functions as are devolved to them. Urban planning and environment, planning for economic and social development, poverty alleviation and the provision of amenities have remained with parastatal agencies controlled by state governments. In some states, for example, urban and town planning is the responsibility of the Town and Country Planning Department, while housing functions are sometimes entrusted to a separate Housing Board. Sectoral programmes also create confusion at the local level as responsibilities lack clarity while administration is ridden with duplication and overlap.

It has been widely noted that one of the principal reasons for lack of control by corporations over the Twelfth Schedule functions is the extensive range of parastatal agencies with broad powers over municipal services with overlapping responsibilities. This is certainly true for the three cities under consideration, as shown in Table 4.1. In Mumbai, for example, the Municipal Corporation of Greater Mumbai (MCGM) shares responsibilities with the MMRDA, the Maharashtra State Road Development Corporation (MSRDC) and a host of other parastatal service providers, and a similar picture emerges in Kolkata and Hyderabad. In short, it is hard to find a report on urban issues in Indian cities that does not attribute the city's disappointing quality of life at least in part to the proliferation of parastatals.

Table 4.1 Parastatal agencies in Mumbai, Kolkata and Hyderabad

City	Agency	1. Urban Planning Including Town Planning	2. Regulation of Land Use and Construction of Buildings	3. Planning for Economic and Social Development	4. Roads and Bridges	5. Water Supply for Domestic, Industrial and Commercial Purposes	6. Public Health, Sanitation Conservation and Solid Waste Management	7. Fire Services	8. Urban Forestry, Protection of the Environment and Promotion of Ecological Aspects
Mumbai	MMRDA	■		■					■
	MCGM		■	■	■	■	■		
	BEST								
	MFS							■	
	UDD		■						
	MSRDC				■				
	MSEDC								
Kolkata	KMDA	■	■		■				
	KMC						■		■
	KMWSA					■			
	WBFS							■	
Hyderabad	HMDA	■		■					■
	GHMC	■	■	■	■		■		■
	AP Disaster Response and Fire Services							■	
	HMWSSB					■			

Source: compiled by Janaagraha (2013).

However, international experience reveals that the presence of multiple agencies does not necessarily result in poor service outcomes. Many high-functioning cities have separate bodies for water, electricity, street construction and other services. A driver in a metropolitan area in the United States could easily travel across roads built and maintained by the city, county, state or

9. Safeguarding the Interests of Weaker Sections of Society, Including Mentally and Physically Challenged
10. Slum Improvement and Upgradation
11. Urban Poverty Alleviation
12. Provision of Urban Amenities and Facilities such as Parks, Gardens, Playgrounds
13. Promotion of Cultural, Educational and Aesthetic Aspects
14. Burials and Burial Grounds; Cremations, Cremation Grounds and Electric Crematoriums
15. Cattle Pounds; Prevention of Cruelty to Animals
16. Vital Statistics Including Registration of Births and Deaths.
17. Public Amenities Including Street Lighting, Parking Lots, Bus Stops and Public Conveniences
18. Regulation of Slaughter Houses and Tanneries

federal government, or by a special-purpose corporation or authority. There are over 1,100 public authorities in the State of New York whose oversight and accountability is subject to ongoing reform. These authorities are not uncontroversial: they often lack elected representation and are often subject to accusations of unaccountability and insufficient transparency. However, their existence in high-functioning cities shows that there is not necessarily a direct link between multiple municipal service providers and poor outcomes.

Economic growth in urban areas is highly dependent on adequate resource management; that is, by efficient service delivery such as quality transport, water supply, waste management, public health and so on. The infrastructure for such services has to be developed with geographic and population considerations that are rarely under local jurisdiction. It is often the case that central, state and local governments carry out activities in the same sectors, such as building roads and public transport systems, and therefore it becomes important to delineate the nature and structure of their relations in each sector. The CAA was meant to rectify the uncertainties in the distribution of planning functions amongst ULBs and state governments but, despite repeated efforts, these bodies still find themselves responsible for only a limited number of functions. Yet, it is the local governments of these cities that bear the brunt of the local populaces' displeasure even though they have no power to counter the actions of parastatal agencies, as this would imply opposing the decisions of the state government (Kasturirangan Committee, 2008).

The CAA provides a basis for state legislatures to transfer responsibilities to municipalities and strengthen municipal-level governance. Under the act, local governments should perform 18 functions, ten of which are deemed as important, particularly when compared with municipal governments in other global cities. The extent to which municipalities have control of these functions is distinctly patchy (see Table 4.2), with the only function controlled by all three cities under study being roads and bridges.

While a significant factor responsible for this is the reluctance of states governments to accord sufficient financial autonomy to the ULBs, there are other impeding factors, as the report of the 13th Finance Commission highlighted:

> While the issue of providing additional funding support to local bodies is significant, all the building blocks of the third tier structure deserve attention. These include entrusting local bodies with implementation and expenditure responsibilities consistent with their mandate; enhancing their capacity to meet these obligations through assigning necessary revenue raising powers as well as providing adequate transfers; making them accountable for their performance, including delivery of services as per previously notified standards; strengthening the functioning of the State Finance Commissions; and providing focused support to the scheduled and excluded areas.
> (Government of India, 2009: 38)

The 13th Finance Commission called for greater decentralisation and the 'need to put in place a stronger incentive mechanism aimed at persuading State Governments to decentralise further' (Government of India, 2009: 38–39).

Table 4.2 Spread of functions across the municipal corporations of Mumbai, Kolkata and Hyderabad

Critical civic functions and services	Mumbai	Kolkata	Hyderabad
Urban planning including land use and management			
Planning for economic and social development			√
Roads and bridges	√	√	√
Water supply (domestic, industrial and commercial)	√		
Fire and emergency services	√	√	
Promotion of cultural, educational and aesthetic aspects			√
Public health, including community health centres/area hospitals	√		
School education			
Traffic management and civic policing activities			
Urban environment management and heritage			
Total	4	2	3

Note: Out of the 18 functions listed under Schedule XII to the Constitution (Seventy-fourth) Amendment Act, 1992 and the five functions recommended by the Second Administrative Reforms Commission for inclusion under the remit of Urban Local Bodies, Janaagraha selected for analysis ten critical functions and services.

Source: ASICS (2013: 63–64).

Financial autonomy of ULBs

Urban local finance registers a small presence in the overall public finance in India. The total municipal revenue in India accounts for about 0.75 per cent of the country's GDP as against a figure of 4.5 per cent for Poland, 5 per cent for Brazil and 6 per cent for South Africa. In terms of both revenue and expenditure, the Urban Local Bodies account for just above 2 per cent of the combined revenue and expenditure of central government, state governments and municipalities (Government of India, 2012: 15).

Municipal revenues

For all ULBs, typically, the income falls under two broad categories – own revenues and income via grants, loans, state and central transfers. Own revenues can be further classified into tax revenues (including property tax, professional tax, water and sewerage tax) and non-tax revenues (user fees, parking fees and other charges). The primary expenditure of ULBs is on salaries and establishment expenses, operations and maintenance relating to urban service provision and capital expenditure relating to asset creation. This income and expenditure comprise the municipal budgets and are broadly captured and reported under accounting categories of revenue and capital accounts.

The surplus/deficit on the revenue account is a crucial indicator of the financial strength of the ULBs – the core city, municipalities and town panchayats. The revenue composition of most ULBs is largely skewed towards their tax revenue sources, in particular, property tax, followed by professional tax. The core cities meet the majority of their revenue expenditure commitments through their own revenue sources rather than transfers from other levels of government. On the other hand, municipalities and town panchayats depend heavily on the upper tiers of governance for sustaining their revenue expenditures – on State Financial Corporations and assigned revenues. For municipalities, the contribution of these corporations and assigned revenues towards their total revenue receipts stands at 45–50 per cent, approximately the same as their income from tax and non-tax sources. Grants from the State Financial Corporations enable municipal bodies to create physical infrastructure for civic services like water supply, street lighting, sewerage and drainage, road construction, slum improvements and the development of health infrastructure. All such schemes are expected to be prioritised by ULBs in consultation with local ward committees.

Salaries dominate revenue expenditures across all categories of ULBs, followed by operation and maintenance expenditure on civic services such as roads, drains, street lighting and solid waste management. Expenditure on water supply and sewerage is handled mostly by the water supply and sanitation boards, and is not the responsibility of the core city, but in some cities, certain municipalities and town panchayats incur considerable expenditure towards operations and maintenance of water supply and sewerage. Despite the increased scope and scale of their engagement, the fiscal space of ULBs is lessening. Their combined expenditure fell from 1.74 per cent of GDP in 1998–1999 to 1.56 per cent in 2002–2003 and 1.54 per cent in 2007–2008. While internal resources provide for less than half the total expenditure, local bodies have been unable to exploit property tax as a major source of revenue. Grants from the centre provide additional support, but as the report of the finance commission noted, these transfers have not been adequate for local bodies to provide the desired level of services. A significant part of resource transfer is tied and non-discretionary, limiting the abilities of ULBs to match resources to local needs (Government of India, 2009: 154–155).

Local spending as a percentage of total spending and local government's own revenue as a percentage of total own revenue of the state are commonly used as fiscal measures of decentralisation. A recent study found that the share of ULBs' own revenue is more than 50 per cent of the total in the states of Punjab, Maharashtra, Gujarat, Andhra Pradesh, Goa and West Bengal, whereas others such as Tripura, Uttar Pradesh, Bihar, Chhattisgarh, Madhya Pradesh and Orissa raise less than 20 per cent. Those states with the higher percentage of own revenue are in a better position to take investment decisions and prioritise appropriately, while those more reliant on external sources of funds find themselves tied to specific projects and bound by conditions and constraints (IDF, n.d.):

> The states with the higher percentage of own revenue are in better position to take investment decisions as they have to rely less on external sources of funds. This is also because external sources of funds are released with a time lag. This is due to a plethora of conditionalities imposed on the release of funds to ULBs and/or because the funds are tied to specific projects. One such condition is that ULBs need the provision of utilisation certificates for their previous instalments to be passed by the State government within 15 days. Since most of the ULBs do not maintain an account and also have a very slack attitude towards getting their accounts audited, they face difficulty in getting the utilisation certificate, which affect their financial position and hence their ability to perform better. If the ULBs are self-sufficient they are in a better position to prioritise their investments. But to generate own revenues ULBs need well-defined powers for proper functioning. And it is possible only if there is more devolution of powers to the ULBs by the states.
>
> (IDF, n.d.: 7)

According to the study, Hyderabad has the largest number of devolved functions, with 19 out of the 29 functions assigned by the SFC; the city also enjoys the highest percentage of its own revenue in the total revenue when compared with other cities in the same category. In Hyderabad, the GHMC has sought greater devolution of funds from state government to take control of assigned revenues. About 66 per cent of revenue income comes from GHMC's own sources – a growth rate of 12.74 per cent per annum over the last decade. The revenue sources include property tax (41 per cent), town planning (14 per cent) and public health and sanitation (2 per cent). The most significant increases have been in property tax collections, with property tax rates in Hyderabad Municipal Corporation (HMC) ranging from 17 to 30 per cent of the annual rental value (ARV). External sources of revenue are in the form of shared taxes/transfers and revenue grants from the state government, with assigned revenues contributing about 33 per cent of revenue income, which include entertainment tax (4.5 per cent per annum), professional tax (8.56 per cent) and stamp duty (20 per cent). The first two of these taxes is collected by the state's commercial tax department, which transfers the tax collected to GHMC, while the last is collected by the registration department, which transfers 95 per cent of the tax collected to the Municipal Corporation of Hyderabad (MCH). Others sources of urban finances include parastatal finances from Hyderabad Metropolitan Water Supply and Sewerage Board (HMWSSB) and Hyderabad Metropolitan Development Authority (HMDA), JNNURM funds routed through Andhra Pradesh Urban Infrastructure and Finance Corporation, and other projects involving private and public investments routed through various governmental agencies.

Kolkata has shown significant growth rates in its own sources of revenue and in the expenditure met by ULBs from these sources, demonstrating the efficient operation of its ULBs. Data from the most recent Kolkata CDP showed an increase from 57.8 per cent to 68 per cent between 2001/2002 and 2004/2005 in ULBs' own source revenue as a percentage of total revenue. Likewise, ULBs' own source revenue as a percentage of revenue expenditure increased from 72.5 per cent to 122.8 per cent during the same period. The growth rates have shown a continuous increase with own source revenue at 20.3 per cent, property tax at 10.3 per cent, and non-tax revenue at 17 per cent. Revenue expenditure stood at 98 per cent in 2003/2004, while expenditure on salaries and wages showed a negative fall of -2.77 per cent (KMDA, 2007: 54). The plan reveals that the majority of the population of the KMA are serviced by ULBs that are functioning effectively in terms of improving their services and taking steps to enhance their revenue from their own sources through improved collections and realisations (KMDA, 2007: 59–60).

In the case of Mumbai, MCGM's own sources account for 97 per cent of the ULB's income, while the proportion of own source income is significantly lower in the case of municipal councils at 75 per cent. Most of the revenue income of ULBs in the metropolitan regions is from tax sources. MCGM's share of expenditure among all ULBs is over 80 per cent, other municipal corporations 14 per cent, and municipal councils account for only 2 per cent. Investments made by ULBs also throw light on the extent of their financial autonomy. In Mumbai, investments made by ULBs constitute around 44 per cent of total public investments.

One of the major problems confronting Indian cities is the poor collection of municipal revenues. Most cities have leveraged only a fraction of their potential to collect property taxes, and continue to face difficulties with revenue collection for such basic services as water supply and garbage collection. Inefficient management practices, poor financial planning, and lack of periodic revision of municipal tax rates and user charges, together with the low degree of financial decentralisation and limited borrowing powers, remain some of the principal weaknesses in India's city-systems. Another issue relates to the devolution of service-delivery responsibility in the absence of commensurate financial resources and increased capacity. While the CAA set out the expenditure responsibilities of ULBs, it failed to specify the legitimate sources of revenue for these authorities. Put simply, it stated that the legislature of a state may, by law, authorise a municipality to levy, collect and appropriate such taxes, duties, tolls and fees; assign to a municipality such taxes, duties, tolls and fees levied and collected by the state government; provide for making such grants-in-aid to the municipality from the consolidated fund of the state; and provide for the constitution of such funds for crediting all moneys received. Thus, while the municipalities have been assigned the responsibility of preparation of plans for

Table 4.3 The constitution of State Finance Commissions: Maharashtra, West Bengal and Andhra Pradesh

	Maharashtra	West Bengal	Andhra Pradesh
First State Finance Commission (SFC)			
Date of constitution	23 April 1994	30 May 1994	22 June 1994
Period covered	1994–1995 to 1996–1997	1996–1997 to 2000–2001	1997–1998 to 1999–2000
Second SFC			
Date of constitution	22 June 1999	14 July 2000	8 December 1998
Period covered	1999–2000 to 2001–2002	2001–2002 to 2005–2006	2000–2001 to 2004–2005
Third SFC			
Date of constitution	15 January 2005	22 February 2006	29 December 2004
Period covered	2006–2007 to 2010–2011	2008–2009 to 2012–2013	2005–2006 to 2009–2010
Fourth SFC			
Date of constitution	Not constituted	30 April 2013	Not constituted
Period covered		2013–2014	
Total number of SFCs constituted	3	4	3

Source: Compiled by Janaagraha based on the 13th Finance Commission, State Finance Commission Reports. Published in ASICS (2013: 61–62).

a wide range of matters, from economic development to promotion of cultural, educational and aesthetic aspects, the power to raise resources by identifying taxes and rates to implement the plans have been vested in the state legislature. This has created what is sometimes referred to as vertical imbalances – constitutionally built-in mismatches in the division of expenditure liabilities and revenue-raising powers of the union, states and local bodies.

The role of SFCs is crucial in strengthening the finances of ULBs. State governments are required to constitute their finance commissions once every five years to review the financial position of ULBs and make appropriate recommendations to the state on the distribution of funds between the state and local bodies. With the exception of West Bengal (Kolkata), the other two states have not constituted the fourth SFC (see Table 4.3). In so far as they exist, experience shows that the functioning of these institutions with regard to rationalising the fiscal relation between the states and local governments has been far from effective. The quality of SFC reports is patchy and their 'recommendations do not follow a uniform pattern, thus detracting from their usability' (Government of India, 2009: 171).

In addition to the timely constitution of SFCs, the requirement is for an *Action Taken Report* to be placed in the concerned state legislature within six months of submission and followed by an annual statement on the devolution, grants given to individual local bodies, and on the implementation of the recommendations. According to the 13th Finance Commission Report, none of the states under study had submitted their reports for the last constituted SFC. The commission noted the enormous variations in data provided by the state governments, while some furnished good quality data, most of the data was sparse, and frequently inconsistent with the data provided to previous commissions. In addition, the SFC reports submitted to the commission were widely 'divergent in the quality of their analyses and the scope and scale of their recommendations' (Government of India, 2009: 165).

Tax revenues

Municipal bodies in India at present can levy and collect only those taxes that state governments choose to devolve from their powers as specified in the State List in the Seventh Schedule to the Constitution. In general, states are reluctant to devolve taxes, demonstrated by the fact that the only revenue collection devolved to all three study cities is property tax (see Table 4.4).

Taxes on advertising, entertainment and profession are rarely under the control of local government. There is a vertical imbalance in the distribution of taxing powers that has worsened over time. As the report of the 13th Finance Commission concluded:

> While in the total revenue expenditure there has been long term stability in the relative shares of the Centre and the states after implementation of the transfers recommended by the Finance Commission, the buoyancy of central taxes has been higher than those of the states and such a trend is expected to continue, given the nature of tax assignment to the Centre and states ... To maintain constancy in the share of states in post-devolution total tax revenue, this share would need to increase by the margin by which the buoyancy of central tax revenue exceeds the buoyancy of combined tax revenue. The argument for using post-devolution tax shares to maintain consistency, as against altering tax assignments, is based on the premise that most schemes of assigning resources in different country settings tend to be biased in favour of the Centre in assignment of tax collection powers on efficiency grounds.
>
> (Government of India, 2009: 32)

It has long been argued that city governments should be allowed to levy their own sets of taxes. It is striking that the share of taxes collected locally is generally greater in more highly developed countries than those in the developing world and that the level of local taxation broadly correlates with levels of efficiency and accountability.

Table 4.4 Tax regimes in Mumbai, Kolkata and Hyderabad

	Mumbai	*Kolkata*	*Hyderabad*
Property tax	√	√	√
Entertainment tax	X	X	√
Profession tax	X	X	X
Advertisement tax	X	√	√

Source: ASICS (2013: 5).

Box 4.1 Levels of autonomy in local taxation

In most developing countries, central governments have been reluctant to confer powers of taxation on sub-national governments. There are potentially sound and productive taxes that sub-national governments could use: property taxes, personal income tax surcharges, taxes on the use of motor vehicles, payroll taxes, value-added taxes and local 'business value' taxes. But the sub-national tax share in total taxes in developing countries is only about 10 per cent in comparison to 20 per cent in developed countries. These figures have changed little in the last 30 years. The present assignment of taxes in countries such as India, Brazil, Pakistan and Russia is far from ideal. One common problem is that there is a significant vertical imbalance between expenditure and revenue, with implications for autonomy, efficiency and accountability. This, in turn, results in significant costs of administration and compliance as well as those arising from tax-induced inefficiencies in the allocation of scarce resources.

Important lessons can be learnt from developed countries. Local governments in the United States and Canada have almost complete autonomy in choosing any tax base as long as there is no interference with inter-state commerce. In Denmark and Sweden, local taxes account for nearly one-half of local government spending. Revenues from sub-national government taxes in Switzerland are greater in amount than revenue received from grants. Japan introduced a local financial system reform called the 'trinity reform' in 2002, under which three reforms have been carried out as a package: (1) reform in the transfer of tax revenue sources from the central government to local governments, (2) reform of the 'national treasury subsidy and obligatory share', and (3) reform of local allocation tax.

Source: Bird and Bahl (2008).

Typically, the most important tax levied at local level is the property tax. The responsibility for designing the property tax system in India rests with state governments, which allow ULBs to fix tax rates within a band and prepare their own strategies for collection. In other words, property tax is controlled by state governments, effectively removing the prime funding instrument from the control of the municipality, as was evidenced recently when the states of Haryana and Rajasthan abolished their property taxes in

92 *Devolution of power to cities*

Table 4.5 International experience on property tax collections (percentage of GDP)

	1970–1980	1980–1990	1990–2000	2000–2009
OECD (number of countries)	1.24 (16)	1.31 (18)	1.44 (16)	2.12 (18)
Developing countries (number of countries)	0.42 (20)	0.36 (27)	0.42 (23)	0.60 (29)
Transition countries (number of countries)	0.34 (1)	0.59 (4)	0.54 (20)	0.67 (18)
All countries	0.77 (37)	0.73 (49)	0.75 (59)	1.04 (65)

Source: Government of India (2009: 163).

all their cities on two separate occasions. Such arbitrary decisions by the state creates political risks that can be damaging to ULBs in terms of their ability to access market finance.

Property tax constitutes 23.4 per cent of the total municipal revenue and 28.5 per cent of own source revenues. There are inter-city variations in the property tax collection, coverage, tax rate and in the valuation of property, with the MMC registering a per capita annual revenue of Rs 1,334 (£13.52) as against Rs 25 (£0.25) for the Patna Municipal Corporation (Government of India, 2009: 162). Currently, property tax revenues in different states of India are in the range of 0.16 to 0.24 per cent of GDP. By contrast, many developing countries collect around 0.6 per cent of the GDP from property taxes (Mathur *et al.*, 2009). In developed countries such as Canada and the United States, property tax revenues can reach up to 3 to 4 per cent of GDP (OECD, 2010).

Certain properties are exempt from taxes and these incur substantial losses, but for assessed properties, the coverage is very low in any case and, as noted above, varies considerably between states. A recent study based on a survey of the 36 largest cities in India showed that the major factors contributing to poor realisation from property tax include poor assessment rate (56 per cent of the properties covered), weak collection efficiency (37 per cent of the property tax demand raised), flawed methods for property valuation, loss on account of exemptions (11.7 per cent) and poor enforcement (Mathur *et al.*, 2009). It acknowledged that the use of geographic information systems (GIS) to map properties could significantly improve coverage by providing municipal administrations with a visual spatial tool for identifying locations. Bangalore, Surat, Ahmedabad, Hyderabad, Delhi and Mumbai have recently concluded GIS mapping exercises and are beginning to use the data for property tax assessment, although it needs to be supplemented with an updated register of assets, on which the progress is seemingly slow. While cities such as Kolkata and Chennai are lagging behind, the National Urban Information System (NUIS), within the MoUD, is engaged in an effort to develop GIS maps of the scale of 1:10000 and 1:2000 and utility maps for 152 cities (HPEC, 2011: 131). Another recommendation is that collection efficiency would be greatly enhanced if property records were digitised. Cities such as Mumbai, Nasik, Pune and Nagpur that enjoy electronic databases of property records have demonstrated greater efficiencies compared with areas reliant on manual systems.

An important issue relates to the periodic revaluation of properties. While countries such as Brazil and South Africa have centrally mandated capital value system to assess properties, and require all properties to be revalued periodically, such periodic assessments are lacking in India. Until about five years ago, most cities in India used an ARV system for property valuation, while the Rent Control Acts in operation in most states locked the value of the rental to unrealistically low levels.[1] Many states have redesigned their property tax regimes to an Area Based System (ABS) – the prescription of unit values (per square foot) based on the area in which the property is located, and the type of construction of the property. Ahmedabad, Hyderabad, Bangalore, Delhi, Pune and Indore are some of the ULBs that have introduced an ABS for assessing property values. Property Tax Boards in some states are attempting to put in place an independent and transparent procedure for assessing property values.

Box 4.2 Area Based System of property valuation: the Patna model

The Patna Municipal Corporation was the first in 1992–1993 to introduce an ABS for assessment of property values in a relatively high income area covering 0.3 per cent of the total area of the city. It linked valuation to the norms of location, usage, built-up area, and type of construction, and simultaneously reduced the tax rate markedly from 43.75 per cent to 9 per cent of the annual rental value. The property tax reform was challenged in the High Court of Patna but was endorsed by the Supreme Court on the grounds that it was simple, transparent and reasonable. It resulted in a fourfold increase [from about Rs 1 crore (£101,380) in 1992–1993 to Rs 4.2 crore (£425,796) in 1993–1994] in tax revenue in the small area where it was applied. While the reform could not be sustained in Patna over time because of political opposition, many states and cities have adopted the Patna model with modifications to suit their local requirements. Karnataka, Andhra Pradesh and Tamil Nadu are some of the states in which the Patna model has been refined for use in some cities and linked to self-assessment.

Source: HPEC (2011: 133).

The 13th Finance Commission argued that an appropriate strategy might also include establishing a Central Valuation Board in each state, along the lines of the West Bengal Central Valuation Board, in order to standardise property valuation, which would also be charged with setting guidance values and subsequent updating, improving collection efficiency, identifying tax evasion and enforcing penal clauses (Government of India, 2009: 164). Since its establishment in the late 1970s, the West Bengal Valuation Board has sought to bring about a uniform and rational system of valuation of municipal properties throughout the state. Its primary function is to enumerate and assess the value of properties in all the municipalities in the state and through a transparent approach to its functioning.

Non-tax revenue

If own tax revenues of ULBs are well below their potential, the performance with respect to user charges is equally poor, if not worse. User charges are the first-best instruments for meeting the cost of public services, and these are far below their operating costs in India. As municipal finances cannot bear this subsidy, it results in poor service delivery and inadequate maintenance, thus decreasing asset life and adding to the pressures for further asset creation.

The importance of user charges for municipal finances cannot be emphasised enough. Urban services such as water supply, sewerage and garbage collection require not only major investments in urban infrastructure assets but also regular maintenance for efficient operation and effective delivery. User charges for these services ensure that the assets are maintained and delivery of services sustained. As the services are delivered directly to households, and there are no 'spillover' effects, levying user charges is highly desirable. Given the proximity to the population and the predominance of 'private goods' characteristics of many of these services, levying user charges on the beneficiaries is also feasible. They are especially important as they signal to consumers the scarcity value of the services, and to service providers the quantum of demand that needs to be met. But all the evidence suggests that user charges have typically not been used by ULBs in India to cover costs (HPEC, 2011: 139–140). Strikingly, Hyderabad introduced the principle of 'users and polluters pay' and has been in the process of identifying direct and indirect users and beneficiaries of the services it provides in order to levy user charges and benefit taxes Rao, 2007: 133).

A study by Mohanty *et al.* shows cost recovery to be higher in cities in which the estimated normative under-spend was lower. There are various potential explanations for the correlation, but it is not unreasonable to assume that poor service quality is associated with low cost recovery. While periodic revisions in user charges are required in order to recover the costs incurred in service provision, this will need to be accompanied by perceptible improvements in service delivery in order to ensure that the fee increase is acceptable to the paying public (Mohanty *et al.*, 2007).

ULBs are required to seek the approval of state governments for levying user charges, which can potentially limit their autonomy and impair their ability to deliver urban services. The case has often been made for an independent Municipal Service Regulator, assigned with the responsibility for revising user charges. It is also argued that, where different segments of the population are charged differently, cross-subsidisation has to be at a level that would enable the cost of Operations & Maintenance (O&M) to be recovered and a modest surplus generated. The ability to build a stable internal revenue base, critical for accessing external sources of funding, is currently limited. Certain investments at municipal level, such as the improvement of slums, urban roads, sewerage networks, waste water treatment and sanitary landfills require at least partial subsidies. Independent commentators have argued that states should create programmes for subsidising priority investments and that these subsidies be delivered in a form that is easy to access for smaller cities and towns with weak technical and financial capacity. Such dedicated municipal funds, with government support, have often been used in this way in European countries during their urban transitions.

The complex institutional and fiscal framework at the urban level in India has been less than conducive to accessing funds in the debt market. There are multiple authorities with overlapping jurisdictions, at the levels of both city and state, and 'urban development' remains a 'state subject'. This has created a problem of *moral hazard* in the municipal debt market, where much of the regulatory responsibility lies with municipal borrowers (ULBs and parastatals), while the borrower–lender interface lies with states, and responsibilities affecting lenders remain with the Government of India. In the event of municipal insolvency or bond default, it is difficult to comprehend who would protect the interests of the ULB.

Financing urban services and infrastructure

Inter-governmental transfers constitute an important source for financing projects within the megacity regions. There are various types of such transfers: untied grants from state governments to local governments, based on the recommendations of the respective State Finance Corporations, investments by the state government through state agencies and development authorities, investments by the national government through programmes such as JNNURM, and those made by agencies of the national government, such as major ports, the Airport Authority of India, National Highways Authority of India, Indian Railways and the more recent Metro Rail projects.

Development authorities are primary investment vehicles in the megacity regions. Land and land-related revenues, such as development charges, form a large proportion of the revenue for most authorities. In Hyderabad and Mumbai investments in projects are mainly funded from surpluses on land related revenues, such as the HMDA's investment in the outer ring road project. The HMDA, for example, holds 74 per cent of equity in the Hyderabad Growth Corridor Ltd, a special purpose vehicle of the Government of Andhra Pradesh, which has a distinct role in regional infrastructure. The KMDA is an exception, being almost entirely dependent on grants from projects under schemes such as JNNURM. Unlike other development authorities, KMDA has limited sources of revenue, and land development has been primarily through state government agencies or other departments. Even so, KMDA has successfully carried out investment programmes to develop basic infrastructures and facilities such as water supply, transport, housing and commercial developments, and other municipal activities in the region.

Across India, urban services have substantially under-performed, particularly in urban water supply and sanitation. An assessment of the JNNURM programmes has shown that the water sector accounts for the single largest share (41 per cent) of the funds disbursed under the JNNURM for infrastructure development, while water, sewerage and drainage together account for over 70 per cent. Solid waste management claimed 3 per cent of the funds disbursed. Most states prioritised their investment plans in these two sectors.

For several decades, state governments, through their own departments, state level boards, and statutory and non-statutory bodies at the city level, had responsibility for providing these services. Capital investments for these services have come mainly from state governments, normally financed through a combination of loans and grants from government owned financial institutions. That decentralisation would reduce the fiscal burden of the various state governments has not quite matched the expectations (Bagchi, 2001).

Although financed by state governments, the maintenance of water and sanitation remains the responsibility of city governments. Substantial investment is required to strengthen ULBs and augment the facilities to keep pace with the demand (Bagchi, 2001). In a study analysing the financing of urban services in the immediate post-decentralisation period, it was found that out of 17 states, eight experienced decline in the growth rate of per capita expenditure on urban water supply in the first few years. Tamil Nadu, West Bengal, Rajasthan and Assam registered significant declines in the growth rate, while Andhra Pradesh, Goa, Gujarat and Orissa recorded an increase in the real per capita expenditure on water supply and sanitation. No expenditure was incurred by states such as Karnataka, Kerala and Punjab specifically for these purposes, although states that do not spend on water supply and sanitation-sewerage facilities, do provide some assistance to their local bodies.

A number of bureaucratic problems often inhibit effective infrastructure developments. The case of the Lions Club-MCGM-Sulabh Friendship Project is illustrative. Undertaken in 2000, the Mumbai project spent Rs 1.5 crore (£152,070) on constructing 27 public toilets between Bandra and Dahanu. But delays in obtaining permissions from the civic authorities led to delays and budget overrun. In this respect, MMR compares most unfavourably with other metropolitan cities in India; its high transaction costs disadvantages the city relative to others. The city's own development plan attributes the lack of efficiency and effectiveness to the complex system of laws, institutions, procedures. The non-ULB investments, for example, come from a range of institutions lacking coordination, which include the MMRDA, Maharashtra Housing and Area Development Authority (MHADA), Maharashtra Industrial Development Corporation (MIDC), City and Industrial Development Corporation (CIDCO), as well as through projects such as the Mumbai Urban Transport Project (MUTP), Mega City

Scheme, Mumbai Urban Development Project (MUDP) and the Mumbai Metropolitan Development Fund.

Since the 1980s, external funding, mainly from the World Bank and other foreign agencies, has been used to finance urban infrastructure projects. A substantial portion – more than 53 per cent – has been for the urban water supply and sanitation programme (NIUA, 1998). The more developed states have generally turned out to be the major recipients of this assistance. A study showed that 15 of the 18 externally aided projects for urban development were in state capitals, and six of these were in the capitals of developed states such as Karnataka, Maharashtra and Tamil Nadu (Bagchi, 2001). Alternative modes of finance, including private sector initiatives, have also been largely confined to the developed southern and western states of Maharashtra, Gujarat, Karnataka and Tamil Nadu. Of the 28 water and environmental sanitation related projects involving PPPs, the majority were in the developed states, and the same was true of PPP projects in solid waste treatment and disposal facilities (Bagchi, 2001).

A similar pattern is apparent in the case of investments arranged through HUDCO, which finances up to 85 per cent of public sector project costs and 100 per cent in the case of direct borrowing by the government, with the structure of interest rates depending on the type of urban infrastructure schemes. The primary areas of operation for HUDCO have been urban water supply and sanitation, although since the late 1990s there has been a shift towards other infrastructure projects. Again those cities with strong economic bases are able to attract investments, whether from within India or elsewhere, and appropriate a disproportionate share of the subsidised HUDCO funds.

The major national urban programme providing funding for infrastructure development is JNNURM, which focuses on the basic services to the urban poor, development schemes for small and medium towns and integrated housing and slum development programmes. In Kolkata, water supply and roads were allocated 48.5 per cent and 25.4 per cent of the share of the total funding that KMA received in 2012 for infrastructure development which stood at Rs 6,318 crore (£640.52 million). During the same period, the amount allocated for basic services to the urban poor was Rs 3,955 crore (£400.96 million). Alongside JNNURM, there were other schemes designed to improve urban planning and governance. In 1999, the Government of West Bengal and the Department for International Development (DfID) collaborated on the Kolkata Urban Services for the Poor (KUSP) programme to provide access to basic services and promote economic growth in the 40 ULBs in KMA. Thirty projects were approved under this programme, which had an allocation of almost Rs 3 crore (£304,140). Another project involving collaboration with the Asian Development Bank and DfID was the Kolkata Environment Improvement Project (KEIP), which aimed to improve the slum districts and the drainage system and underground sewerage system for the extended areas of KMC.

Power of ULBs to raise borrowings

As mentioned above, city governments are largely dependent on transfers of resources from the higher levels of government, with cities having little access to capital markets. For a city to credibly access capital markets, some of the prerequisites include a basic double-entry accounting system, a sound financial position, and management capacity at the municipality. Another consideration is the nature of projects to be undertaken. These factors form the basis for the credit rating process, which assesses the underlying capacity of the local government to take on debt and to determine the probability of default. The higher the underlying strength of a municipality and the revenue-generating capacity of the projects undertaken, the higher the rating of the debt issued. A higher rating indicates lower cost of debt to the municipality.

UBLs across India have been aiming to achieve efficiencies so as to maximize their potential for accessing funds from the market, involving efficient allocation between capital and current expenditures, and at the same time delivering quality civic services at low costs. Attaining both goals would not only maximize the net revenue earning potential but also boost 'debt capacity' (via credit enhancement) and thus ease the constraints on financing projects involving capital expenditure. This depends on a number of factors, including the ability of the municipal corporations to carry out the designated functions independently, organisational structure for production, the planning and implementation of municipal services, and political stability (Banerji *et al.*, 2013).

As with other aspects of finances, cities in the more developed states are in better position to raise funds in the open market, as they are able to demonstrate robust systems and a greater capacity to manage projects, although even the most advantaged cities experience shortages of expertise and appropriately qualified people in key areas of urban development.

Devolving human resource management

Empowering local governments with appropriate functions is just one aspect of devolution, necessary but not sufficient. The ability of ULBs to deliver urban services depends on their capacities to fulfil their responsibilities. The Megacity Programme for Infrastructure Development in the Ninth Five Year Plan and the Urban Reform Incentive Fund (URIF) in the Tenth Five Year Plan were attempts at building capacity, but both proved to be ineffective and short-lived. Municipalities need suitably qualified skilled personnel, and the present shortcomings of municipal corporations in their ability and capacities to meet their service obligations are well recognised. India has an acute shortage of urban planners – one for every 100,000 urban residents, compared with, for example, one for every 5,000 urban residents in the United States (Janaagraha, 2013). While several capacity building initiatives have been undertaken through JNNURM and other

Table 4.6 Key recommendations: SARC, HPEC and the Working Group on Capacity Building for Twelfth Five Year Plan

Second Administrative Reforms Commission (SARC)	High Powered Expert Committee (HPEC)	Working Group on Capacity Building for the Twelfth Five Year Plan
Train elected representatives and personnel on a continuous basis	Train 300 officers from the Indian Administrative Services (IAS) and other central services annually as urban specialists and place them systematically through deputation in cities and towns	
	Build/reform municipal cadres in all states with recruitment into the cadre at entry level through a competitive examination	Create a municipal cadre, monitor performance of Capacity Building Development Plan, take mid-course correction, evaluation and assessment of effectiveness of the Capacity Development Plan
Outsource specific functions to public or private agencies, as may be appropriate, through enabling guidelines and support. In addition, focus on in-house training and capacity building measures	Provide flexibility in lateral hiring of professionals with special skills into the cadre	Evolve a Comprehensive Capacity Building framework which would address issues such as staffing, training and skill development, institutional issues and financing
	Put in place a transparent search and selection process in the appointment of the municipal commissioner	
	Tenure of the management team to be a minimum of three years	
	Develop dedicated IT cadre with a chief information officer for the larger cities	
Establish a network of institutions concerned with various subjects such as financial management, rural development, disaster management	Set up five Indian Institutes of Urban Management either anchored in existing IIMs or as stand-alone institutions of excellence	

Table 4.6 (cont.)

Second Administrative Reforms Commission (SARC)	High Powered Expert Committee (HPEC)	Working Group on Capacity Building for the Twelfth Five Year Plan
Maintain a pool of experts and specialists (e.g. engineers, planners, etc.) Create enabling provisions in municipal legislations	Promote think tank initiatives in urban policy through Centres of Excellence/ Innovation Create a Reform and Performance Management Cell (RPMC) in the Government of India (and at state level and in large cities) Infuse funds and new talent into existing Schools of Urban Planning	

Source: SARC, HPEC and Report of the Working Group on Capacity Building (2012–2017).

initiatives, the challenge is one of sustaining and building adequately trained manpower. As such, with serious deficiencies in personnel, the state of urban governance in India is in a relatively weak position to raise resources, promote PPPs or implement service level benchmarks. The implementation status of key mandatory reforms under JNNURM across the country, for example, is not encouraging. During the period 2005–2012, only 60 per cent of the total allocation of Rs 66,080 crore (£6.7 billion) was released, with just 9 per cent of the 2,815 approved projects having been completed. In respect of all JNNURM cities and ULBs receiving project assistance from central government, FICCI recommended the appointment of transaction advisors and for central government to maintain a panel of advisors, whose would be involved in the preparation of the financial road map for the ULBs, and advise on the feasibility of undertaking and implementing projects (FICCI, 2011: 14).

Both the HPEC and the Working Group on Capacity Building for the Twelfth Five Year Plan (WGCB) identified inadequate capacity as the principal reason behind the poor implementation of reforms and projects. Their reports revealed that nearly 33 per cent of ULBs and parastatals had not implemented the accrual based double-entry accounting system; more than 40 per cent of ULBs had failed to meet 85 per cent coverage of property tax by 2010–2011; out of 39 cities audited, only seven cities had implemented the user charge collection mechanism for water supply; and only five cities

Table 4.7 Key capacity building initiatives in India

Name of the initiative/institution	Objective	Coverage	Budget (INR Cr)
Pre-JNNURM[a]			
Regional Centres for Urban and Environmental Studies	Providing training and research needs in the urban sector in various states	-	21.2
National Institute of Urban Affairs (NIUA)	Providing policy prescriptions, innovations for better local governance, information and training inputs to improve quality of life of urban residents	-	10.6
Training of Elected Representatives	Training elected representatives in the ULBs	-	4.2
Public Health Engineering Training Programme, MoUD (1956)	Providing training to in-service engineers and para engineering staff of state public health engineering departments, water supply and sewerage boards, ULBs etc.	2,610 persons participated in the post-graduate programme, 25,94 in the short-term course and 30,319 in the refresher courses (until 31 March 2011)	1.9
JNNURM[b]			
Rapid Training Programme (RTP)	Upgrading the skills of municipal and parastatals staff involved in service delivery in 56 cities (all Mission cities excluding seven megacities) and orientation programme for elected representatives	1,800 ULB officials and 2,000 elected representatives from 56 Mission cities	7.8
Regional Capacity Building Hubs	Second phase of the RTP	Entire country divided into six regions with Regional Capacity Building Hubs in each region	5.51

Table 4.7 (cont.)

Name of the initiative/ institution	Objective	Coverage	Budget (INR Cr)
Other capacity building initiatives			
North Eastern Region Urban Development Programme (NERUDP)	Providing technical assistance for project design, monitoring and implementation through appointment of design supervision and monitoring consultants	Five capital cities of the North East region	1300
Scheme of Urban Infrastructure Development in Satellite Towns	Developing infrastructure	Eight satellite towns in the vicinity of seven megacities	500
Capacity Building for Urban Local Bodies (CBULB)	Establishing Centres of Excellence (CoEs) in ten institutions of repute. These institutions are working on different areas that expose urban sector related issues to senior urban managers in the government sector	Capacity building programmes have been sanctioned for Chhattisgarh, Madhya Pradesh, Karnataka and Odisha	87.5
Total			1,938.7

Notes: [a] The budget for these initiatives is for the period of the Eleventh Five Year Plan up to 31 March 2011. [b] The budget for these initiatives refers to the total cost over the period of implementation.

Source: Report of the Working Group on Capacity Building (2011).

had implemented the user charge collection mechanism for solid waste management. Table 4.6 shows the range of measures proposed by these bodies to address the problem.

Urban management is, therefore, yet to emerge as a specialised professional domain in India. Municipal corporations in India lack the comprehensive and well-defined set of roles and job descriptions to ensure that there are appropriately staffed across all urban services and functions. While it is recognised that the devolution of powers in respect of human resource management would take time, interim solutions are recommended that might be appropriate in the short term such as appointing search committees for the appointment of municipal commissioners. Proposals have been advanced to combine the role of the chief executive with that of the chairperson of ULBs and for the combined post holder to have complete authority to fill positions in city administration. As a transitional arrangement, it has also been recommended that for designated senior positions the state government might offer a panel of names to the urban local body for consideration and selection.

Beyond the position of commissioner, calls for establishing appropriate mechanisms for the recruitment of senior staff in urban management have been made that would ensure a time-bound, fair and transparent process. Proposals to develop Key Performance Indicators with appropriate benchmarking – both metric (to establish different levels of performance) and process (to assess performance) have been considered. The proposals of the working group on capacity building identified a number of initiatives, including training for elected representatives and administrators, and enabling local bodies to outsource specific functions to public or private agencies through appropriate guidelines, supported and backed by development of in-house capacity for the monitoring and oversight of outsourced activities (Table 4.7). The group also recommended that state governments create an empanelled List of Urban Practice Professional Institutions whose services could be accessed contractually by ULBs without having to go through cumbersome and repetitive procurement procedures.

The role of state governments is crucial as they are ideally placed to contribute effectively to human resource management and to improve the quality of urban development through dedicated funds for urban capacity building, as seen in other countries such as Mexico, China and Brazil.

Digital governance

A recent survey of India's city systems concluded that:

> there is a total absence of institutional mechanisms that would empower the ULB to manage its affairs efficiently and effectively such as performance management systems, robust digital governance, emergency management systems and most importantly appropriate supervisory powers with respect to functioning of other civic agencies operating in its jurisdiction.
>
> (Janaagraha, 2013: 14)

A crucial resource relates to modern technological systems as cities increasingly need access to modern tools and the technology of urban management in order to respond to the complex challenges of rapid urbanisation. While Mumbai and Hyderabad have set up a range of modules under e-governance initiatives under JNNURM, Kolkata lags far behind (HPEC, 2011: 196). Noting the wide variations between states, the committee emphasised the importance of support infrastructure and issues relating to telecommunications links, band connectivity, and skills including IT literacy with local language content and applications as crucial for making e-governance effective (HPEC, 2011: 105). The committee's recommendations included the requirement for state governments to develop standard and comprehensive urban e-governance packages setting out specifications, applications, hardware, software and service level assessments, and to have in place the key services relating to accounting, payroll, procurement and tendering, works management and property tax (HPEC, 2011: 106).

While some ULBs have migrated to double-entry accounting systems, there has been a lack of effective integration with the regularly audited financial statements, service-level benchmarking and credit rating mechanisms, all of which are central to effective financial management. Insufficient use is made of GIS, a powerful tool, set to become an increasingly vital element of good urban governance, both at the metropolitan level and at the level of each local body. However, currently there exists little usable GIS data for the various metropolitan regions in India, both at macro and neighbourhood levels. A number of initiatives have been recommended, which include the establishment of a GIS service level agreement by ULBs with a data centre covering mutual deliverables, the production of a base map for the entire metropolitan area and maintained by the data centre, and for the urban body to generate such primary data as property tax and water distribution relevant to its own area. The aim is for each ULB to have web-based access to view all data in the data centre with updated access to its own layers of data. Undoubtedly the application and development of such modern technological systems of governance requires large infrastructure and the expertise of professionals, but in cities around the world it has been shown that such investment pays dividends. A comprehensive policy to include capacity building for ULBs, information infrastructure, and applications and access would facilitate more effective urban governance.

*****

Recent decentralisation initiatives and the increasing pace of urbanisation have considerably increased the fiscal obligations of the third tier of government, without commensurate devolution of human and financial resources to discharge these obligations. Estimating the investment requirements for urban infrastructure services, HPEC recommended empowering ULBs with 'exclusive' taxes, for state governments to share with ULBs a pre-specified percentage of their revenues from all taxes on goods and services, and provide for formula based transfers and grants-in-aid from the divisible pool. To date, none of the recommendations have been implemented. There has been much discussion about reforming the indirect tax system to move towards value added tax and subsequently to a consolidated goods and services tax, which would enable sharing of service tax revenues, currently retained with the national government. The 13th Finance Commission attempted to create a buoyant source of revenue for local bodies in general, but progress is impeded by lack of reliable and consistent data from both the SFCs and states themselves.

A weak tax base, inadequate taxing and poor recovery have remained the salient features of ULBs in India. The balancing of budgets is generally at the cost of essential municipal services. There is considerable mismatch between the functions and finances of municipalities, with very few functions having corresponding financing sources. The Twelfth Schedule of the Constitution had envisaged important functions such as slum improvement and urban poverty alleviation to belong legitimately to the functional domain of ULBs.

However, the devolution of functions as envisaged has not happened and the commensurate resources have not been made available for institutions to discharge effectively those limited functions that have been devolved. Since ULBs have only limited powers to levy taxes and duties, and several of these are inflexible and unproductive, they have to depend on resources from the Government of India and state governments to perform the tasks assigned to them by the constitution and state legislatures.

The parastatal agencies are often criticised in the decentralised governance framework, but in reality these bodies play a vital role in the planning, implementation and management of important functions such as urban and town planning, water supply, construction, and maintenance of roads. One of the main justifications of having these functions with the parastatal agencies is the dedicated human resources and technical competencies they possess, which ULBs lack. Their role in managing India's urban governance is likely to continue until such time as Urban Local Bodies are themselves empowered with the necessary financial, functional and human reources.

Notes

1 The ARV system gave enormous discretion and provided a basis for corruption by tax collectors as they determined the value at which the property may 'reasonably' be expected to be rented. Under the JNNURM, some states have amended their Rent Control Acts.

5 The reach of metropolitan power

The classic metropolitan problem of growth spilling beyond municipal boundaries is as prevalent in India as elsewhere. The peripheral expansion has taken place rapidly beyond the formal administrative boundaries, with smaller municipalities and large villages surrounding the core city sometimes becoming part of the large metropolitan area. There are huge challenges facing Indian cities in identifying new ways of planning and managing such expansion and, as such, governance arrangements are currently confined to limited, often socially and spatially distinct, areas.

This chapter considers metropolitan growth and expansion in Hyderabad, Kolkata and Mumbai, all of which are undergoing considerable strains of expansion. These cities experience considerable problems of growth and sprawl that have undermined their ability to plan for, direct and control the development process. Master plans have been the principal tool by which cities have sought to steer and channel the pressures of growth and, though ambitious, they have inescapably been limited in scope. Expansion has continued to be haphazard which together with uncoordinated planning has led to the development of urban peripheries, areas that pose immense challenges for city planners in their attempts to produce spatially integrated plans and pursue a comprehensive urban reform agenda. The chapter examines the opportunities and challenges of managing these spatially dispersed regions in the context of the changing landscape of metropolitan governance.

Metropolitan growth and expansion

Scattered and fragmented forms of urban land-use have long characterised the phenomenon of urbanisation in sustainable development. Problems of sprawl, the urban fringe and peri-urban areas or, more appropriately, defined as semi-urban areas have been subject to much analysis in recent years (Dwyer and Childs, 2004).[1] The Garden City Movement in the UK in the early twentieth century represented a movement against sprawl, with the aim of preserving open spaces and providing coherence to the growing edge cities on the urban fringe (Lee and Ahn, 2003; Talen, 2005; Walmsley, 2006). Much of the development in the inter-war era had been on greenfield land, along roads that run out to the suburbs. All this came to an end with the outbreak of war in 1939, and subsequent years saw the introduction of the 'green belt' and other modern town planning arrangements aimed at halting city-edge development. It provided a solution to create sustainable semi-urban and peri-urban areas. In the United States, Smart Growth became a popular planning tool for containing sprawl by directing development towards existing communities and enabling development decisions to be predictable, fair and cost-effective. At the core of the concept was the promotion of green belts, mixed land-use, compact building design, rural developments near urban fringes and multifunctional land-use to provide attractive housing and transport opportunities (Walmsley, 2006).

Another important trend in urban form has been polycentricity, associated with growing socio-spatial polarisation. This form of development, aimed at providing proximity to services and employment opportunities, is increasingly acknowledged as an ideal pattern for very large cities, driven largely by private investments rather than deliberate planning. Against the backdrop of these different approaches emerged a broad consensus amongst metropolitan planners on the nature of strategic ambition, which Foster summarises as 'containment, consolidation and centres'. He captures the compact city vision, for example, which now informs all metropolitan strategies in Australia:

> In 20–30 years time, if the plans come to fruition, our major cities will be characterised by limited suburban expansion, a strong multi-nuclear structure with high density housing around centres and transport corridors, and infill and densification throughout the current inner and middle suburbs. Residents will live closer to their work in largely self-contained suburban labour sheds, and will inhabit smaller, more energy efficient houses. Regeneration programs will have broken up large concentrations of disadvantage, and a diminished public housing sector will only house welfare dependent households in acute need.
>
> (Foster, 2006: 179)

Indian cities manifest multiple problems of urban sprawl, congestion and high infrastructure costs. Several factors have contributed to sprawl, including population growth leading to spatial expansion of the city and rising incomes demanding larger space for housing and quality of life. Recent decades have witnessed heavy suburbanisation caused by the 'flight from the city' and improvements in transport, which have enabled and encouraged people to move to the suburbs. Structural and other related issues such as improper fringe area planning and weak enforcement of planning norms have been other contributory factors that have exacerbated the problem of uncontrolled growth of peripheral areas.

Low density developments, developments along transport corridors and discontinuous development of areas (leapfrog development) have resulted in high infrastructure costs, traffic congestion, social segregation and environmental hazards (Siddiqui, 2003). For many years, growth and expansion was largely directed to big cities, and, to a lesser extent, to a few new towns where large-scale industries developed. More recently, this pattern has changed significantly, with an increasing trend towards movement into the periphery of metropolitan and other large cities. The lateral spread of cities has resulted in an increase in the use of urban area, with the decadal rate of growth of urban land area rising from 8.72 per cent during 1961–1971 to 20.54 per cent during 1971–1981 and 21.81 per cent between 1981 and 91 (Shaw, 2012).

In Hyderabad, while such peripheral spread has occurred at the expense of the old city, growth and expansion has resulted in development that has not always been contiguous with the city limits (Neelakanthan *et al.*, 2007). Some pockets of development within the metropolitan area are densely built but infrastructure deficient because of their remoteness and the lack of capacity in existing civic services. Here and in other rapidly growing urban centres, such settlements are emerging spontaneously and remain virtually untouched by formal governance (Sivaramakrishnan, 2008: 28). Planning in these circumstances has become a somewhat abstract exercise, as urban form becomes more or less uncontrollable and infrastructural problems continue to increase (Roy, 2013: 2).

Such haphazard and unregulated increases in peripheral areas have prompted state governments to devise new strategies for renewal and redevelopment. They necessitated the first master plan for the Hyderabad Development Area in the 1980s, which aimed at achieving a greater synthesis between the rural hinterland and the metropolitan region through balanced development. Detailed Zonal Development Plans (ZDPs) were prepared during this period, which formed the basis for land-use, conversions, conservation and recreation areas. The subsequent revised master plan advocated clustering of areas for compact development in conjunction with the development of transport corridors.

The spatial distribution and patterns of growth, however, have not always been uniform. Smaller metropolitan cities in India continue to expand within city limits, while the large ones experience declining growth in the core and outward expansion. Population densities in and around the largest metropolitan areas are very high. They average 2,450 persons per square kilometre in the 50-kilometre radius of the seven largest metropolitan areas (with populations above four million), and in a third of India's new towns developed in a 50-kilometres radius of existing cities with more than one million people.

A recent World Bank study concluded that:

> If these trends are any indication of how the future will unfold, much of India's urbanisation challenge will be to transform land-use and expand infra-structure in its largest metropolises and their neighbouring suburbs – places that are not pristine or greenfield but that already support 9 per cent of the country's population and provide 18 per cent of the employment on 1 per cent of the land area. The challenge so far is that these high population densities have not been supported by commensurate

policies and investments to enable residential and commercial development, infrastructure services, and connectivity.

(World Bank, 2013: 1)

As such, managing densities has been a key challenge in trying to accommodate urban expansion. Floor space capping is much more restrictive in India compared with other countries where the practice is to raise the permitted Floor Space Index (FSI) to accommodate growth. Such regulations have forced businesses and residents out of urban cores to suburbs, which in turn has impacted on house prices and commuting costs for workers. The rationale for restrictive FSI practices has been justified in terms of protecting existing infrastructure that would otherwise collapse under the weight of densities. Nevertheless, many have argued the case for high density vertical development, while the missed opportunities through regulated densities and the consequent problems of sprawl were identified by the World Bank:

> Density regulations through low FSIs generate sprawl as development is forced to the periphery of urban areas. In Bangalore, for example, FSI-induced sprawl causes welfare losses of 2–4 per cent of household income due to higher commuting costs. Another striking feature of density regulations is that Indian cities have blanket FSIs that cover large areas – thus missing opportunities to strategically increase densities around infrastructure networks. In fact, 'granularity' – or extremely local variations – in FSI design and in coordination of land-use to exploit infrastructure placement is the bedrock of good urban planning. Best international practice in cities such as New York, Seoul, and Singapore suggests that planners need to keep in mind that while density should not overwhelm infrastructure capacity, neither should it sub optimally use infrastructure networks.
>
> (World Bank, 2013: 5)

Several states decentralised their planning to contain high densities and sprawl and achieve a spatially balanced urban growth. The imbalanced distribution of urban population across West Bengal prompted the state to adopt a policy of decentralised urban development involving small and medium towns and growth centres to discharge urban functions, and municipal towns to disperse activities from the metropolitan core to other areas within the metropolis. Mumbai adopted a similar approach to manage its expansion, with polycentric developments involving satellite towns serving as counter-magnets to draw people away from the centre to the periphery.

The planning process

The process of managing urban change goes directly to the heart of governmental systems. The need for area-wide structures that enjoy legal

110 *The reach of metropolitan power*

capacity and authority has been well recognised for some years now and a number of attempts were made during the 1970s and 1980s to achieve better land-use planning and improved coordination through the creation of appropriate boards and agencies at all levels of decision making. The State Town and Country Planning Acts set out the various stages of the planning process, including the requirement to produce regional plans. In Mumbai, the Maharashtra Regional and Town Planning Act, 1966, governing the physical and land-use planning of the city, provides for regional plans for metropolitan regions, development plans (DPs) for individual cities, town planning schemes for parts of the cities, and proposals for undeveloped areas through special planning authorities. The state's special Township Policy for development of new towns is designed to prevent growth of population in large cities, disperse population away from bigger cities by planning a spatial dispersal of economic activity, and attract direct foreign investment and the private sector. In Andhra Pradesh, the Town and Country Planning Act of 1920, revised in 1988 (governing all districts), and the Andhra Pradesh Urban Areas Development Act, 1975 (for Declared Urban Development Authorities and Municipalities, and constituent municipalities), have been the two principal planning related laws. More recently the Andhra Pradesh Municipalities Act, 1994, and Hyderabad Metropolitan Development Authority Act, 2008 (for establishing HMDA) have also been instrumental in the governance of HMR, the metropolitan region. The Municipal Corporation Urban Development Authorities exercise powers to plan and regulate development as vested in them by the act of 1975, but the presence of multiple agencies in planning and administration often undermines zonal regulations prepared by these authorities.

Regional plans, as strategic spatial plans, have an important role in guiding the development, but have not been very effective in recent times. The years immediately following the implementation of the CAA saw a peak in the work undertaken on regional planning, but little has been done on the subject since then. The slow pace of regional planning has had implications for the development of city regions, compounded by the failure of states to constitute effective metropolitan planning committees, whose task it is to review regional plans and define appropriate procedures for the expansion of urban limits. Regional plans also have an important role in guiding district plans. Again, in reality, district plans have generally superseded regional plans in almost all cities. Mumbai's first district plan was produced in 1967, with a regional plan following in 1973; the second district plan was completed in 1994 and the regional plan in 1999. The same pattern holds for the current, third, district plan, due in 2014, with the regional plan expected to follow at a later date. More fundamentally, as regional planning authorities have no responsibility for district councils, their effectiveness as instruments of development control have been questioned (Phatak and Patel, 2005). The district development plans have themselves been subject to considerable delays. The Region and Town Planning Act requires every municipal corporation to prepare a development plan to be implemented over 20 years. The last development plan for Mumbai was prepared in 1981 but adopted 13 years later, in 1994. A new plan that is valid for 20 years is now scheduled for 2014, to be in force until 2034. Such inordinate delays are not specific to Mumbai.

The weaknesses in the planning system lie not in the legislation, but in its administration. Although states may direct local authorities to prepare plans, the municipalities are not always willing to carry out the edict, nor do they have the capacity and the expertise. Financial burden is often cited as a deterrent and few municipalities undertake comprehensive planning programmes. This argument is not without substance, for local revenues are stretched, especially in smaller towns without any industrial base. Funds continue to be controlled and dispersed from the centre, which in recent years has led states to compete with one another to attract funding, largely independent of policies and strategies at the state or national level (Sridharan and Razak, 2003; Sridharan and Yadav, 2001). A recent study showed just how such competitiveness led to unintended or unplanned growth and problems of regional inequalities leading to unplanned expansion and territorial conflicts within the metro regions (Kundu and Sarangi, 2009). The case is made for better working relationships and cross-departmental cooperation, linking plans with funding opportunities at state and national level, together with equitable distribution of funds to meet the development needs of cities and towns.

Put simply, the challenge of urban growth and the inability of local bodies to plan for, direct and control the development process has led to continued dependence on specialised planning bodies, such as the state government nodal agencies – agencies with the state's chief minister acting as the chairperson, and comprising representatives from various constituent bodies. Although there are variations in the way they integrate into the different devolution models adopted by each state, they carry out their own planning programmes, subject to minimal checks, principally in the form of budgetary control of development projects, involving central funds. They have the power, in the public interest, to modify, revoke or annul any part of the plan. The extent to which states should enjoy the right to amend, revoke or refuse plans has been the topic of much debate and discussion. The Kasturirangan Committee, set up to consider a governance framework for Bangalore metropolitan area, expressed the view that it may not be necessary for a plan prepared by a local self-governing body to be reviewed by the state government for formal approval (Kasturirangan Committee, 2008).

Planning requires governance, and to that extent the problems of managing urban change go directly to the question of structures. The CAA called for a more decentralised and collaborative system that respected the sensitivities of local authorities. Although well conceived, the success of reform has been limited. There is widespread duplication of functions and an absence of effective coordination between municipal, metropolitan and state level agencies. Urban development authorities remain responsible for planning, while municipal corporations have the task of implementing, often without adequate resources, resulting in poor governance and management of urban areas. Coordinated enforcement of the plan is made difficult by the presence of multiple planning authorities with overlapping roles and responsibilities.

Master-planning the cities

The limits to the planning of India's cities are readily apparent. The metropolitan areas will continue to grow, and new – if scarcely adequate – infrastructure will be laid down even in the absence of any plan. Most Indian urban master plans have been used only as a framework for development control. They set the parameters within which development and improvement of the entire plan area is to be carried out and regulated. The plans are required to anticipate how the city's population and boundaries might grow, and what the city needs to do to absorb this growth, function effectively and remain liveable. The scope and content of master plans across the states are broadly similar: designed to contain growth and limit the territorial expansion of the core city, and to identify areas adjoining the existing core city with a view to developing them.[2]

The process of developing city master plans involves several stages, including economic and demographic surveys to take stock of population, employment and the local economy, projections of the overall population, demographics and economic growth for the next 20 years, land-use surveys, and land-use planning for housing, commerce and public amenities to accommodate the projected increases in population. The process takes two to four years in a major city and results in a draft master plan, which is then shared with local citizens to elicit their suggestions and comments. Changes, if deemed necessary, are made to the draft master plan based on public input and then submitted to the state government for approval. Following close scrutiny, the state government makes further modifications, if necessary, and gives final approval. This review, refinement and approval of the final master plan can take a further two to four years.

Despite the clarity of the process, master planning has not worked to expectations. Cities have not kept pace with the growth that urban areas have experienced, resulting in poor amenities and infrastructure and problems of overcrowding. Structural plans and zoning regulations aimed at controlling density and dealing with environmental issues have proved more appropriate for the management of urban sprawl, while master plans are criticised for not having adequately addressed the growing demand for space by households and commercial organisations (Sarkar *et al.*, 2013: 64).

The lengthy time frame for the preparation of a master plan, which can run into several years – sometimes up to ten years – has been subject to much criticism. The Hyderabad Master Plan for 2001–2021 was not completed until 2005 and notified only in 2008. Almost half the plan period had passed by the time the plan was notified and ready for implementation. If the purpose of the planning is to project how cities would develop in the foreseeable future, such delays often mean the actual population or economic growth turns out to be different than that projected. The master plan, then, is often divorced from the actual development of the city. A classic example of this is the establishment and growth of the IT industry since the mid-1990s in Pune, in the State of Maharashtra. The industry was almost non-existent when the city developed its 1987–2007 Master Plan. However, the boom in the IT industry led to the creation of large technology parks on the outskirts of the city, which in turn gave rise to highly populated fringe development without adequate infrastructure, roads, water and sewage facilities. The master plan had clearly not envisioned this type of growth in these areas.

The master plans are further criticised for placing undue emphasis on land-use without giving adequate consideration to other aspects of city development such as transport and mobility, environmental preservation, and regional linkages. Some commentators have called for a more dynamic and flexible master plan to guide and direct the growth of cities, a high level 'macro' plan explicitly setting out a vision for the city with implications for transportation, public services, amenities, housing environment and economic growth. This was acknowledged by Hyderabad's previous comprehensive master plan of 2003, which accepted that any indicative plan is vulnerable to changes in the international and national environment as well as to state and local policies and priorities. 'In this globalized world', commented the document, 'Hyderabad is no longer only the capital of Andhra Pradesh. It is an international city' and as such open to exogenous influences beyond any planner's control (HUDA, 2003: 147).

Most cities underestimate the cost of implementing their master plans and tend to be overly optimistic about implementation. The plans are not accompanied by financial estimates of developmental costs. As the regional plan for the MMR acknowledged:

> Sanctioning of the regional plan could not establish any linkage with the formulation of Five Year Plans and consequent resource allocation. No conscious efforts are made in annual budgetary exercise either to allocate resources for the implementation of plans. Investment programming has thus remained isolated from land-use planning and also uncoordinated across the agencies.
>
> (MMR, 1996: 98)

A robust business plan setting out the development activities envisioned in the master plan and sources of financing – whether in the form of new taxes or charges, PPPs, or loans from multilateral agencies –would to some extent address the existing gap between planning and implementation.

Implementing the master plan in Hyderabad

A common feature of expansion in the main large corporations of the State of Andhra Pradesh is the growth away from the city core. The population growth in the surrounding municipalities of Hyderabad, for example, during 1981–1991 was 158 per cent as against 42 per cent in the MCH. In the following decade the population growth in surrounding municipalities stood at 72 per cent as against 19 per cent for the MCH area. The low rate of growth in the MCH was attributed to poor access to land, the high cost of land, rental values and restricted building regulations (HMDA, 2010). The MCH is the core city area and is divided into five zones, including the recently merged 12 municipalities, designed to enhance service provision and achieve an integrated civic development strategy. The municipal corporation comprises only 27 per cent of the GHMC area, but accommodates around 60 per cent of the population of GHMC. Likewise it occupies only 2 per cent of the HMDA, while accommodating nearly 50 per cent of the HMDA's population. The city itself is expected to cross five million by 2021.

The HMR enjoys premier status in Andhra Pradesh both in terms of its demographics and economy. Incorporating the two districts of Hyderabad and Ranga Reddy, it covers an area of 7,000 square kilometres. Apart from the GHMC area, the remaining area comprises two municipal councils, 202 block panchayats and 4,340 village panchayats. The boundaries of this region were reconstituted in 2008 when the then Hyderabad Urban Development Authority (HUDA) was extended to create the HMDA. In view of the projected rise in the population in the next two decades, the master plan aims to create multiple growth centres, a series of self-contained zones with employment hubs, and residential and associated amenities to reduce the pressures on the core. Apart from the core, the plan identifies second order developments of *urban nodes*, dispersed across the region, with the potential to grow, and an additional 35 third order development centres – *urban centres* (defined as those interdependent on the urban contiguous pockets and urban nodes). As a transition space, peri-urban zones are identified that would help contain the urban sprawl.

The region is emerging as a concentrated political entity representing diverse political constituencies, both urban and rural. Hyderabad was the first city to develop a CDP, but each of the planning tools currently operational in Hyderabad represents a specific developmental need. There are seven master plans in operation shared by HMDA, GHMC and two municipalities. These include the revised plan for HMC, which is essentially a development control plan and creates new opportunities in the core area through potential reclassification of land-use. The Hyberabad Development Authority, responsible for the expanding IT and advanced producer services sector, has its own master plan that aims to develop entire finance and IT districts and promote institutional infrastructure. The Hyderabad Airport Development Authority (HADA) master plan aims to open up a development zone that is flexible enough to be attractive to investors for new infrastructure projects in the hospitality and retail sector. The Outer Ring Road Growth Corridor plan is to facilitate urbanisation around the new road; the Bhuvanagiri and Sangareddy Municipal Plans are for the rapidly expanding municipalities; and a master

The reach of metropolitan power 115

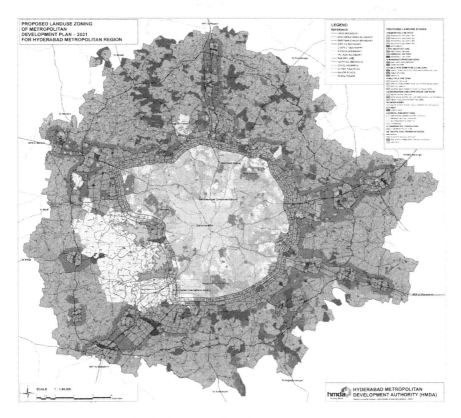

Figure 5.1 Map of Hyderabad Metropolitan Area
Source: Hyderabad Metropolitan Development Authority (HMDA).

plan for non-municipal areas of the original HUDA to devise new land-use categories and reserve zones of conservation.

An analysis of spatial growth patterns indicates saturation of growth in the core area and high growth and densities in the surrounding areas along the industrial growth corridors, with a further concentration of activities along roads (ribbon development). Radiating roads connect the core city with the outer development areas. Apart from a Regional Ring Road (RRR), the development plan proposes arterial roads such as state highways and national highways connecting the inner ring road to the outer ring road. The Inner Ring Road (IRR) is a 50-kilometre city arterial road in Hyderabad, designed mainly to divert heavy vehicle and commercial traffic from city roads. Designed by Nippon Koei of Japan, the project is implemented with assistance from the Japanese International Cooperation Agency (JICA) and had been planned for completion by 2013.

The Outer Ring Road (ORR) and its Growth Corridor (predominantly greenfield areas) constitute almost all the development area, and the master plan aims to regulate development within the green belt. The ORR, a 158-kilometre, eight-lane ring road expressway, connecting national and state highways, was built with substantial funding from JICA and designed to improve connectivity and reduce traffic flows on the existing major arterials between the outer suburbs of Greater Hyderabad. These, together with the new elevated expressways and nodal developments in the north, south and west, comprising the Knowledge Park, international airport, HITECH City and the financial district respectively, provide the new spatial structure for Hyderabad. As a result of these developments, the city region of Hyderabad has acquired a complex character incorporating a mix of rural and urban areas and multiple agencies governing the urban space.

During the mid-1990s, the HUDA had implemented the Hyderabad Greenbelt project, aimed at regulating developments around the twin cities of Hyderabad and Secunderabad and extensive greening of waste lands, industrial estates and residential areas. The current Green Hyderabad project, funded by the Government of the Netherlands, continues to build on the success of its predecessor and focuses on Urban Greening and Integrated Lake Treatment, with the latter having identified 18 lakes as problematic and in need of restoration. The HUDA's plan also makes provision for environmentally friendly non-motorised transport, together with adequate provision for cycle tracks, shaded footpaths and cluster layouts instead of linear layout to reduce vehicular lengths. Other provisions include battery charging facilities in sites over 20 hectares for every one in 50 cars parked.

City development strategy

Andhra Pradesh is set to become the foremost state in the country in terms of economic growth, equity and quality of life. Its plan, *Vision 2020*, envisages that by the end of the decade the state will have well-planned, economically productive, environmentally sustainable, culturally vibrant, and safe cities and towns. The role of the state is to ensure balanced urban development by promoting alternative urban centres as counter-magnets and providing for urban infrastructure through comprehensive and integrated planning, and operating municipal services on a competitive basis. The plan seeks to maintain the central role of PPPs as well as public participation in the delivery of services. Based on *Vision 2020*, the HMC embarked on a city development strategy with the aim of achieving equitable growth by addressing issues of poverty, good governance and service delivery based on community empowerment and decentralised decision making.

The problems associated with urbanisation in the state were acknowledged, including the dominance of urban agglomerations, growth in the number of cities, migration and diversification of economic activities resulting in a shift of towns from mono- to multi-functional categories. In collaboration with multilateral agencies such as Cities Alliance and the UN Centre for Human Settlements, stakeholder consultation was undertaken involving service providers, private sector, NGOs, research and academic institutions, media and resident welfare associations. It clearly established the 'inter-dependence of the several components of planned change, the achievement of which could only be realized by more effective joint working between the many stakeholders' (Rao, 2007: 129).

A strategic plan outlining a strategic vision of the city, taking into account the constraints, opportunities and challenges, provided the basis for a City Assistance Programme (CAP). It set out the short- and long-term high impact programmes requiring coordinated cross-sectoral planning and investment. Other proposals include redevelopment projects for commercial and retail purposes, implementation of innovative development regulations, and improvement of infrastructure through renewal, rejuvenation and redevelopment (HMDA, 2010: 73–75). A positive impact of the city development strategy process in Hyderabad is the realisation of the need for spatial and functional convergence of the roles of the city and state level institutions such as MCH, HMWSSB and HUDA. The strategy acknowledges the importance of taking a 'holistic approach giving equal weight to economic, political, institutional, social, and cultural factors and to democracy, which is seen as a vital component of development, not merely an outcome of the process of economic and social advancement' (CGG, 2003).

Planning the Kolkata metropolitan region

Since 1951, all three major constituents of the metropolitan region – KMC, Kolkata Urban Agglomeration (KUA) and Kolkata Metropolitan District (KMD) – have experienced a decline in the rate of population growth, while urban sprawl, outward from the city core, has continued in all directions. The decadal growth rate of population in the fringe has surpassed that of the city core since the 1980s. Within the city the population declined from 4.57 in 2001 to 4.48 million in 2011, while the metropolitan region as a whole grew by 5.3 per cent during that period, accompanied by growth in the number of census towns.[3] The total number of census towns within the KMA doubled from 80 in 2001 to 153 in 2011.

The number of such census towns is growing at a rapid rate and the state currently has 780 census towns (528 were added in the last decade), the highest in India. Although many of the newly developed towns qualify to be municipalities and nagar panchayats (transitional areas, which will in future become municipalities), only 127 of them are statutorily declared as such. In 2001, the number of census towns was 252, of which only four were recognised as ULBs. The latest census revealed 'non-recognised' urban territories, the term used to denote the territories that have been declared as 'urban' by the Census of India but have not been declared as 'statutory urban' ULBs by the state. This slow process of municipalisation and underreporting of actual urban territorial dimension contributes to the low level of 'recognised' urbanisation in West Bengal. Most of the census towns, especially those that are experiencing rapid growth of industries, mining and commercial enterprises, also experience high levels of inward migration of population either from immediate rural vicinities or from other adjoining areas. These census towns are under the governance of gram panchayat – the lowest level of rural government in India – but the actual built-up areas often cut across different panchayats, thus making the governance as well as provision of infrastructure and services more problematic (Samanta, 2012). The process has sometimes been referred to as 'subaltern urbanisation' in India, denoting autonomous growth of settlements that are generated by market and historical forces, which are dependent neither on large traditional settlements nor planned cities nor industrial townships (Mukhopadhyay *et al.*, 2010: 52).

KMA is the second largest metropolis in India and extends over an area of 1,854 square kilometres with a population of more than 15 million. The metropolitan area comprises 41 contiguous ULBs and over 100 rural local bodies. The city forms a linear pattern along the east and west banks of the River Hooghly, with rural areas serving as protective green belt around the conurbation. The total area has been increasing since 2001, the most recent being the addition of 47 villages to the region in 2009. Despite the dispersal, KMC continues to be the most densely populated in the region, with 24,092 persons per square kilometre, followed by Howrah Corporation. The maximum growth of population has been in the western and southern parts of the KMA, mainly in the districts of Hooghly and Howrah. However, infrastructure developments and investment have focused mainly on the eastern bypass, resulting in a mismatch between population growth and commensurate public services.

The KMA was constituted under the Calcutta Metropolitan Planning Area Control Act of 1965 with the objective of coordinating development planning and the implementation of projects. However, the planned development of the city has a long history. The Calcutta Improvement Trust (CIT), now known as the Kolkata Improvement Trust (KIT), was set up under the Calcutta Improvement Act, 1911, and has played a major role in developing the city. KIT designed and developed most of housing, urban infrastructure and lake development projects over the past hundred years, both within the core city and the suburban areas. The city is one of the most advanced in developing perspective plans, having published its first such plan in 1966. The following decade witnessed rapid population growth and industrial development, which necessitated a new plan in 1976 that proposed the creation of self-contained community groups. The Kolkata–Howrah complex was to be the major centre, supported by a number of sub-centres of varying size and importance. The plan was revised in 1983 with proposals to create 19 new centres for development. In an effort to streamline and coordinate developments KIT was merged with KMC in 2011 and a special officer appointed to oversee development and infrastructure projects.

On the basis of the intensity of spatial development of the city, the metropolitan region was classified into three different groups: areas covering the compactly developed central core; less compact areas surrounding the central core; and sporadic fringe areas that merge into the adjoining rural areas to give rise to urban sprawl. In line with this, the CDP published in 2007 envisaged a hierarchy of centres to include: (1) Kolkata as the metro centre of first order, which would continue to dominate the activities in the metropolis; (2) Howrah as the metro second order sub-centre; and (3) 15 major centres with populations ranging between 0.5 million and 0.75 million. It was estimated that by 2025 about nine million people would reside in these major centres (KMDA, 2007: 21). In addition, five metro city centres were identified together with industrial growth centres of economic activities generating employment opportunities.

KMA's latest *Vision 2025* is much more prescriptive, identifying priority areas for planned development of the region including the Kolkata Metropolitan Region (areas within a 50-kilometre radius of the city), the intermediate metropolitan region (areas within 75 kilometres of the city) and the inner metropolitan region (within 100 kilometres of the city). The vision provides for strategies to sustain Kolkata as 'the strong industrial and intellectual hub' both nationally and regionally. The conservation of natural heritage, space for housing and social infrastructure, the establishment of rapid transportation corridors to ensure accessibility and opportunities, and the creation of economic enterprise zones by providing high intensity industrial establishments are some of the central principles underlying the city's *Vision 2025*.

Managing Kolkata's peripheries

The last three decades have witnessed an expansion of the periphery of KMA. Its area of 1,350 square kilometres in 1991, housing a population of 12.5 million, increased to 1,886.67 square kilometres by 2007, with a population exceeding 15.5 million. It is predicted that by 2025 the population of KMA will increase to 22.04 million, and approximately 5.80 million are likely to settle either in municipalities and non-municipal areas within the KMA or just outside it. Recent years have seen the growth of new towns to accommodate expansion within the metropolitan area, while the growing density of population and land values in the core hubs has resulted in the dispersal of settlements away from the metropolitan core. For decades, the area has been emerging as a poly-nucleated multi-centre metropolis, with Howrah and Kolkata as hubs. The population of the KMC and Hooghly Metropolitan Corporation areas in 1961 was about 57 per cent of the population of KMA, which reduced to 38 per cent in 2001 (KMDA, 2007: 19).

These emerging new spaces in the fringe areas of the sprawling metropolis have given rise to 'new Kolkata', where planning authorities in partnership with the private sector are 'set to redesign and restructure the spatial parameters'

Figure 5.2 Map of Kolkata Metropolitan Area
Source: Kolkata Metropolitan Development Authority (KMDA).

(Podder, 2013: 145). The development in the 1970s of Bidhannagar, popularly known as 'Salt Lake City' due to its location on a reclaimed salt lake, characterised the beginning of the sprawl, with the new township absorbing over half of the wetlands on the city's eastern fringe. The region also witnessed the development of other new towns – East Kolkata Township and Patuli Township – which reclaimed large areas of the remaining wetlands. The East Kolkata township, located nine kilometres from the central business district (CBD), aimed to provide additional housing for a projected population of about 50,000. The Baishnabghata Patuli township, 15 kilometres southeast from the CBD, was also specifically designed for a population of just over 50,000. Both are served by important roads, rail and metro networks. Other new developments in the south and the south-east include the affluent neighbourhoods of Ballygunge and Jodhpur Park, in close proximity to the city centre, and the development of the country's second financial hub at Jyoti Basu Nagar. Spread over 120 hectares, with huge investment, the hub is expected to play a catalytic role as the business gateway to South-East Asia. The financial hub is home to several banking and financial institutions, insurance companies, stock exchanges, hospitality and educational institutions.

Another project which is functionally and spatially integrated with the main metropolitan structure is the Rajarhat New Town development. Located about ten kilometres from the CBD and less than a kilometre from the airport, the project is being developed by the West Bengal Housing Infrastructure Development Corporation (WBHIDCO), and enjoys strong political support. Other initiatives include the South City development comprising shopping malls, residential complexes, schools and clubs, and the Kolkata West International Township at Howrah, on the National Highway. 'Planning for Kolkata has turned into planning for its fringes', commented Arpita Podder, observing that the radical transformation surrounding the city of Kolkata evolved despite the lack of well-defined, well-integrated plans.

Mumbai's regional planning

In 1961, the core of the city, Bombay Island, had a population of 2.7 million, or 65.8 per cent of Greater Bombay's total population of 4.1 million. In 1991, Bombay Island's population of 3.3 million was only 33 per cent of the Greater Bombay total of 9.9 million. In part the dispersal of the population was the outcome of deliberate planning, through restrictive legislation prohibiting the development of industry in the core region. The Regional Plans of 1973 and 1999 provided for managing the city's growth through supporting inter-regional dispersal of industries, the development of new towns, and confining urban growth to well-defined areas based on desirable densities and population distribution. The plans were essentially aimed at the management of growth through polycentric urban structure as opposed to planned and controlled growth.

Selective development of new sites aimed at reducing congestion in the built-up area, including Navi Mumbai and the Bandra-Kurla complex. The latter was the first in the series of new growth centres designed to serve as a counter-magnet and contain growth of commercial activities in South Mumbai. The MMRDA had oversight of all developments of private and public offices, banks, shopping complexes and wholesale establishments in the 370 hectares of the Bandra-Kurla complex (Shaw, 1995). On the other hand, the attempt to ease the pressures by developing Navi Mumbai was impaired by the continuing migration of people into the city, which has necessitated a second overspill. Navi Mumbai's population had already surpassed a million. The resulting new city, to be constructed 80 kilometres away in Uran on a 100-square kilometre site across Mumbai's Dharamtar Creek, is expected to grow to a quarter of the size of Mumbai itself. Uran has a major port and Maharashtra housing authority's plans for new housing estates and the development of roads and boat links to Mumbai are designed to ensure that the new city becomes an effective part of metropolitan Mumbai. In setting out his vision for Uran, the Minister of State for Housing remarked that 'we're trying to create a new satellite city for the people who come here but never want to go back. They will be able to live their Mumbai dream in Uran' (*Telegraph*, 2013).

The decentralisation and diversification of industries in Mumbai has to a large extent succeeded in taking the pressure off its cities. However, new commercial and office developments continue in the island city mainly through 'illegal land-use conversions' while, at the same time, despite high land values, large areas remain derelict due to land-use restrictions (MMR, 1996: vi). The number of urban centres in the region has continued to grow, more than doubling since the 1960s. As with West Bengal, although the state experienced a phenomenal increase in the number of census towns, the growth in the number of statutory towns has been low compared with the country as a whole. During 1991–2001, while India saw an increase of around 26 per cent in the number of statutory towns, it was a mere 2 per cent for Maharashtra (Bhide and Waingankar, 2011: 4). The population residing in census towns increased from 1.37 per cent in 2001 to 2.72 per cent in 2011.

Despite the drive to modernity, which encouraged the rise of a sophisticated and highly qualified planning profession in these megacities, actual achievements in terms of liveability have been modest. The state government set up a task force in Mumbai to identify, implement and pursue the reform agenda outlined in its vision document, *Vision Mumbai*, which recommended an eight-pronged approach to improving urban services and put in place effective and responsive governance arrangements. Its aims include decentralisation, environmental sustainability, slum management, reform of municipal finance and municipal management, improving transparency and civic engagement, and capacity building. As the key service provider in the city MCGM has the overall responsibility for management and delivery and a number of recommendations were made to strengthen its resource base and leadership capacity

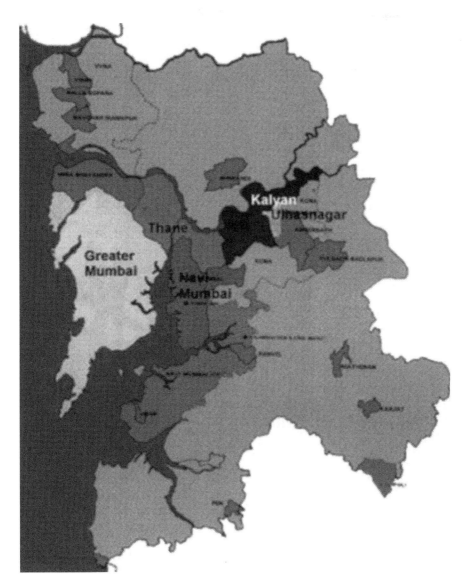

Figure 5.3 Map of Mumbai Metropolitan Region
Source: Mumbai Metropolitan Regional Development Authority (MMRDA).

to enhance its accountability and coordination with other departments and agencies. The World Bank mission in March 2005 endorsed the above agenda and underlined the need to strengthen the authority and responsibility of local government. It recommended procedural and organisational changes to streamline decision making, establish service standards, and devolve services and functions to autonomous bodies. The follow-up consultative process initiated through the Citizens' Action Group (CAG) and the governance sub-group identified key issues relating to improving city governance and putting in place an efficient, transparent and responsive system suited to the needs of the community.

The challenges of urban fringe and peri-urban areas

The continuous outward expansion of cities has thus resulted in changes in land-use patterns and linkages between the core and surrounding areas. Industry and housing may be located in satellite towns some way distant from the main urban area or close to transport zones within the urban periphery. Waste processing may be in urban centres close to where the waste is generated or outside the urban area where it is economically and environmentally feasible. While occurrences of this nature suggest that there may not be a distinct land defined as urban periphery, the term peri-urban interface has been used to denote the place where the urban and rural activities co-exist (Bowyer-Bower, 2006: 152). These areas provide both opportunities and challenges. Captured in McGee's concept of the 'desakotta', where both regions gain – the rural areas through increased earnings and extended markets, and the urban areas through reduced congestion in the core built-up areas (McGee, 1991) – the fabric of a peri-urban area is neatly described by Allen and Davila as:

> a mosaic of agricultural and urban ecosystems, affected by material and energy flows demanded by urban and rural areas. They are socially and economically heterogenous and subject to rapid change. Small farmers, informal settlers, industrial entrepreneurs and urban middle class commuters may all co-exist in the same territory but with different and often competing interests, practices and perceptions. Few institutions can address both urban and rural activities. Local government agencies have either an urban or a rural focus. Few metropolitan governments include rural jurisdictions. District and regional governments fail to bridge urban and rural concerns.
>
> (Allen and Dávila, 2002: 1)

Developmental opportunities

Such areas, while posing immense challenges, also provide several development opportunities. Migration to the periphery is principally driven by housing needs and availability of cheap land. High rates of land transactions and land conversions are of great interest to land developers. They are gaining in importance, particularly in terms of their economic and social links with the central city and are therefore emerging popular sites for the location of airports, hospitals, hotels and educational institutions, the construction of which is dependent on land availability, not readily available in the cities, and removed from regulations and controls (Nangia, 1976; Ramchandran, 1988; Sen, 2011). With increasing economic activities and industrial resurgence, peri-urban areas are popular locations for new developments and industrial growth centres, special economic zones, satellite towns and knowledge cities. They are also useful sites for the establishment of water and sewage treatment plants, thermal power stations and regional bus terminals (Mitra, 2007: 136). The Kolkata peri-urban area, where waste-water fish farming is practised, supports the livelihood of a large number of people through waste recycling and natural resource use; some 15,700 households comprising 70,750 individuals depend on wetland based activities in East Kolkata (Mukherjee, 2006: 106).

A recent study showed the extent of opportunities for farm enterprises, in particular, in the early stages of urban influence on the outer parts of the peri-urban interface. Those who benefit tend to be the larger farmers, while those who are least able to take advantage of the opportunities are smaller farmers who lack capital and surplus land, leading to increased polarisation. In the later stages, however:

> the threats to farm enterprises from declining labour availability and higher labour costs outweigh the opportunities, leading to increased abandonment of farming. Those who benefit from this process are those who can either sell land to speculators or developers or have the capacity to develop it. Those who lose tend to have little or no land, are dependent on wage labour in other farms for all or part of their incomes, and are unable to take advantage of alternative economic opportunities in the urban labour market. This is because their households and its members lack labour, skills, contacts, capital, or freedom of movement. Those who have insecure rights to land, or who have little to sell, and who are excluded from urban labour market opportunities may be impoverished and, in any case, polarization between the rich and poor is likely to increase.
> (Brook *et al.*, 2003: 16)

Others have identified benefits of these areas beyond the 'efficient urban governance mechanism for certain groups:

> As long as this anarchist rule ... prevails, the running system is good for some groups – big land developers and real estate agents, industrial houses, politicians and police, who can earn a lot from non-legal and non-formal activities.
> (Samanta, 2012: 15)

Clearly, peri-urban areas are seen in different terms and are valued in different ways by diverse groups of people and organisations. For the poor, these are places for building homes and occupying land for agriculture, while for the middle classes these are potentially residential zones for homes in a rural setting with recreational facilities. These areas remain protected sites for the conservationists, but for local government, the fringes are often sites for locating landfills, waste dumps, peripheral freeways and toxic industries. And for industry they may be sources of materials essential for urban life. The case of the HITECH City development below presents a striking example of how targeted industrial and economic policies can transform peri-urban regions.

Targeted development: the case of HITECH City

Around Hyderabad metropolitan area, large tracts of peri-urban spaces are being transformed by infrastructure led growth and specialised business and technology parks. HITECH City (Hyderabad Information Technology Engineering Consultancy City) is a large-scale industrial park dedicated to IT. Situated about 20 kilometres from the centre of Hyderabad, it is a classic illustration of peri-urban development. Located on a large campus, nearly 65 hectares, the concept is modelled on successful international examples of Hsinchu Science-based Industrial Park in Taiwan, and Research Triangle Park in North Carolina.

Several national and international firms, including Infosys, Wipro and Microsoft, have established their offices on land given to them by the Andhra Pradesh Industrial Infrastructure Corporation (APIIC), which until recently managed infrastructure facilities including roads, water supply, drainage, street lighting and provision for data connectivity. APIIC was the 'deemed local administrative body' for this entire zone, providing the interface between the firms and various utilities, regulatory bodies, and branches of government. The area has also witnessed the development of a range of other new industrial and service activities, large projects involving state of the art infrastructure, housing colonies and commercial centres.

A recent study of the impact of industrial policies on peri-urban dynamics in Hyderabad attributes this development to the loosening of central control of the economy since the early 1990s, which resulted in the state government taking initiatives to promote growth and investment. The state developed its own strategies, prioritised its investments, and liaised directly with foreign investors. Between 1995 and 2004, Andhra Pradesh proved itself one of the most proactive states and took economic reforms further than any other. The rapid growth of this region is also due in part to the new information and communication technology (ICT) policy, adopted in 2002, that provided for a range of incentives designed to attract investment to the IT sector. These included exemptions from statutory zoning regulations, inspections and the granting of permissions and other special rebates for which companies may apply in relation to registration fees, stamp duties, transfer of property duty and cost of land (Kennedy, 2007).

The spatial and environmental impact of such projects can be immense. As the study of HITEC City showed:

the architectural style of HITEC City and of the large office buildings built by IT firms, the vast landscaped campuses, and the remarkable quality of the roads mark a striking contrast with the surrounding environment, which is generally dry and rocky and poorly equipped in basic infrastructure. In this way, HITEC City is actively contributing to the formation of highly differentiated 'mixed spaces' midway between urban centres and rural spaces that characterise peri-urbanisation.

(Kennedy, 2007: 100)

The private sector played an important role in the development of HITEC City. It set up the internationally renowned Institute of Information Technology (an engineering school that offers world-class training in engineering) and other educational institutions, including the Indian Business School, established in partnership with internationally recognised management institutions such as the Kellogg School of Management, the Wharton School and the London Business School.

Yet, in governance terms the region continues to be a challenge, with central and state government agencies dictating institutional arrangements. In January 2001 the state government of Andhra Pradesh created the Cyberabad Development Area (CDA) with a view to developing the area around HITEC City by providing high quality water and sanitation services, waste management, electricity, housing and transport. A master plan for CDA defined land-use zoning regulations and building regulations. To finance the creation of capital infrastructure such as road and urban amenities, the plan provided for raising revenues through user charges and changes in the structure of property tax and recovery rates. The area around HITEC City now enjoys the presence of other commercial and residential buildings and road networks to the city supplemented by a mass transit commuter train and a new ring road connecting to the international airport at Shamshabad, south of the city. The region between the centre of Hyderabad and HITEC City comprises affluent residential areas, which provide attractive housing opportunities and other amenities including luxury hotels, restaurants, shops and entertainment. Despite these developments, the presence of a multiplicity of institutional arrangements and special regulatory frameworks set by CDA and HADA appear to diminish the prospects for effective governance at the metropolitan scale.

More recently, 14 Industrial Area Local Authorities (IALAs) were merged with the GHMC to provide for a more robust and coherent governance. The IALAs were formed in 1994 in the industrial zones of the suburbs, with responsibilities divided between APIIC and municipalities. Tax collection resided with the former while the provision of civic facilities was the responsibility of the municipalities. Since the merger in 2010, governance is more unified, with the municipal corporation maintaining roads, providing infrastructure facilities, administering building permissions and collecting property tax from residential colonies under IALAs.

Stresses and strains: governing the peri-urban areas

More often, the positive benefits of settlements in peripheral areas are eclipsed by the negative consequences (Bentinck, 1996). Some of the problems that arise are unusual and unexpected. A study of the Hubli–Dhariwal interface, for instance, found that farmers leading essentially rural lifestyles, but within the municipal boundary, were deprived of access to rural credit schemes on favourable terms, resulting in greater impoverishment of the poor peri-urban populations that fall within the municipality (Brook *et al.*, 2003). Environmental implications can be significant, according to Shaw, whose study shows that such areas are particularly vulnerable because of their proximity to the city. Land and water resources are vulnerable to degradation through the dumping of solid and liquid wastes, and as population growth spills beyond municipality limits, it exacerbates the pressures on adjacent areas. The problems are wide ranging, from pollution to land speculation to negligence of basic services such as water, sanitation, health and education.

More importantly, these sites lack the institutional capacities and governance structures to enable them to respond to the processes of change in a positive way. Located at the fringe of the city, these areas are 'far from the corridors of political power and often without any official urban status' (Shaw, 2005: 130). The basic infrastructure networks that cover the built-up areas of the city do not reach the outskirts:

> Peri-urban areas often lie outside the legal jurisdiction of the city and sometimes, even outside the legal jurisdiction of any urban local body. They are thus not provided with many of the basic services taken for granted in the city. Peri-urban areas could be situated within the larger metropolitan region and yet not have any basic services other than electricity. This makes them no different from the villages of rural India but unlike these villages, they face a bigger environmental burden stemming from their transitional nature.
>
> (Shaw, 2005: 130)

Joka, on the south-western fringe of the KMA, provides a classic illustration. It is part of the urban agglomeration and yet, as it lies outside the KMC, it lacks all the basic urban services such as water supply, sanitation, garbage collection and disposal, all of which are provided by the corporation. The town faces problems that epitomise the state of much of peri-urban India. In spite of lacking in basic services, the area has attracted new housing developments and is home to the prestigious Indian Institute of Management. Schools, hospitals and a range of small and medium sized industries are also located there (Goswami, 2001). It has long been argued that peri-urban settlements, such as Joka, should be given town panchayat status to enable the management of their environmental services through an elected committee and funding from the state. An alternative is to entrust the existing metropolitan development authority, in this case the KMDA, with the responsibility of providing the basic infrastructure (Shaw, 2005: 136).

In most regions these newly urbanising areas are almost always outside the planning jurisdiction of the central city, in municipalities that are suddenly confronted with huge development pressures and infrastructure demands:

> Such conditions mean that larger scale patterns of regional growth are extremely difficult to plan and adequately service. The outcome is in part a function of fragmented governance in megacity regions, which often include several municipalities, each with its own planning functions ... In addition to jurisdictional fragmentation, the difficulty of planning is compounded by the fact that most areas in suburbs are settled informally, through organised and unorganised invasions of available space.
> (Roy, 2013: 1)

Peri-urban developments are profoundly contested. In India, the CAA, for the first time, granted such areas the civic status of nagar panchayats or town panchayats, with the aim to give them the much needed authority and status to carry out their functions. However, it was discretionary and largely left to state governments to take the lead in configuring areas and creating the legal framework for providing infrastructure services either through panchayats, their own departments or other agencies and private organisations (Shaw, 2005). While some states took the initiative, others have been slow to implement the framework.

Where attempts have been made – and a number of settlements in the fringes do qualify for such a status – the process of transformation has been slow. Several factors have contributed to resisting change to municipal status, foremost among which is a desire to avoid the taxation that such a change would entail. Municipal areas not only have higher taxation, but are also subject to a wider range of taxes and charges. Electricity charges and tariffs are also significantly higher than in rural areas. In addition, rural areas also benefit from free water supply, primary education and healthcare. On average, gram panchayats generate a little over 15 per cent of their revenue from their own sources, compared with almost 70 per cent in the case of municipal bodies. Gram panchayats survive primarily on development grants provided by state governments and little effort is made towards generating their own resources (Aziz, 1998; Sen, 2011). Thus in the absence of larger benefits for the fringe areas there is little incentive for them to seek to qualify for the status of municipalities. Yet, where such a status has been designated, they are found to be lacking in the expertise required for programming investments and expenditure, design, construction, and maintenance and implementation of projects. Nor do they have the requisite trained personnel to carry out these functions (Datta, 2007). The weak institutional structure of the panchayats and the acute shortage of manpower and financial resources are the main constraints in extending appropriate facilities and services to these areas (Mitra, 2007: 135).

Several corporations proposed mergers as solutions, but their attempts met with considerable opposition. In Mumbai, the decision to create the Vasai-Virar Municipal Corporation by merging 53 villages was opposed by local residents, who campaigned to protect their villages under the banner of *Gaon Vachva Jan Andolan* (People's agitation to save villages). Local leaders across party lines joined the campaign to save the last remaining green belts of Vasai from imminent urbanisation following the merger with the municipal corporation. They demanded the exclusion of all 53 villages from municipal corporation limits. Although the state government initially accepted the exclusion of some villages, all were finally amalgamated with the Vasai-Virar Municipal Corporation. Similar proposals put forward by the state government of Andhra Pradesh in 2013 to merge 36 new villages with the municipal corporation of greater Hyderabad met with similar opposition. Protests by local villagers, members of legislative assemblies, GHMC corporators and other public representatives led the government to withdraw their proposals for merging. Instead, they sought to convert the villages into municipalities or nagar panchayats, taking into consideration the population, revenue and geographical area (*Times of India*, 2013).

Planning for the peri-urban regions, then, is far from straightforward. One study went so far as to say that 'India cannot plan its cities', claiming that Indian cities defy all norms of rational planning, based as they are on informal systems of deregulation, exceptions and absence of mapping to any prescribed set of regulations. The 'systems are neither anomalous nor irrational; rather they embody a distinctive form of rationality that underwrites a frontier of metropolitan expansion' (Roy, 2009: 86). Roy's work examined the way in which forms of deregulation and informality on the peri-urban fringes of Kolkata enable the state government to have considerable territorial flexibility to acquire, redevelop and alter land-use and undertake various forms of urban and industrial development, often against its own prohibitions against such conversions (Roy, 2003).

Metropolitan planning committees are the only constitutionally recognised multi-jurisdictional bodies best placed to provide for coherent planning. While they have not attracted the necessary support, some state governments have created Joint Planning Boards to bridge urban and rural planning within each district. But fundamentally there is lack of cooperation and coordination between the planning authorities, in spite of the fact that their realms overlap to a certain degree. Comprehensive Development Plans, revised every ten years, are intended both to guide land-use and ameliorate the impact of urban expansion on peri-urban areas, and more specifically designate green belt that is earmarked for agriculture and future expansion of existing rural settlements. But the means by which these ideas have been implemented have taken little account of environmental considerations and also lack a broader vision of regional development to promote a more efficient use of renewable natural resources in the peri-urban interface (Brook *et al.*, 2003: 23–24):

> Those states that have not yet developed [planning committees] are perhaps failing to recognise that an holistic approach to planning and administration of peri-urban areas is needed, especially given the non-static nature of the peri-urban interface. Today's peri-urban area will be tomorrow's suburbs; today's rural area will be tomorrow's peri-urban interface. Thus, for a given locality, the peri-urban interface is a temporary state. It is important to recognise that the extent of the effects of urbanisation depends on the nature of the various influences. Any administrative mechanism developed must be allowed to expand and change over time, or risk becoming fossilised as another anachronistic tier of administration.
>
> (Brook *et al.*, 2003: 144)

Mumbai appears to have grasped this need to adapt to changing circumstances. Recently a committee, constituted under the chairmanship of the Additional Chief Secretary (Revenue), was set up tasked with the responsibility of finding solutions to 'the issues of unauthorised development in peri-urban & rural areas and to suggest appropriate remedies to the Government'. The committee's report recommended the establishment of an Area Development Authority to oversee planned development in peri-urban areas and called for suitable infrastructure. Although the work of the committee is yet to be seen, other cities, working with their relevant state governments, must be equally prepared to find new approaches and mechanisms to tackle the rapid growth and change expected in the next decades.

*****

In summary, clearly the impact of metropolitan planning is contingent upon the tendency of the urban system as a whole to make timely decisions and to carry them through to execution; hence it varies with the effectiveness of leadership, as well as with manpower and fiscal resources, and with the functional relationships among local, metropolitan and state policies and authorities. At its root, the planning challenge is essentially one of more effective governance, something which none of the cities has found easy to achieve. The strains and costs of metropolitan growth have proved a powerful argument for area-wide planning, and all the three cities considered here subsist within a more or less ambitious framework for shaping future development.

Planning cities is, of course, about more than just the regulation and control of development. It is also a matter of concept and vision, of setting out the framework within which major developments are to take place, and beyond the plans themselves lies the capacity of governments to bring about the large, strategic developments they envisage. The examples of the three case study cities highlight the extent to which coordinated planning is a prerequisite for effective metropolitan governance. It is not solely a matter of effective integration of land-use planning with economic, social and environmental planning, but greater coordination among federal, state and local governments. The roles of the MPCs, DPCs and ULBs in economic, social and land-use planning cannot be underestimated.

Notes

1 There is little consensus around the concepts of 'sprawl', or the 'urban fringe' or peri-urban landscapes. Fringe is defined as the densely settled territory surrounding one or more urban cores and is often characterised by relatively strong pressures for growth compared with more distant rural areas. According to some, the fringe is the continuing expression of global to local impacts on prices and of the relative costs of conflicting land uses and commodities. While a fringe denotes a specific place, just outside the limits of the core area, this is less true for sprawl, which is often used to describe perceived inefficiencies of development through disproportionate growth of urban areas and excessive leapfrog development (Irwin and Bockstael, 2004). The most commonly used definition of sprawl refers to the kind of urban expansion characterised by scattered, unplanned, low-density development that is not functionally related to adjacent land uses (Sengupta and Thiagarajan, 2013: 21).
2 Proposals to contain growth through green belt (an approach that was influenced by Abercrombie's London plan) were incorporated as early as 1958 in the master plan for Delhi. The metropolis was the first in the country to recommend green belt by specifying agriculture and low-density norms for several of the fringe areas of the Union Territory. However, the designated 'green belt' failed to be protected, and it reduced over time, as developers managed to buy land for building residential accommodation and industries.
3 The census of India defines two types of towns: (1) statutory towns – all places with a municipality, corporation, cantonment board or notified town area committee; and (2) census towns – places which satisfy the following demographic criteria: (i) a minimum population of 5000; (ii) at least 75 per cent of male working population engaged in non-agricultural pursuits; and (iii) a density of population of at least 400 persons per square kilometre.

6 The structures of metropolitan authority

Charles Merriam's telling comment that 'the adequate organisation of modern metropolitan areas is one of the great unsolved problems of modern politics' is perhaps more pertinent today than when it was first made in 1942. While this is true of all large urban agglomerations, its relevance to the Indian metropolises is particularly appropriate. Concerns about the growth and expansion of Indian cities have once again called into question the appropriateness of administrative structures for service delivery – especially of basic civic amenities – while the need for greater coordination among metropolitan agencies has become all the more acute. Independent commentators and policy makers alike warn of the importance of effective management of growth and the serious implications of the failure to do so in a sustained and consistent way (Planning Commission, 2012b; Raje, 2013).

Variations abound in the quality and distribution of services across cities and between the different states in India. Although decentralisation, as noted in the previous chapters, is acknowledged to be the more efficient way of promoting accountable and effective service delivery, there remain substantial inter-jurisdictional spill-overs and overlaps in administrative roles, potentially leading to issues of coordination and sub-optimal outcomes (Azfar et al., 1999; Bardhan and Mookherjee, 1999). Cities stand in striking contrast to one another, with some lacking any form of defined mechanisms for service delivery and others incorporating clearer accountabilities drawn across administrative structures.

This chapter examines the institutional and administrative structures in the three cities of Kolkata, Mumbai and Hyderabad and explores the ways in which they address the basic needs of housing, water and sewerage, transport and planning. It highlights the disparate and fragmented nature of decision making and argues for a streamlined and coordinated system of service delivery to meet the growing challenges of urban governance.

Institutional arrangements

Institutional arrangements are key to determining the quality and delivery of services. They comprise the totality of policies, systems and processes on which organisations depend to legislate, plan and manage their tasks (UNDP, 2011). Although the Constitutional Amendment Act mandated municipal corporations in India with clear and streamlined responsibilities for urban planning, the system remains complex, involving a mix of elected members, selected members, technocrats and state appointed bodies with varied roles and responsibilities.

Kolkata's municipal organisation is unique in India and stands out against the rest in the powers and responsibilities it vests in its mayor. The mayor-in-council, comprising the mayor, deputy mayor and ten elected members, discharges the functions of the KMC, the city's apex municipal body. As the chief executive officer the mayor holds significant administrative and executive powers and supervises the work of a municipal commissioner, who functions as the principal executive officer. This core team is further supported by bureaucrats, engineers and accountants. The mayor-in-council enjoys the powers and attributes of a cabinet government.

The KMC is grouped into 15 boroughs, which are further divided into 141 wards. Each borough is managed by a committee of elected councillors from their respective wards. This committee is responsible for services such as water supply, drainage, health and sanitation, road repairs and maintenance of parks. KMC's functional domain includes urban planning, building rules and regulations, town planning, urban poverty and slum rehabilitations, amongst others. In spite of the apparent clarity in governance and theoretical benefits of an empowered mayor, lines of responsibility and accountability for Kolkata are overly complex, with supporting agencies lacking autonomy and the mayor's executive function somewhat constrained.

The city of Mumbai, administered by the Municipal Corporation of Greater Mumbai (MCGM), the largest in South Asia, presents a different institutional structure. Its titular head is a mayor with few executive powers. The municipal corporation and mayor are voted in every five years and the corporation's real executive power resides in the municipal commissioner, a civil servant appointed by the state government. Additionally, there is provision for the office of the deputy mayor in the Mumbai metropolitan corporation and the leader of the opposition enjoys statutory status. Best described as a polycentric governance system, the MMR is a complex structure comprising eight municipal corporations and nine municipal councils, which are responsible for the civic affairs of different cities and towns in the region. An assistant municipal commissioner oversees each municipal division for administrative purposes. The MCGM is the city's key service provider responsible for basic civic amenities, health, sanitation, solid waste management, roads, education and transport in the city of Mumbai. In addition, several parastatal agencies are responsible for specific services such as affordable housing and planning for infrastructure. There are also independent agencies providing public goods and services in the MMR.

In Hyderabad, the MCH is the apex urban planning agency overseeing civic planning and is responsible for sewerage and drainage, solid waste management and the maintenance of roads and hospitals. The three main authorities constitute the corporation, the standing committee and the municipal commissioner. The mayor is a titular head, directly elected by the councillor body for five years, while a municipal commissioner, appointed by the state government, holds executive power in the corporation and directly supervises the MCH function. The city is divided into 150 municipal wards and each is overseen by an elected corporator. The Hyderabad Municipal Corporation (HMC) Act, which governs MCH, assigns 'obligatory and discretionary functions' to the corporation subsumed under 'public health, public welfare, public security and public works'. The municipal commissioner holds overall charge of the wards' performance (Yadav, 2013).

India's layered urban administrative organisation, then, comprises a mix of managers, bureaucrats, government agencies and elected representatives. While it is widely accepted that governance is a collective and interactive process involving various forms of collaborations and partnerships, acknowledging power dependence in such collective action also requires the recognition that plans do not often match outcomes. The current institutional framework for urban planning and governance in India fails to provide clarity in the roles and responsibilities of the various bodies involved in the preparation, implementation, enforcement and monitoring of the plans. In the absence of clearly defined roles there is greater room for the different stakeholders to behave opportunistically, thus adding to complexity and unpredictability.

India's rapidly expanding economy calls for effective governance and planning for urban services that go beyond core cities to address the issues of provision brought about by expansion and overspill. The UN warns that developing economies like India will have to increase their capacity by a staggering 65 per cent to produce and manage urban infrastructure services to ensure that newly expanded regions maintain at least present living conditions. In many countries, this has to be achieved under severe economic stress and the pressure of rising expectations (UN, 1989).

The urban expansion in India has significantly outpaced the ability of governance structures to deal with the consequences. It took over 20 years for the MMR to develop to its present form which effectively incorporates the satellite towns with the city government. As the country's most populous city, the challenge of accommodating growth and expansion is immense. As Hyderabad expanded its jurisdiction over peripheral areas and became the GHMC in 2007, the stated rationale for the integration was to combine the variety of independent administrative services under a cohesive administrative structure to coordinate various civic systems including drainage, sewerage, urban transport and environment management. The aims appear not to have been realised and the current planning is criticised for lacking the vision and strategy for integrating peri-urban and rural areas (Kennedy, 2007). This is as true for other Indian cities as it is for Hyderabad. The lack of a regional approach to planning among India's cities has led to haphazard growth and an inadequate supply of civic amenities in and around industrial locations and

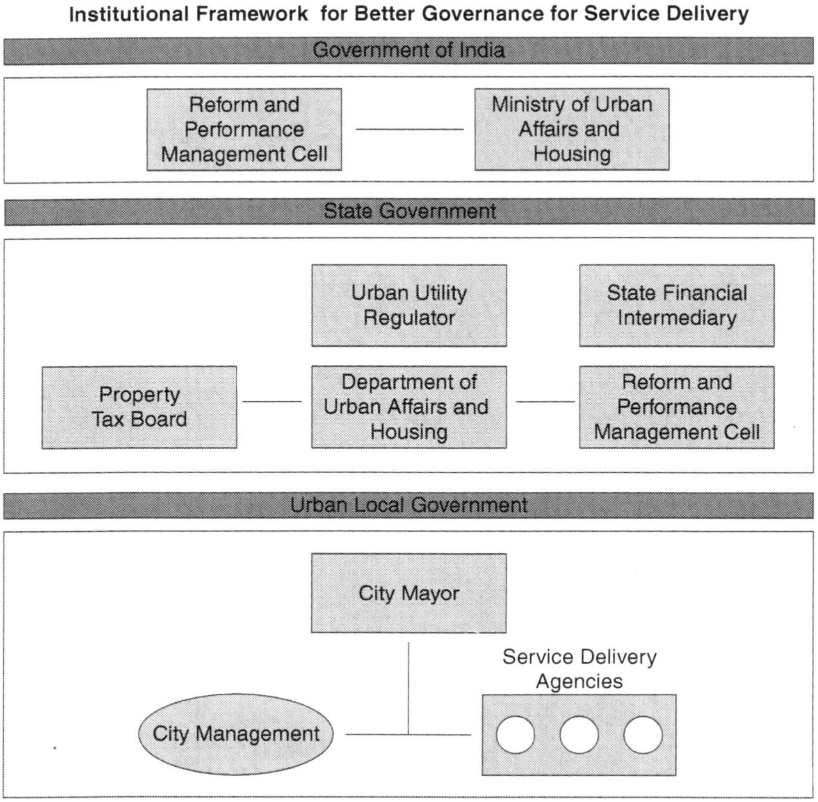

Institutional Framework for Better Governance for Service Delivery

Government of India
- Reform and Performance Management Cell
- Ministry of Urban Affairs and Housing

State Government
- Urban Utility Regulator
- State Financial Intermediary
- Property Tax Board
- Department of Urban Affairs and Housing
- Reform and Performance Management Cell

Urban Local Government
- City Mayor
- City Management
- Service Delivery Agencies

Figure 6.1 Institutional framework for better governance for service delivery
Source: HPEC (2011: 91).

peri-urban areas (Twelfth Five Year Plan, 2012). 'The institutional framework for urban governance in India needs a major overhaul if cities are to play a dynamic role in the next phase of India's development', concluded the report by HPEC. Arguing that 'the present institutional structure is politically weak and administratively cumbersome', the committee set out a more streamlined framework for better governance (see Figure 6.1) (HPEC, 2011: 89).

Planning for cities

The CAA called for the creation of regional planning platforms like the DPCs and MPCs, with responsibilities for draft development plans. Each MPC is required to prepare a draft development plan taking into account the plans prepared by the municipalities and the panchayats in the metropolitan area and matters of common interest between the municipalities and the panchayats, including coordinated spatial planning of the area, sharing of water and other physical and natural resources, integrated development of infrastructure and the nature of investments likely to be made in the metropolitan area by agencies of the Government of India and state governments. In addition, the twelfth schedule of the constitution lays down the functions of ULBs, lists urban planning including town planning, regulation of land-use and construction of buildings and the planning for economic and social development. Yet, not all states have established DPCs/MPCs or incorporated the lists of functions set out in the twelfth schedule into the State Municipal Acts. They have been less than enthusiastic in implementing the constitutional provision and the planning scope of MPCs, where they have been established, is restricted. The recommendations to transfer land-use planning to ULBs has been poorly implemented, and responsibility continues to remain with development authorities and town planning departments, which are accountable to state governments. State legislation for urban planning invariably provides an overriding role for the state government. Most decisions at the local level are subject to approval by the state government, which has the power to alter plans presented by ULBs.

The MPCs operate with varying effectiveness in the cities of Hyderabad, Mumbai and Kolkata. In the case of Hyderabad, the Government of Andhra Pradesh passed the necessary legislation in relation to the CAA, but elections to local bodies encountered delays due to a range of technical difficulties and litigation. The municipal corporation, elected in 2002, was dissolved in 2007 and elections postponed for several years as the contentious issue of the amalgamation of surrounding municipalities into GHMC, as noted in the previous chapter, superseded all other matters. Although the appropriate legislation has now been passed, the MPC has not yet been constituted. Instead, the District Development Review Committee, chaired by a minister, and comprising members of the legislative assembly (MLAs) and parliament (MPs), meets regularly to review progress made in the planned development and welfare activities of the area. In its current form it is without resource and appropriate support structures and, given the current political uncertainties in the State of Andhra Pradesh, it appears unlikely that the MPC will be accorded a role in metropolitan planning in the immediate future.

The planning committee in Mumbai has also been largely redundant. Now in existence for about four years, it is reported to have held one formal meeting and a few thematic sessions. While the Maharashtra state legislature enacted the Maharashtra Metropolitan Planning Committee (Constitution and Functions) (Continuance of Provisions) Act in 1999, the MPC was not constituted until a decade later, in 2008. The Mumbai MPC comprises 64 members, with two-thirds of the total members elected from the municipalities and other nominated members, ex-officio, special permanent invitees and representatives from various other government and parastatal agencies.

138 *The structures of metropolitan authority*

Kolkata was the first city in the country to set up an MPC, in 2000, following amendments to the state's Municipal Acts in 1993. The committee when first constituted consisted of 60 members – two-thirds elected by and from amongst the elected members of the 41 municipalities and around 100 chairpersons of the village councils in the KMA. The remaining 20 were nominated members, including representatives of the Government of India, the state government, and of organisations relating to urban development and infrastructure. They included local MPs and MLAs and a representative of the KMDA. The secretary of KMDA also serves as secretary of the Kolkata MPC. The MPC was reconstituted in 2006 after local elections and the newly formed committee held its first meeting in 2007 under the chairmanship of the Chief Minister. However, since the election of a new government in 2011, the MPC has not yet been reconstituted. The framework adopted by Kolkata (see Figure 6.2) is relatively more advanced and rightly places the metropolitan and district levels of governance at the centre of the process, bringing together formal and informal processes. As McKinsey remarked:

> With the chief minister leading the committee [MPC], there is strong political legitimacy for its work. This is further bolstered by four key committees that report to the MPC (planning, traffic and transportation, sewerage, and program monitoring), in which state bureaucrats from the relevant state government ministries coordinate between the state government and the metropolitan government. The presence of the Kolkata Metropolitan Development Agency (KMDA) as the secretariat to the MPC gives heft to implementation. The metropolitan government also wields the power of coordination across municipalities by stipulating that all municipal plans need to conform with metropolitan development plans.
>
> (McKinsey, 2010: 92)

At lower levels of India's urban governance, the ward committees, responsible for providing a legal framework of decentralised municipal governance and community participation, have been noted for their ineffectiveness. The constitution, while generally providing for the ward committees, has remained silent about the extent of their functions and administrative and financial powers, leaving the details to the discretion of state governments. Additionally, the administrative and financial base of the ward committees is too weak to enable them to implement their plans effectively. The absence of delegated budgets to ward committees have not enabled them to function effectively. The Kerala model is often cited as an exemplar that takes municipal administration to the grassroots, where there are as many ward committees as there are elected councillors. At the other extreme, the upper limit of 25 ward committees in Maharashtra, irrespective of size and population, is criticized for its arbitrariness and is seen as too remote and inadequate to effectively reflect the voice of the common citizen (Mumbai Transformation Project Support Unit, 2006).

The structures of metropolitan authority 139

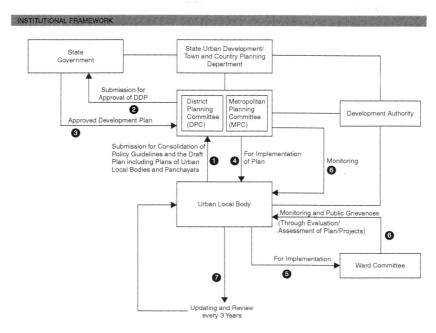

Figure 6.2 The institutional framework for Kolkata.
Source: Institute of Town Planners (2013: 96).

The nature of urban planning and development in India, then, reflects a high degree of exclusion of key players tasked with developing plans and promoting growth. While the bottom-up MPC structure does not appear to have performed well, and has become an effete body, the development authorities established to consolidate and implement development plans in all major cities have continued to remain responsible for development of the metropolises. While these authorities are undeniably complex, there is greater contractual completeness in the projects they undertake and with easier enforcement. The KMDA, the development authority for KMA, formed in 1970, coordinates all development activities undertaken within the geographical boundaries of the metropolitan area by different state and central agencies. The development authority has an 11-member board which includes elected representatives and nominated officials. It works in tandem with KMA to prepare official Land-Use Maps and Registers (LUMR) and a Land-Use and Development Control Plan (LUDCP). KMDA also works in collaboration with a range of private sector firms to modernise the city.

Likewise, the MMRDA, as the apex policy-making body responsible for planning and administering the city of Mumbai, is primarily responsible for steering the regional development through infrastructure planning and expansion. Chaired by the Minister for Urban Development, the authority comprises 17 members and a number of representatives of government departments and other independent experts. It has an executive committee chaired by the state's Chief Secretary, beneath whom a metropolitan commissioner, appointed by the state government and independent of the corporation, is responsible for policy implementation. MMRDA's notable successes include the Bandra Kurla Complex, Backbay reclamation and the Oshiwara district centre. Over the years, the authority has been able to foster new capabilities in functional areas, including the development and marketing of land, project formulation and coordination (especially for externally funded projects such as the Mumbai Urban Infrastructure Project and MUTP), providing loans to ULBs and promoting PPPs. In 2003, the responsibility and administrative power of the Slum Rehabilitation Authority was transferred to MMRDA.

Delivering services

Poor civic infrastructure characterises most large Indian cities, with overcrowded public transport, poor sanitation and health, and pollution related problems. Housing shortages have resulted in the growth of slums, while inadequate road networks have led to problems of traffic and congestion. The inadequate access to basic services such as drinking water, health services and education for the urban population in Indian cities is well documented (Figure 6.3) (McKinsey, 2010; Shaw, 2012).

Housing

India's housing sector is an urban predicament marked by innate Indian socioeconomic and political problems of poverty, marginality and uncontrolled growth (Zeiderman, 2008). The unprecedented migration of people in recent years has led to an acute housing crisis and shortage in the provision of basic services. Almost a third of India's population comprises internal migrants. This manifests itself in the form of overcrowding, homelessness and slums.

In Hyderabad, during the period 2001–2012, around 22,000 housing units were estimated as necessary to address the housing deficit, with additional 20,000 units by 2031 to keep up with projected growth (HMDA, 2010: 62). The housing needs statement of KMDA similarly shows a current average annual housing need of 70,000 units, projected to rise to 90,000 units by 2025 (KMDA, 2007: 73). These estimates do not take into account those living in unauthorised settlements around Kolkata, where an additional five million people live on the streets or in cardboard and bamboo makeshift homes (Christensen, 2004). Evidence suggests that Kolkata offers some of the worst quality of life to its residents. Within the KMC area, about 49 per cent of households live in single-room units and only 8 per cent live in units of five or more rooms, while the comparable figures for the metropolitan area are 37 per cent and 8.8 per cent respectively (KMDA, 2007: 70).

The structures of metropolitan authority 141

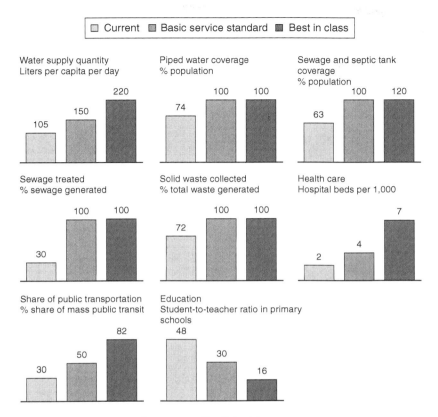

Figure 6.3 The current performance of India's cities
Source: McKinsey (2010: 54) – compiled from City Development Plans, the Energy and Resources Institute, Planning Commission, Census 2001, Central Pollution Control Board, McKinsey Global Institute Analysis.

Though one of the worst in terms of living conditions, Kolkata is not an exception. McKinsey predicts that for the country to meet its urban demand for housing the economy has to build between 700 million and 900 million square meters of residential and commercial space a year (McKinsey, 2010). The Planning Commission recommends that the government develop a set of policies and incentives to bridge the gap between price and affordability. This is especially important as building standards continue to rise. Between 2010 and 2025 the number of *kutcha* houses – built from unimproved materials such as clay and straw – is expected to remain broadly static, while the number of *pucca* houses – using improved materials such as fired bricks and sheet roofing – is expected to double.

The role of central government and external agencies in recent years has been instrumental in shaping housing policy. Greater resources are allocated

142 *The structures of metropolitan authority*

to state governments through centrally sponsored schemes, while national urban development and housing schemes also enjoy the support of external assistance programmes. During the 1970s, a number of housing finance institutions were established. The Housing Development Finance Corporation (HDFC), set up in 1978, took the lead in establishing a market-driven housing credit instrument and developed a viable home ownership market, while HUDCO developed credit packages for poor and disadvantaged groups. The establishment of the NHB in 1988, as a premier refinancing institution with regulatory functions, was significant in promoting and developing the housing finance system through housing finance institutions, commercial banks and cooperative banks.

Following the CAA and the JNNURM, India adopted measures for urban reforms on a major scale. The national housing policy, developed in the mid-1990s, envisaged a role for the government as a facilitator and provider of affordable housing. Subsequently, in the Ninth Five Year Plan, a Working Group on Urban Housing of the Ministry of Urban Affairs and Employment was set up to address estimated shortfalls of around seven million units by 2001. Table 6.1 shows the group's predictions of housing shortage between 2001 and 2025.

In Kolkata, specific programmes were launched to improve the housing conditions and quality of life of the urban poor – DfID-funded KUSP and the central-government-funded JNNURM. The former aimed at improving infrastructure and supporting the social and economic development for specifically the urban poor, while the JNNURM was wider, covering improvements to basic services as well as housing for the slums. Both projects are implemented by ULBs within KMA. JNNURM is monitored by the Urban Development Department while KUSP is the responsibility of the Municipal Affairs Department of the Government of West Bengal. In addition, the national government has developed a housing scheme, Rajiv Awaas Yojana, which enables *in situ* development of slums in urban areas. The state government also promotes different housing projects in partnership with the private sector. Other major reforms in Kolkata's housing sector include privatization of public rental housing, development of new towns and deregulation of the financial sector. Critics argue that these reforms are far from holistic, and have helped provide homes to upper and middle income groups rather than the poor, who continue living in slums and *bustees*.

A federal structure for policy making and the planning process in India, together with the presence of several agencies and stakeholders working on similar policy issues, characterises much of housing provision. Two central ministries of the national government are entrusted with tasks related to urban development, housing and urban poverty alleviation: (1) the Ministry of Housing and Urban Poverty Alleviation – the national apex authority of the Government of India that formulates policies, sponsors and supports programmes, coordinates activities of various central ministries, state governments, and other nodal authorities, and monitors national programmes for

Table 6.1 Projections for housing stock, households and housing shortage (2010–2025) (in million units)

Category	Trend rate (%)	2010	2020	2025*
Pucca	4.99	75.8570	123.4454	157.4760
Semi Pucca	1.16	7.7213	8.6652	9.1795
Kutcha	0.76	3.6933	3.9838	4.1375
Households	3.40	77.7148	108.5698	128.3252
Housing shortage	-	1.6586	0	0

Note: * Computed.
Source: Ministry of Urban Affairs and Employment, Government of India (1996).

urban employment, poverty and housing; and (2) the MoUD responsible for formulating policies, supporting programmes, monitoring and coordinating activities of various central ministries and state governments, and other nodal authorities related to urban development issues.

At the level immediately below are state departments responsible for urban development, housing, transport and tourism. It is the urban development departments of the state that take responsibility for ULBs. Besides this two-tier structure, numerous other agencies within the city play a role in planning and facilitating housing. City governments play a key role in planning housing projects, with direct responsibility for policies, which drive public and private development activities. They maintain responsibility for providing basic services at the city scale. As with other aspects of urban governance, there remains a lack of coordination among the several agencies responsible for housing, and this is evident across the cities of Mumbai, Hyderabad and Kolkata.

Water supply and sewerage

India's cities face immense pressure on their civic infrastructure systems for water supply, sanitation, solid waste management and sewerage. Providing a steady water supply is increasingly becoming a challenge for local and state governments in many large cities of India, while an equally serious problem epitomises the collection, transportation and disposal of solid waste in the form of sewerage. A recent study shows that, on average, a water supply is available for 2.9 hours per day in cities and towns across India (Vaidya, 2009). Nearly 75 per cent of the population living in urban cities have no access to human waste collection either. While less than half of the total sewerage is collected, only 30–40 per cent is treated properly. Tables 6.2 and 6.3 exemplify the state of water supply and its management across various cities. The provision of a sewerage system continues to be expensive, particularly at the point of collection and conveyance. With weak management, solid waste often ends up in open spaces, sanitary landfill or drainage systems, threatening both surface water and ground water quality (Sivaramakrishnan and Singh, 2003).

Table 6.2 The state of water supply and waste water treatment in selected cities in India

City	Water supply				Waste water	
	Capacity (MLD)	Hours per day	Consumption (LPCD)	Unaccounted (%)	Generated (MLD)	Treatment capacity (MLD)
Bangalore	965	4		34–44	772	
Chennai	198	4		20	158	264
Delhi	4,346	4	78	26	3,800	2,330
Hyderabad	578	0.5–4	96	33	462	593
Kolkata	1,625	9	116	30–40	706	172
Mumbai	3,000	5	90	18	2,400	2,130

Source: Vedachalam (2012).

Kolkata performs better than other cities in India in relation to water supply. It has several sources, both public and private, including treated water through underground piped-networks, public wells owned by KMC as well as those that are privately owned and managed by local residents. Yet, several ULBs in the metropolitan areas do not receive piped water supply, which is attributed in large part to a combination of inadequate resources to implement an adequate water distribution system and the lack of clarity in delegating administrative responsibilities. The task for water distribution is divided between the state and the municipalities. KMC is responsible for the overall management of the water network in the city, while state organisations bear the financial responsibility. At the metro level, the responsibility for water provision is shared between KMWSA (Kolkata Metropolitan Water Supply Authority), KMC and other municipalities. KMWSA is responsible for source development and bulk transmission of water in KMA, and ULBs are responsible for operation and maintenance.

Different institutions handle drainage and sanitation with significant inter-jurisdictional overlaps. The responsibility for sewerage lies jointly with KMWSA, KMDA and the West Bengal government's Public Health Engineering (PHE) Department. Sewerage and drainage systems are planned by KMDA, while respective ULBs are responsible for their operation and maintenance. All core KMA cities have a sewerage system, yet the overall coverage stands at only 45.2 per cent of KMA. Solid waste management through door-to-door collection is on the increase, either through the corporation's own personnel or private agencies. To streamline waste management in urban areas, the state government recently established the West Bengal Solid Waste Management Mission in collaboration with USAID.

Compared with other cities, Kolkata exemplifies low levels of decentralisation. There is 'no concern for locally and technically decentralised solutions' within the administrative framework such as taking up measures to promote

Table 6.3 Water management in selected Indian cities

Indicators	Delhi	Mumbai	Kolkata
Demand–supply gap (MGD)	230	317	290
Water loss	Production loss at treatment plants, high leakage in the distribution system (40%), theft, in sufficient leak detection	Leakages, theft, plant losses	Leakage in transmission and distribution line, illegal connections, theft, metering inaccuracies
Non-revenue water (%)	52	20–25	97
Unaccounted flow of water (%)	42	20	42 (based on a study of 62 wards)
Coverage/households connected to pipe network (%)	72	100	88
Metering of connections (%)	55 (many non-functional and defective meters)	100 (only 54% are working)	0.08% (functional metered connections as % to total connections); 200 metered connections for bulk users
Per capita supply (lpcd)	191 (intra-urban disparities)	180 (unequal supply)	133 (imbalances in distribution)
Average supply/day (hours)	2–3	2–4	10
Cost recovery (%)	42	95% of the population clear their bills regularly	90 (for billed connection)

Source: Aijaz (2010: 4).

local recycling, disposal of waste at lower costs, and sustainable ground water management (Ruet *et al.*, 2002: 23).

Revenue collection for water systems in the city is at sub-optimal levels, with users not charged, neither volumetrically (as connections are unmetered) nor based on estimated consumption figures. Revenues from the water system are subsumed within the larger property tax, which is characterised by poor collection rates and irregular assessments. Attempts made in 2013 to install water meters in institutional, commercial and privately owned buildings met with fierce opposition by residents on the grounds that installing water meters, albeit on an experimental basis, would lead eventually to levying water usage charges. The corporation had to withdraw its proposal, despite the recommendations of the working group on urban water supply for the Twelfth Five Year Plan, for water and sewerage to be charged to enable the state to recover its costs and improve service delivery.

Mumbai, similar to Kolkata, experiences wide variations in the standards of water supply throughout the region. A number of government agencies – MJP, MIDC, MCGM – and irrigation departments are involved, although in Greater Mumbai, the overall responsibility lies with the municipal corporation. The responsibility for water, sewerage and solid waste is split between different departments in MCGM. The deputy municipal commissioner (special engineer), the additional commissioner (projects) and the municipal commissioner supervise the water supply and sewerage department, while the water supply project department, accounts department and the assessment and collection department work in collaboration with the hydraulic engineer. This division of responsibility is not uniform across all constituent units of the MMR. Water supply and sewerage functions are undertaken by respective ULBs and water supply sourced from multiple channels.

The ULBs source bulk water from either MIDC or use ground water. Some municipalities, such as the Navi Mumbai Municipal Corporation, source part of their water from CIDCO. The Maharashtra Jeevan Pradhikaran (MJP) is the state water agency responsible for conceiving, preparing and implementing water supply schemes in both urban and rural areas of Maharashtra, although it is not responsible for Greater Mumbai. MJP operates under the aegis of the Water Supply and Sanitation Department.

Coordinated mechanisms for overall planning and implementation of sewerage facilities at the metropolitan level are also lacking. Sewerage services across MMR's urban areas are currently the responsibility of ULBs and, with the exception of the recently established Vasai Virar Municipal Corporation, all municipal corporations have an underground sewerage system. Vasai Virar depends upon on-site arrangements. Sewerage treatment capacities are reported to be inadequate and are currently being upgraded under the JNNURM scheme in some cities. Unlike in Kolkata, Mumbai's water supply and sewerage is a good source of revenue. Charges and cross-subsidies apply to all users, with industrial and commercial establishments paying higher charges than domestic users. Those living in slums are not exempt from charges.

The city of Hyderabad suffers from serious water shortages and it is predicted that the current water deficit could more than double by 2021. One of the key issues affecting its provision at the metropolitan level is the location of water sources well beyond the jurisdiction of the core city. Although transport connectivity transcends municipal or metropolitan limits, organisational arrangements remain inadequate and the proliferation of parastatal agencies limits the corporation's functional mandate. The HMWSSB is the statutory authority providing and maintaining water supply and sewerage facilities in Hyderabad and surrounding areas. The water distribution system for MCH is divided into 20 distribution zones which are further subdivided for operational convenience. Seventy per cent of MCH has piped water supply and 95 per cent of the connections are estimated to be metered (HMDA, 2010: 102) for volumetric water charges. The sewerage system is also extremely inadequate, covering only 70 per cent of the MCH area, and this figure falls significantly in peripheral municipalities and urban areas, where the majority of the population does not have access to sanitation facilities.

Although the provision of water in cities such as Kolkata, Mumbai and Hyderabad is vastly better than in others, the inequities in access and problems of intermittent supplies and contamination remain acute. In some cities, user group networks have taken control of water services management, but their long-term survival is highly dependent on securing preferential rates and cross-subsidies from the municipal system (Desfeux and De Bercegol, 2011). Local governments have limited scope across all three cities, and the governance varies considerably. While Kolkata and Hyderabad have metropolitan water agencies, Mumbai has different municipalities and corporations to provide water and sewerage services. Within the three cities, only KMWSA has a metropolitan structure with a board which includes local representatives; the other two are state agencies. There is a growing trend towards greater private participation, but there remain considerable, unresolved problems of accountabilities.

Traffic and transport

Issues of traffic and transport are equally acute and present enormous challenges for Indian cities. High volumes of traffic and lack of comprehensive fiscal strategies have contributed to congestion, overcrowding and poor environment. The annual rate of growth of the motor vehicle population in India is estimated to be around 10 per cent and, between 1999 to 2009, the number of vehicles per 1,000 people in metropolitan cities increased more than twofold, from 132 to 286. During 2009, there were nearly 15 million vehicles in the four big cities of Delhi, Bengaluru, Chennai and Hyderabad alone, which constitute 16.6 per cent of all motor vehicles in the country (Singh, 2012: 3).

The rapid development of satellite towns, which have increased long-distance commuting, has made public transport much more important for the urban poor in recent years. Yet, public transport is inadequate and received little financial assistance from the government (Table 6.4). The lack of policy support for such measures as road pricing, cycle lanes and traffic priority schemes for public transport exacerbates the problem. Delhi's Bus Rapid Transit (BRT) corridor is an exception to this (Pucher *et al.*, 2004).

Urban sprawl around the core cities and dependency on the core have been other contributory factors, which, together with narrow roads, rapid growth in private car ownership and the poor infrastructure network has made it difficult for transport to meet the needs of growing urban commuters. This is evident in all of the large cities in the country. The heavy traffic flow into

Table 6.4 Number of vehicles and share of public transport in selected Indian cities

City	No. of vehicles – 1998 (in lakh)	Share of public transport (%)	Share of suburban railway (%)
Mumbai	8.60	88.0	44.0
Calcutta	6.64	79.0	14.0
Chennai	9.75	67.0	16.0
Delhi	30.33	62.0	1.0

Source: NIUA (1998).

Hyderabad, generated by the growth of the surrounding municipalities and the concentration of economic activity within the city, leads to severe blockages and congestion. In the absence of alternative routes, substantial flows across the core area exacerbate the problem and contribute to very low average journey speeds and road traffic accidents. Inadequate buses and the proliferation of para-transit modes, such as three-wheelers, which do not effectively complement the public transport system in the city, place additional strain on traffic. The absence of lane discipline, growth in the density of population, encroachment on to pavements and streets by hawkers and vendors and an absence of effective traffic management are additional contributory factors to an unsatisfactory situation (HMDA, 2010: 122–128). Against this backdrop, the National Urban Transport Policy (NUTP) recommended the adoption of measures to restrict the use of motor vehicles through measures such as higher fuel taxes, parking fees and reduction in the availability of public parking spaces.

Despite measures to restrict private vehicles, the use of public transport has been on the decline, with the utilisation rate of bus transport falling from 74 per cent in 1996 to 59 per cent in 2002. Private transport, particularly two-wheelers, currently accounts for 60 per cent of the traffic, yet carries only 32 per cent of all commuters. The share of public transport in Hyderabad, currently at 44 per cent, stands well below the optimum. Buses constitute 42 per cent of all transport, rail-based Multi Modal Transport (MMTS) 1.7 per cent, autos around 10 per cent and other form of private vehicles nearly 50 per cent. The Hyderabad Metro, a mass rapid transit system (MRTS), was established with a mission 'to create an efficient, safe, reliable, affordable and world class public transportation system' which would facilitate the city's transformation as a 'competitive global city with high quality of life' (HMDA, 2010: 132). Phase I of the MRTS, nearing completion, involves three corridors, two of which cut across from east to west, while another connects north to south. The southern corridor is close to the international airport and well placed to provide good connectivity. The Bus Rapid Transit System (BRTS), currently in development, is to be integrated with MMTS and other modes of transport. Dedicated bus corridors and road widening schemes are some of the recommendations in the master plan.

The structures of metropolitan authority   149

In Mumbai, a number of transport plans and projects, including the MUTP, have been implemented in collaboration with the World Bank. The project funded new rail lines, urban expressways and the conversion of public buses to eco-friendly gas power, while also supporting investments in improving the road system, developing bus depots (through BEST), signal improvements and, through MCGM, the construction of flyovers, pedestrian bridges and tunnels. A number of other traffic management schemes were also introduced during this period on the recommendation of a government appointed committee, chaired by Chief Secretary K.G. Paranjape. This was followed by a comprehensive transportation study for MMR, undertaken in 1994, which recommended a longer-term strategy. More recently, the principle of user charges was recommended to encourage mass transport services and discourage the use of private vehicles. It was proposed that these measures should be further supplemented by charging parking fees at strategically placed parking lots, from which travellers would be offered substantial concessions on public transport such as buses and taxis (MTSU, 2006). In a recent submission on the *Mumbai Sustainability and Corporate Citizenship Protocol*, the Asian Centre for Corporate Governance and Sustainability (ACCGs), together with the Indian Merchants' Chamber (IMC), called for corporates to improve mass commuting systems and to encourage employees to avail themselves of these facilities so as to reduce road congestion and air pollution. The adoption of green technologies and investment in a variety of infrastructure projects such as flyovers, sea link and metros are being further encouraged to reduce travel time, congestion and improve the quality of life (ACCGs, n.d.).

Despite the substantial investment of around $2 billion in the city's transportation infrastructure over the last decade, the problems of traffic and congestion remain. Traffic growth in Mumbai has been exponential, primarily driven by increases in private vehicles even though the majority of peak passenger trips are still undertaken by public transport. The road network is dominated by major north–south corridors, which not only carry high volumes of traffic, but also function as 'parking areas for vehicles, sites for hawkers, hutment dwellers, and other commercial activities' (MMR, 1996: 227). These activities severely reduce the traffic capacity of the roads. The strategy set out in the revised regional plan focuses on improved connectivity, development of expressways, trans-harbour links and the construction of by-passes.

About 88 per cent of all travel in Mumbai is by bus and train. BEST is by far the largest provider of bus services in MMR, carrying around five million passengers every day. All routes within Mumbai are provided by BEST, including radial routes to and from main centres, trunk routes linking main centres and feeder services connecting to the trunk routes and to railway stations. It offers smart cards for better fare collection and is currently introducing low-floor buses in a bid to be user-friendly to physically disabled travellers (Brihanmumbai Electric Supply Transport Undertaking, 2011). The suburban trains of the Mumbai Railway Vikas Corporation (MRVC) are popular and robust means of transportation, primarily because of their moderate fares, which make travel

150 *The structures of metropolitan authority*

affordable for those with lower incomes. The two main zonal railways that serve the city of Mumbai are the Western and Central Railways, but the rail system suffers massive overcrowding, most clearly seen during peak hours, when the average occupancy of trains is 4,000 despite a designated capacity of only 1,750 passengers. Mumbai's transport strategy aims to double the rail system's capacity. A number of challenges face the MRVC, including technical delays and the need for continuous maintenance work resulting from high usage. The introduction of new technologies is designed to make for safer, faster, efficient and more eco-friendly systems. Other measures include the construction of new lines, additional corridors and the expansion of rail services to new towns and the central business district. More recently, the MMRDA established the Metro rail system, the first PPP project, providing east–west connectivity with world-class features and facilities, designed to carry approximately six million commuters per day and expected to reduce travel time from an average of 90 minutes to about 20 minutes. The system aims to reduce traffic congestion in the city, and is planned for development over a 15-year period, with completion expected in 2021. Outside of the state, there is a recognised need for state governments to build synergies with national-level transport planning in preparing their state plans.

Kolkata's elaborate transport system comprises trains, trams, buses, ferries and taxis, and privately owned vehicles. With the highest car density and second highest car ownership in India, the region suffers from high traffic congestion on roads for, in common with other large metropolises, the existing road and highway network remains inadequate. While the national highways and the state and district roads provide links with the region, a number of roads function as arteries of the metropolis. About 40 such arterial roads function as the major arteries within the cities of Kolkata and Howrah in the metro core area.

Rail transport within the region comprises suburban railway, circular railway and the metro railway line, with infrastructure developments along the growth corridor. The Kolkata Metro's MRTS serves the city of Kolkata and the districts of South 24 Parganas and North 24 Parganas. The railways are complemented by effective water transportation facilities. The Kolkata Port Trust operates the Kolkata Port, while the Central Inland Water Transport Corporation (CIWTC), a Government of India undertaking, operates river services carrying goods between Kolkata and the neighbouring states of Assam and Bangladesh. The West Bengal Inland Water Transport Corporation (WBIWTC), set up by the Government of West Bengal, operates ferry services. WBIWTC also has oversight of infrastructure and terminal facilities and is responsible for the promotional activities for growth and development of inland water transport in the state.

Passenger volume on public transport is expected to rise significantly in the next decade. On the expanding metro rail, for instance, official estimates suggest that passenger numbers could almost quadruple by 2025 (Table 6.5). Given the range of multiple agencies involved in delivering transport (Table 6.6), a Comprehensive Mobility Plan (CMP) was designed by the Infrastructure

Table 6.5 Projected passenger volume for public transport in Kolkata Metropolitan Area (in millions)

Modes	2009/2010	2014/2015	2019/2020	2024/2025
Metro rail	4.5	10.1	19.8	38.7
Bus service (South Bengal State Transport Corporation)	768.2	799.0	831.1	864.5
Ferry service	2.4	2.6	2.8	3.1
Total	775.1	811.8	853.8	906.3

Source: Infrastructure Development Finance Company (IDFC, 2008).

Development Finance Company with a view to developing a 'balanced, integrated and multi-modal transportation system' accessible for all users (IDFC, 2008: 89). The plan proposed a multi-pronged approach combining land-use planning with public and freight transport requirements to strengthen the transport system by promoting mass transit systems and connecting key nodes such as the port with national highway terminals. A single ticketing system for different modes of transport has also been proposed to improve intermodal transport systems.

More importantly, the mobility plan proposed:

> A comprehensive single authority for all transportation issues ... The objective of the apex body would be to promote and secure the development of transport system of the KMA and provision of transport services ... The apex body would have the power to hold, manage and dispose of land and other fixed and movable assets and other property to carry out building, engineering and other operations to provide or cause to provide, transport service, to execute works in connection with development of transport facilities and supply of transport service and amenities, and generally to do anything necessary or expedient for purposes of such development and for purposes incidental thereto.
>
> (IDFC, 2008: viii)

Kolkata's transport strategy is forward looking and sophisticated, with development needs of the metropolis assessed up to 2025 and projects identified for investment. The strategy proposes a number of recommendations including the setting up of a centralised information system to hold all the data and information in respect of traffic and transportation systems and route rationalisation studies to cover all the mass transit and para-transit modes. The establishment of a high powered committee to coordinate and monitor activities of development projects undertaken by the various organisations operating in the area is also proposed for consideration.

To provide for greater coordination of public transport services across all cities, in 2006, the Government of India established the Unified Metropolitan

Table 6.6 Main agencies for transport in Kolkata Metropolitan Area

Name of the agency/unit	Related government Department	Main functions
Kolkata Metropolitan Development Authority	Urban Development Department, GoWB	• Acting as Technical Secretariat of Kolkata Metropolitan Planning Committee (KMPC) • Planning and Development Authority for KMA including KMC area • Design and implementation of transportation projects
Transportation Planning and Traffic Engineering Directorate	Transport Department, GoWB	• Planning and traffic engineering design for entire West Bengal
Kolkata Municipal Corporation	Municipal Affairs Department, GoWB	• Statutory local authority • Repair and maintenance of roads belonging to KMC • Implementation agency for planning regulations • Coordination and supporting all utility diversion work related to road infrastructure construction
West Bengal Transport Infrastructure Development Corporation	Transport Department, GoWB	• Developing transport infrastructure including bus terminals, truck terminals and traffic engineering and traffic
Hooghly River Bridge Commission	Transport Department, GoWB	• Implementing agencies for roads, bridges, bus stands, flyovers, etc.
Directorate of Movements	Transport Department, GoWB	• Coordination with South Eastern Railways and Eastern Railways with respect to passenger transport • Coordinate with Metro Railway for restoration of public utility services and related matters
Kolkata Improvement Trust	Urban Development Department, GoWB	• Planning and implementation of general improvement scheme, • Planning and implementation of street alignment schemes • Planning and implementation of road infrastructure projects including bridges, flyovers

The structures of metropolitan authority   153

Name of the agency/unit	Related government Department	Main functions
Public Works Directorate	Public Works Department, GoWB	• Repair and maintenance of roads belonging to PWD in KMC area. • Planning and implementation of transport infrastructure project like roads, bridges, parking structures, terminals • Street lighting
Kolkata Police and West Bengal Police	Home Department, GoWB	• Traffic operation and enforcement of traffic regulation • Road user and driver training and education programme
Kolkata Tramways Corporation	Transport Department, GoWB	• Provides and operates tram services and bus services
West Bengal Surface Transport Corporation	Transport Department, GoWB	• Provides and operates ferry services and bus services
Calcutta State Transport Corporation	Transport Department, GoWB	• Provides and operates bus services
South Bengal State Transport Corporation, North Bengal State Transport Corporation	Transport Department, GoWB	• Provides and operates long-distance bus services with Kolkata as one of the terminal points
Inland Water Transport Corporation	Transport Department, GoWB	• Managing inland water transport
State Transport Authority	Transport Department, GoWB	• Issue of permits and regulate procedures for buses plying inter-district and inter-state routes
Public Vehicle Directorate	Transport Department, GoWB	• Registration of all motorised vehicles operating in the state and issuing permits to all commercial vehicles and penalising violation
Kolkata Port Trust	Ministry of Shipping, GoI	• Maintain and operate Kolkata Port • Construction and maintenance of roads and bridges in port area • Regulatory body relating to water transportation, construction of ferry stations

Table 6.6 (cont.)

Name of the agency/unit	Related government Department	Main functions
Eastern Railways, Indian Railways	Ministry of Railways, GoI	• Planning, construction, operation and maintenance of suburban railway system and circular railway system (in addition to long-distance railway system)
Metro Railways, Indian Railways	Ministry of Railways, GoI	• Planning, construction, operation and maintenance of Metro Railway System
Hooghly Nadi Jala Paribahan Samity	Transport Department, GoWB	• Operating the ferry services
Private Bus Operators	Transport Department, GoWB	• Provision, operation and maintenance of bus services
Taxi Operators	Transport Department, GoWB	• Provision, operation and maintenance of taxi services
Auto Rickshaw Operators	Transport Department, GoWB	• Provision, operation and maintenance of auto rickshaw services
Truck Operators	Transport Department, GoWB	• Provision, operation and maintenance of truck services.

Source: IDFC (2008).

Transport Authority (UMTA) for cities with populations over a million. UMTA was expected to ensure coordination between the different institutions delivering transport service and to recommend integrated traffic plans, including modal priorities, integration of infrastructure facilities, investment planning, PPP initiatives and training for the transport sector. Core committees were established on strategic planning, finance, traffic engineering, regulations, safety and environment, parking, legal issues and research. While UMTA succeeded in addressing local issues, it failed to address problems of strategic and regional importance, which is partly attributed to inconsistencies in its structures and the lack of representation of regional development authorities.

Modernising service delivery

Evidence and experience have demonstrated the benefits of well-coordinated and modernised systems of public service delivery for good governance. In the context of growing demands for greater accountability and better quality of life, many of the policies require reconsideration, and engaging professionals and the wider public is perceived as critical to getting it right. The Planning Commission of India recently recommended the strengthening of managerial and technical expertise in city administrations, while the steering committee for the Twelfth Five Year Plan on water, sanitation and sewerage outlined specific proposals to change institutional arrangements in municipal administration (Planning Commission, 2012c). The proposals to improve urban sector performance are based on enhancing the financial and service-delivery capacities of ULBs, cities, states and parastatal agencies. Investments in skilled personnel and a cascaded planning structure, in which large cites will have binding 20- to 40-year municipal plans at the metropolitan level, are acknowledged as key to achieving innovative urban forms. In outlining the ways in which these reforms could be implemented, the steering committee recommended various phases in which governments could support local bodies, with the first phase involving the ring-fencing of water and sanitation operations to enforce the bare minimum, and subsequent phases focusing on target setting over a five-year period. Shortfalls in governance and performance would result in the state government recommending appropriate steps, including options to transfer operations to a third party through PPPs.

More specifically, the commission's recommendations were directed to address the growing deficits in public transport through the monetising of land assets, improving the collection of property taxes and raising user charges to reflect costs. In some of the largest cities in India, the combined operating deficit in the bus system has quadrupled during the last decade, while the annual operating deficit tripled for the Indian Railways (Pucher *et al.*, 2004). Kolkata is said to have the most unprofitable bus service, covering only 42 per cent of the costs. The bus services in Mumbai and Hyderabad, on the other hand, which have followed more progressive models, recover 80 per cent and 92 per cent of the costs respectively. Both cities have contracted their publicly owned bus firms to privately operated companies and are experimenting with reforms to improve performance (Pucher *et al.*, 2004).

The PPP model is increasingly being discussed in policy debates as a viable model of urban financing and a potential mode of delivery for infrastructure services in a variety of sectors. The roads sector took the lead as part of the National Highways Development Program (NHDP). Other sectors, such as water, solid waste management and housing have also experimented with PPPs, and the Hyderabad, Delhi and Mumbai Metros are some of the highest-value transport projects in the world. Although PPPs in water and sanitation sectors have generally shown greater success in terms of enhanced connectivity, increased productivity and improved quality of service, the country's urban systems pose particular challenges for building these partnerships. As we have seen from previous chapters, the devolution of funds, functions and finances from state to local bodies has not been effective and without the necessary autonomy in finance and administration, ULBs are in no position to negotiate PPPs. The presence of multiple agencies complicates matters further, as obtaining permission from the various parties involved can be time-consuming, often requires regulatory change, and generally leads to considerable delays. The Rajiv Gandhi Salai Road, or 'IT Corridor', in Chennai illustrates this problem sharply: the first stretch opened three years after the scheduled completion and project costs tripled as permissions had to be issued by a range of agencies.

Among the more successful PPP projects is the new international airport at Hyderabad, commissioned in 2008. Recently ranked the sixth busiest airport in the country in terms of international and overall passenger traffic, its current capacity is estimated to be over ten million passengers. Located at the heart of the HMDA, the development covers over 2,000 hectares of land and is planned to become an international transit hub with convention centres, shopping malls and resorts. The development authority, HADA, is connected to other premium real estate projects and is expected to change the dynamics of urban development in Hyderabad significantly over the next few years.

For India as a whole, the World Bank's mission of March 2005 was a turning point as it underlined the need to strengthen the authority and responsibility of local governments. Following its recommendations, aimed at streamlining decision making by government agencies and the devolution of services and functions to autonomous bodies, many states adopted an ambitious reform agenda. In Maharashtra, the reform agenda for Mumbai, Vision Mumbai, listed amongst its aims decentralisation, environmental sustainability, slum management, reform of municipal finance, civic engagement and capacity building. The Mumbai Transformation Support Unit (MTSU) worked in parallel in collaboration with the World Bank, USAID, All India Institute of Local Self Government and the Government of Maharashtra to facilitate the process of Mumbai's transformation. MTSU spans a wide range of initiatives covering issues such as physical and social infrastructure, strategic planning, health, education, sanitation, the environment and beautification.

Similarly, the KMDA has undertaken a number of ambitious projects to transform the city, some funded by the central government sponsored JNNURM. One such project, BSUP, focuses on building housing for the poor in seven districts across the state by 2015. Another project, the Kolkata Environment Improvement Programme, sought funding from the Asian Development Bank to upgrade the sewerage and drainage network, improve solid waste management and alleviate some of the poor conditions in slums (Sanhati, 2010). Other poverty reduction schemes to address the employment, housing and service needs of the poor include Swarna Jayanti Sahari Rozgar Yojana (SJSRY), Valimiki Ambedkar Awas Yojana (VAMBAY), Wage Employment Programme, National Slum Development Programme (NSDP), Integrated Low Cost Sanitation (ILCSP) and Sishu Siksha Kendra (SSK).

The World Bank's recommendations led the State of Andhra Pradesh to draw up its *Vision 2020*, in which key issues included building capacity, focusing on high-potential sectors as engines of growth, and transforming governance to ensure accountable and transparent decision making. The objective was to integrate the local economy with the national and global, and seizing opportunities created by new knowledge-intensive technologies. The capital investment required for the restructuring was to be provided by the private sector, while the role of the state was to enable suitable conditions in which businesses could thrive. Governance reforms, underpinned by administrative transparency and strong legal institutions, were integral to the overall strategy for making the city an attractive place for business (Kennedy, 2007: 98).

Despite taking steps in the right direction, urban service delivery is yet to be linked to a viable model, and improved professionalisation is required to enhance its effectiveness and ensure robust and coherent accountabilities.

Blurred accountabilities in governance

Multiple institutions within a metropolitan region typify much of urban governance in India. These institutions have overlapping responsibilities, and lack accountability to a single body. Tables 6.7–6.9 offer a brief overview of some of the complexity in the three study cities.

In Mumbai, a range of agencies and organisations operate which are accountable to different ministries and departments. The MMRDA was set up as the planning agency for MMR under the department of urban development, while the affordable housing and slum rehabilitation was the mandate of the MHADA and the Slum Rehabilitation Authority, created under the Department of Housing. Similarly, Maharashtra State Road Development Corporation under the Department of Public Works is in charge of road networks, bridges and flyovers, while other agencies such as the Port Trusts, Airport Authority of India, National Highway Authority of India and Mumbai Railway Vikas Corporation operate in certain jurisdictions in MMR that are outside the control of the relevant ULBs. A number of government agencies – MJP, MIDC, MCGM and the irrigation department – likewise are involved in water resource development and supply. The lack of effective coordination between these various agencies often results in faulty and expensive execution of projects.

A recent study assessing the conditions for effective governance identified 'active participation, indeed, overbearing interference, by the Government of Maharashtra in the governance of MMR via the para-statals established by it under different departments' (Pethe and Gandhi, 2011: 190). Instances of cooperation between MCGM (in charge of administration of civic affairs) and MMRDA (the planning and development agency) within MMR were found to be rare and the study concluded that 'the two are at loggerheads over various issues due to implicit (assumed) hierarchy, lack of coordination, differences in ruling political parties as well as considerable ambiguity regarding their respective roles and responsibilities' (Pethe and Gandhi, 2011: 191). The study illustrates numerous instances of tensions, frictions and failures in the relationship between the two organisations and identifies political rivalries between ruling parties at the state and local level as responsible for the

Table 6.7 Institutional arrangements for governance, infrastructure and services in Kolkata Metropolitan Area

Sector	Agency	Governing department	Legislation
Local level planning and governance	Kolkata Municipal Corporation (KMC)	Department of Municipal Affairs, GoWB	Calcutta Municipal Corporation Act, 1980
	Howrah Municipal Corporation (HMC)	Department of Municipal Affairs, GoWB	Howrah Municipal Corporation Act, 1980
	Chandannagar Municipal Corporation (CMC)	Department of Municipal Affairs, GoWB	Chandannagar Municipal Corporation Act, 1990
	38 municipalities	Department of Municipal Affairs, GoWB	West Bengal Municipal Act, 1993
Planning, development and big infrastructure provisions	Kolkata Metropolitan Development Authority (KMDA)	Urban Development Department, GoWB	West Bengal Town and Country Planning Act, 1979
	Kolkata Metropolitan Planning Committee (KMPC)		West Bengal Metropolitan Planning Committee Act, 1994
Urban development	Kolkata Metropolitan Development Authority (KMDA)		
Water supply and sewerage	Kolkata Metropolitan Water and Sanitation Authority (KMWSA)	Urban Development Department, GoWB	Calcutta Metropolitan Water and Sanitation Authority Act, 1966
Housing and slum development	West Bengal Housing Board	Housing Department, GoWB	West Bengal Housing Board Act, 1972 (ACT XXXII, 1972)

Transport, ecology and environment	Transportation Planning and Traffic Engineering Directorate (TP&TED)	Transport Department, GoWB	
	West Bengal Transport Infrastructure Development Corporation (WBTIDC)	Transport Department, GoWB	1969
	Hooghly River Bridge Commissioners (HRBC)	Transport Department, GoWB	
	Kolkata Improvement Trust	Urban Development Department, GoWB	Kolkata Improvement Act, 1911 (K. I. Act).
	Public Works Directorate		
	Eastern Railways		
	Indian Railways		
	Kolkata Metro Rail Corporation Limited (KMRCL)	A special purpose vehicle of Government of West Bengal and Government of India	1978
	Calcutta Tramway Company Limited (CTC)		
	Hooghly Nadi Jala Paribahan Samity		
	West Bengal Surface Transport Corporation (WBSTC)		
	South Bengal State Transport Corporation and North Bengal State Transport Corporation		
	Calcutta State Transport Corporation (CSTC)		
	Kolkata Port Trust		
	State Transport Authority		
	Public Vehicle Directorate		
	Department of Environment, Government of West Bengal		
	West Bengal Pollution Control Board (WBPCB)		Water (Prevention and Control of Pollution) Act, 1974

Table 6.7 (cont.)

Sector	Agency	Governing department	Legislation
	West Bengal Biodiversity Board (WBBB) East Kolkata Wetland Management Authority (EKWMA) West Bengal State Coastal Zone Management Authority (WBSCZMA)		
Power and energy	Calcutta Electric Supply Corporation Limited		Electricity Supply (1948) Act
Industries and commerce	West Bengal Industrial Development Corporation Limited	Commerce and Industries Department, GoWB	West Bengal Industrial Development Corporation Ltd. (WBIDC) Act 1967
Economy and finance	Finance Department		The West Bengal Finance Act 2012
	Finance Department		The West Bengal Fiscal Responsibilities and Budget Management Act, 2010

Source: Centre for Policy Research, New Delhi (2013).

Table 6.8 Multi-level (central and state) agencies functioning in Mumbai Metropolitan Region

Sl. No	Sector	GoI ministry/ GoM department	Quasi-government agency	Functions
1	Urban development	Ministry of Urban Development	Central Public Works Department	MoUD implements JNNURM Development of GOI land and buildings
			National Building Organization	Research and deciding norms for building construction
		Urban Development Department	Town and Country Planning Organization	Technical advice to Ministry
			Directorate of Town Planning	Technical advice to department and preparing development plans of cities
			Mumbai Metropolitan Region Development Authority	Planning, coordinating and executive agency for MMR
			City & Industrial Development Corporation of Maharashtra	NTDA for Navi Mumbai and SPA for Vasai Virar
			Directorate of Municipal Administration (Municipal Councils)	Controlling and regulating affairs of municipal councils
2	Housing	Ministry of Housing and Poverty Alleviation		Ministry implements centrally sponsored schemes
			Housing and Urban Development Corporation (HUDCO)	Financing housing and urban infrastructure
		Housing Department	Maharashtra Housing and Area Development Authority (regional Boards for Mumbai and Konkan)	State level agency for public housing operating with regional boards
			Mumbai Slum Improvement Board	Environmental improvement of slums in Greater Mumbai
			Mumbai Building Repairs and Reconstruction Board	Repair and reconstruction of cessed buildings in the Island City
			Slum Rehabilitation Authority	Regulating authority for slum rehabilitation

Table 6.8 (cont.)

Sl. No	Sector	GoI ministry/ GoM department	Quasi-government agency	Functions
3	Water resources development	No central agency Water Resource Department	River valley development agencies Water Resource Regulatory Authority	Development and management of water resources (dams) and irrigation system An independent statutory regulatory authority
4	Water supply and sanitation	No central agency Water Supply and Sanitation Department	Maharashtra Jeevan Pradhikaran	State level agency for water supply and sewerage development
5	Transport	Ministry of Civil Aviation Ministry of Shipping, Road Transport and Highway Ministry of Railways Public Works Department Home (Transport) Department	Airports Authority of India National Highway Authority of India Port Trusts Railway Board and the Zonal Railways Mumbai Railway Vikas Corporation Maharashtra State Road Development Corporation Maharashtra State Road Transport Corporation Maharashtra Maritime Board Road Transport Authority	Development and management of airports Development of national highways Development and management of major ports Development and operations of railways/ suburban railways Planning and coordination of development of suburban railways and commercial development of railway land State level agency for development of roads, flyovers and privately financed bridges Intercity bus services Developing and regulating minor ports Registration of vehicles and drivers

6	Environment	Ministry of Environment and Forest	Stipulating environmental regulations and granting environmental clearance
		Central Pollution Control Board	Prescribing environmental norms and their monitoring
		Environment Department	Enforcing environmental legislation and rules and monitoring environment
		Maharashtra Pollution Control Board	Promoting development of SEZs
7	Commerce and Industry	Ministry of Commerce Industries and Energy Department	Formulating state wide policies for industrial growth (manufacturing and services), attracting FDI, promoting SEZ
		Directorate of Industries	Regulating industries
		Maharashtra Industrial Development Corporation	Developing industrial estates, along with water resources.
8	Finance	Ministry of Finance	Providing refinance facility to Housing Finance Companies, regulating housing finance and financing rural housing and slum redevelopment
		National Housing Bank	
		India Infrastructure Finance Company Limited (IIFCL)	Supporting private investment in infrastructure through PPP
9	Energy	Industries and Energy Department	Power sector policies and generation, transmission and distribution
		Maharashtra State Electricity Board	
10	Transport	Tourism Department	Promoting tourism and hospitality industry
		Maharashtra Tourism Development Corporation	

Source: Centre for Policy Research, New Delhi (2013).

Table 6.9 Multiplicity of institutions in Hyderabad Metropolitan Region

	Organisation	Legislation	Jurisdiction	Functions
1.	Greater Hyderabad Municipal Corporation	Hyderabad Municipal Corporation Act, 1955	Greater Municipal Corporation Limits (erstwhile Municipal Corporation of Hyderabad and 12 surrounding municipalities)	Municipal functions
2.	Hyderabad Metropolitan Development Authority	Hyderabad Metropolitan Development Authority Act, 2008	Hyderabad Metropolitan Region	Planning, coordination, supervising, promoting and securing the planned development of the area
3.	Special Development Authorities, constituted under A.P. Urban Areas (Development) Act, 1975 designated as functional units Quli Qutb Shah Urban Development Authority	Hyderabad Metropolitan Development Authority Act, 2008	Respective area for which they are constituted	Assist HMDA in the functions specified for HMDA
4.	Hyderabad Metropolitan Water Supply and Sewerage Board (HMWSSB)	HMWSSB Act, 1989	Hyderabad Metropolitan Area	Water supply and sewerage services
5.	AP State Road Transport Corporation.	State-owned organisation	State-wide	Bus transport to the city commuters
6.	AP Housing Board	State-owned organisation	State-wide	Housing
7.	AP Transmission Corporation	State-owned organisation	State-wide	Electricity transmission to the city
8.	Central Power Distribution Company Limited (CPDCL)	AP Electricity Reform Act 1998	Anantapur, Kurnool, Mahboobnagar, Nalgonda, Medak and Rangareddy	Electricity distribution in the city
9.	Andhra Pradesh Pollution Control Board	Water (protection and control of pollution) Act, 1974	State-wide	Pollution control

10.	Hyderabad Metropolitan Water Supply and Sewerage Board	Hyderabad Metropolitan Water Supply and Sewerage Act 1989	Hyderabad Metropolitan Area	Planning, design, construction, maintenance, operation and management of water supply system and all sewerage and sewerage treatment works
11.	AP State Highways Authority	State-owned organisation	State-wide	Highways servicing the city
12.	Andhra Pradesh Industrial Infrastructure Development Corporation	State level organisation	State-wide	Development of industrial infrastructure
13.	Hyderabad Growth Corporation Limited (HGCL)	Companies Act, 1956	Hyderabad Outer Ring Road	To implement urban development around Hyderabad outer ring road
14.	Metropolitan Planning Committee	Andhra Pradesh Metropolitan Planning Committee Act, 2007	Hyderabad Metropolitan Area	MPC not yet constituted; preparation of Draft Development Plan for Metropolitan Area

Notes: A separate Metropolitan Planning Committee as required under Article 243 ZE of the Constitution was also set up under the AP Metropolitan Planning Committee Act 2007. The composition of this Metropolitan Planning Committee as specified in the Act is a repetition of the stipulations contained in Article 243 ZE itself. The present position therefore is that the MPC Act 2007 is only an enabling Act. Additionally District Planning Committees have also been set up as required under Article 243ZD of the Constitution for the District of Ranga Reddy, Medak, Mehboobnagar and Nalgonda. Source: *Centre for Policy Research, New Delhi (2013)*.

lack of cooperation and coordination. The period between 1999 and 2010, in particular, was one of conflicts and tensions between MCGM and MMRDA, as the former was governed by one political party (Shiv Sena), while another (Congress Party) controlled the latter. Beyond politics, even where MCGM and MMRDA undertake similar functions, such as road constructions, the relationships between MCGM and MMRDA 'are riddled with conflicts that fester due to the absence of arrangements for conflict resolutions' and duplication is used 'as an excuse to shirk responsibility and create confusion' (Pethe and Gandhi, 2011: 192–193).

The absence of accountability is also manifested in voluntary cooperation between units of local government with no permanent or independent institutional status. The STEM project in Mumbai is an example of such an arrangement. Established in 1987, the project is a collaboration between the three municipal corporations of Thane, Bhiwandi-Nizampur and Mira-Bhayander and 34 villages within Thane district to manage the region's water supply. STEM recovers costs of operation from the sale of bulk water, metered at the point of supply. Its governing council consists of the mayors and municipal commissioners of the three ULBs, the CEO of Thane representing the 34 villages, the commissioner/deputy commissioner of MMRDA, and the principal secretary/secretary of the Water Supply and Sanitation Department of the Government of Maharashtra. Given the voluntary nature of this project, the scope for its longer-term sustainability is reduced. In some countries federal incentives are used to engage voluntary cooperation. In India, while JNNURM represents such a programme, there have been limited attempts to use this as a lever to facilitate cooperation at the regional level. This is in part because local bodies have little autonomy and JNNURM focuses on the local rather than regional scale.

The involvement of numerous agencies in the delivery of water, sanitation and drainage in Kolkata has already been discussed above, and Tables 6.6 and 6.7 exemplify the multiplicity in respect of other related services and arrangements. In Hyderabad, the issue is most pronounced in the field of transport. The Andhra Pradesh State Road Transport Corporation (APSRTC), a parastatal agency that runs city buses, is in charge of public transport in general. The MMTS is the public train system, which caters for nearly 35,000 passenger trips per day. Developed by the Government of Andhra Pradesh, in collaboration with the South Central Railway, the MMTS builds on the existing suburban South Central Railway system and has helped improve connectivity. Road infrastructure on the other hand is provided by GHMC and HMDA. The police department also regulates and manages the traffic though other agencies such as the National Highway Authority of India (NHAI). The Transmission Corporation of Andhra Pradesh (AP TRANSCO) and HADA have further responsibilities for the transport network system. Recognising that the absence of a single coordinating agency makes accountability difficult, the Hyderabad Unified Metropolitan Transport Authority (HUMTA) was constituted in 2008 as the apex body to address the region's traffic and transport problems. The driving principles set out in the master plan for Hyderabad also have as their objective the attainment of a balanced and steady growth of traffic and transport.

*****

Metropolitan management of India's cities is infused with a range of agencies, parastatal organisations and other voluntary bodies providing similar or related civic services. The poly-governance structure across the cities is further complicated by the presence of private agencies, through PPPs, carrying out various planning and delivery roles for services.

This chapter has highlighted just how the multiple bodies involved in governance and their jurisdictional overspill pave the way for blurred accountabilities. While there exist functional bodies for such services as water supply and sewerage, they are not strategic or metropolitan authorities. Although set up to serve the metropolitan region, their jurisdictions are limited to municipal boundaries. Yet, where strategic authority exists, as is the case of water resource planning in Mumbai, its functioning is weak due to the presence of other providers for developing water resources at that level. The absence of a single, unified, metropolitan institution has resulted in trans-municipal arrangements in all the three cities of Mumbai, Hyderabad and Kolkata.

Another common characteristic across metropolitan management is the lack of incentives to ULBs. Despite powers accorded to them by the CAA, they do not function as autonomous units of democratic government. The current fiscal approach does not require the performance of ULBs to be evaluated against outcomes, while the overlapping and fragmented system weakens the incentives for performance. Proposals to create arm's-length boards for certain functions to maintain independence from municipal corporations have been considered, but dismissed. The current administrative organisation is beset with endemic issues of reduced accountabilities and confusion regarding respective responsibilities, leading to difficulties in coordinating smooth service delivery and maintenance in urban governance.

7 Urban leadership and civic engagement

The cities of the Western world are replete with attempts to represent the urban community through political leadership. Different national systems have developed different mechanisms for managing their cities, reflecting their cultural, historical and constitutional circumstances. City governments are enormously varied in both size and institutional form. Even intra-country variations abound, as in the case of the United States, where the principal forms of government range from the council manager type to mayor-council form and the commission form. The council-manager form of urban government arose from the reform campaigns against corruption and partisanship in the 1920s that centred on the ideal of a professional chief executive accountable to a small council elected city-wide, while the directly elected mayor was designed to give political leadership to both the council and its manager. It was against this cacophonous background that the British debate about institutions, which received considerable attention during the late 1990s, came to be dominated by the urge to import ideas from other countries. The United States provided the most influential model of the elected mayoral system, while Europe offered a number of other interesting variations on the theme.

The different systems and their historical legacies have produced a range of styles, often within the same polity. The way in which mayors seek to lead their communities and shape their cities depends just as much on their own ambitions to drive and innovate as the political and financial resources at their disposal. Thus, a mayor given extensive authority may, in practice, carry little effective power, while a dynamic and energetic mayor can often stretch the formal powers of an office that is inherently weak. Irrespective of the forms of urban leadership currently in operation, the importance and significance of sub-national politics cannot be overestimated.

Local politics has long been recognised for its role in legitimisation and democratisation beyond its boundaries, functioning as a 'training ground for democracy' in the sense that it offers positive socialisation effects for higher levels of politics. In major democracies, city leadership has often been the stepping stone to state and national level office. The mayor can be a dominating figure in national as well as metropolitan politics: Jacques Chirac combined the positions of Mayor of Paris and Prime Minister. A number of Parisian deputy mayors held seats in the national legislature. The mayors of Buenos Aires, Shanghai, Rio de Janeiro and London have been major national figures, often holding national offices.

So too in India, where several major national leaders in the freedom struggle acquired experience and rose to prominence through local government leadership. Jawaharlal Nehru, India's first prime minister, was Mayor of Allahabad during 1924–1926, and Chittaranjan Das, another prominent national leader, served as Mayor of Calcutta in 1924. Much earlier, at the turn of the nineteenth century, Pherozeshah Mehta was Mayor of Bombay.[1] This indeed was at a time when municipal politics was the only form of electoral politics in which urban educated Indians could engage under the British rule. Today, the growing heterogeneity of India's cities and the changing landscape of local and national politics is once again in need of leaders of that calibre to contribute to building cities for the twenty-first century.

The office of the mayor

Many major cities in the world outside of India have a strong and powerful executive mayor. A powerful and directly accountable mayor is seen to bring significant benefits for local communities, in terms of enhancing the local economy and bringing greater prosperity to the city. The case for mayors is founded on their having the potential to make a greater contribution to achieving successful economic, social and environmental outcomes for their cities than other forms of local government. This is particularly important for megacities that have the potential to be key drivers of economic growth. The value of big cities, effectively led by powerful mayors, is demonstrated by a range of international experiences. For example, Barcelona was transformed through the strong leadership of its powerful executive mayor, Pascal Maragall, into a leisure and cultural centre – it is now one of the most prosperous cities in Europe with a GDP per capita 44 per cent above the European average, and is one of the most popular tourist destinations (CLG, 2011). In southern Germany, directly elected mayors enjoy immense public visibility and the possibility of building a strong base of public support, while the French mayorality stands at the centre of a complex system of actors varying in nature and status, but all looking to the mayor as the locus of local power and decision.

India is among a small group of countries that do not have elected executives for their large metropolitan areas (see Figure 7.1). China's major cities have mayors who are powerful political appointees and are held accountable by the central government for delivering economic growth and improvements in the quality of life of their cities. The United States operates distinct types of mayors depending on the system of local government. The first of these is a council-manager system in which the mayor is a first among equals on the city council, which acts as a legislative body. Executive functions are performed by the appointed manager and the mayor may chair the city council, but lacks

170 *Urban leadership and civic engagement*

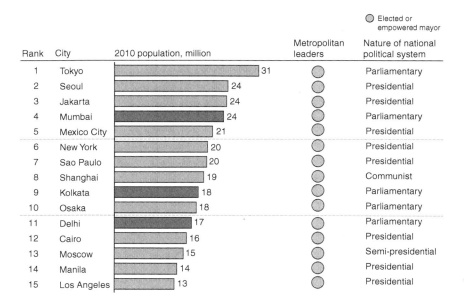

Figure 7.1 Patterns of political systems (cities' rank ordered by population size)
Source: www.citymayors.com; McKinsey Global Institute analysis.

any special legislative powers. The mayor and city council serve part-time, with day-to-day administration in the hands of a professional city manager. The system is most common among medium sized cities from around 25,000 to several hundred thousand, usually rural and suburban municipalities. In the second form, known as mayor-council government, the mayoralty and city council are separate offices. Under a *strong mayor* system, the mayor is usually directly elected and holds executive power, but with the city council exercising legislative powers. The mayor generally selects a chief administrative officer to oversee the different departments and can often engage and dismiss department heads without the need to seek council approval. This is the system used in most of the large cities in the United States, primarily because mayors serve full-time and have a wide range of services that they oversee. In a *weak mayor* or *ceremonial mayor* system, the mayor has appointing power for department heads, but is subject to checks by the city council, sharing both executive and legislative duties with the council.

There are wide variations in local laws and customs regarding the powers and responsibilities and the manner of election for the post of mayor. In many cities, including New York, London, Tokyo, Sydney, Athens, Mexico City and Buenos Aires, mayors are elected by popular vote once every three or four years. In Paris, the mayor is chosen by proportional representation, while the mayor in Rio de Janeiro is popularly elected by a two-round majority system. In almost all of these cities, the city government is a powerful institution with a very real and effective role in the management of most aspects of the city. The mayor is usually the head of the executive branch of the city government, and service functions such roads, water supply, sanitation, drainage and sewerage, the police, airports, ports, fire services, traffic and transport are generally under the city government's control.

The model generally operating in India is commonly known as the commissioner system, taking its name from the role of the city administrator, who is generally a state-appointed officer. In such a system, the mayor in a municipal corporation is chosen by the councillors from among themselves. The mayor generally lacks executive authority. This is due to the British roots of the system, which remain from the time when the administrator was the representative of the colonial power, not to the fact that it operates under a council-manager system, whereby the executive would be accountable to the elected representatives. In this context, the indirect election of the mayor combined with his short one-year tenure renders the role little more than that of a figurehead. Councillors act by committee, the most powerful being the standing committee, which acts as the steering committee exercising executive, supervisory, financial and personnel powers. It is composed of anything between seven and 16 members elected through a system of proportional representation.

The mayor is usually elected for a term of one year, which is renewable. In states such as Assam, Delhi, Haryana, Himachal Pradesh and Karnataka the councillors elect a new chairperson every year by rotation. Exceptions to the system of annual tenure are seen in Gujarat and Maharashtra, where the term of office for the chairperson is two-and-a-half years, while the mayors of Madhya Pradesh, Tamil Nadu and Uttar Pradesh are directly elected with even longer terms of office, typically five years (see Table 7.1)

The system is different in Kolkata. Here, the chairperson and mayor hold two different roles: the former chairs the corporation meetings, and the mayor-in-council exercises executive functions. The aim of this separation of functions was to make the corporation more efficient and effective, and the change in the municipal authority ensured that there would be three authorities including the corporation, the mayor-in-council and the mayor. This experiment with mayor-in-council was tried in Mumbai during 1998–1999 but the decision was reversed immediately. Currently, as elsewhere, the role of Mayor of Mumbai is largely ceremonial and the real powers are vested in the municipal commissioner, who is the effective executive head of the city, but accountable to the state government and not the city. The commissioner is assisted by additional officers on deputation from the state government or sometimes from the municipal cadre. The mayor of Hyderabad is similarly a figurehead and has few administrative powers, and the standing committee and the commissioner are the two main entities representing the legislative and executive branches of government. Although modification of the 1995 Municipal Act provides for a directly elected mayor, it does so without really empowering the position. All of the city's 150 municipal wards are overseen

Table 7.1 Mode of election of municipal chairperson and terms of office

State	Election	Term (in year[s])
Andhra Pradesh	Indirect	5
Assam	Indirect	1
Delhi	Indirect	1
Gujarat	Indirect	2.5
Haryana	Indirect	1
Himachal Pradesh	Indirect	1
Karnataka	Indirect	1
Kerala	Indirect	5
Madhya Pradesh	Direct	5
Maharashtra	Indirect	2.5
Orissa	Indirect	1
Rajasthan	Indirect	5
Tamil Nadu	Direct	5
Uttar Pradesh	Direct	5
West Bengal	Indirect	5

Source: Second Administrative Reform Commission (2005: 214–215).

by a corporator. The administration corporators are elected by popular vote, and almost all the political parties field their own candidates.

The issue currently under debate is whether the existing commissioner system of chief executive is able to provide the coordinated leadership necessary at the city level or whether India's cities should consider other options such as a strong mayoral system in which a directly elected, empowered mayor plays the role of chief executive of the urban local body. Models under consideration include a directly elected mayor and council; a directly elected mayor, but executing through the municipal commissioner and his deputies; or the wider adoption of the indirectly elected mayor and council system, as prevalent in Kolkata. The current commissioner/mayor model, in which the mayor as the chief of the deliberative wing has no executive powers, is increasingly being viewed as ineffective, as accountabilities are diluted and elected representatives appear unable to carry out their roles effectively. It is this perceived ineffectiveness that is driving current concerns about the lack of empowered representatives and the need to achieve a better balance between accountability and empowerment in urban governance.

A directly elected mayor and council

Chosen by the local electorate, a directly elected mayor would serve as the political leader for that community, supported by a council drawn from among the council members. Depending on local political circumstances, the council might be a single party or a coalition. This system is seen to have several advantages, the most important being that the directly elected mayor has the mandate of the whole electorate and can represent and speak for the whole city with greater effectiveness and legitimacy. Such a mayor also has the authority to coordinate with other agencies strategically without being closely involved in the day-to-day administration. The mayor has a fixed tenure and cannot ordinarily be removed from office by the councillors, and is therefore able to bring greater stability and certainty of leadership. The mayor depends for his authority on the electorate at large, and thus has a mandate separate from that of the council.

The system, however, brings with it several political challenges, including situations where a mayor directly elected by the people may represent one particular political party while the majority of the councillors may belong to another.[2] The advantages of having a strong mayoral model have been disputed on the grounds that while such a system focuses public attention, it can lead to undue personalisation and a dangerous concentration of power. Elsewhere, even the advocates of change have recognised the dangers of so great a concentration of power leading to 'elected dictatorship' (Rao, 2000).

A directly elected mayor and commissioner

A directly elected mayor's role would primarily be one of influence, guidance and leadership. The mayor would delegate strategic policy and day-to-day decision making to the commissioner. Such a system, not tried and tested in the Indian context, could carry potential frictions and tensions. Much would depend on whether such a mayor is a strong mayor or a weak mayor. While the former enjoys considerable administrative powers, authority is relatively more fragmented under the weak mayor model. Even though the mayor is directly elected, leads the city and speaks for it, a weak mayor has limited formal powers to ensure his political will. On the other hand, although commissioners are inescapably prominent figures in their communities, they lack the authority that comes with election to leadership.

An indirectly elected mayor and council

This is the Kolkata model, introduced in 1984 and commonly known as the mayor-in-council form of city governance, can be described as a cabinet government replicating the formula operating at the state and national levels. Municipal authority is vested in three entities: the corporation, mayor-in-council and the mayor. The corporation is the highest body, consisting of elected councillors representing the 141 wards, while the mayor-in-council consists of the mayor, the deputy mayor and not more than ten other members of the corporation. Executive power is exercised by the mayor-in-council.

This system is, in essence, a hybrid between a mayor-council system and the integrated federated framework. The municipal corporation groups wards into boroughs, with each one having a committee consisting of the councillors

174 *Urban leadership and civic engagement*

elected from the respective wards of the borough. The councillors elect one among themselves as the chairperson of the borough. The borough committees are subject to general supervision of the mayor-in-council, and look after sub-local functions such as water supply, drainage, collection and removal of solid waste, disinfection and health services, housing services, lighting, repairs of certain categories of roads, maintenance of parks, and drains. The mayor-in-council confers power on the elected representatives rather than the commissioner, as is the case in Mumbai and Hyderabad. The municipal commissioner acts as the chief executive officer and even though theoretically subject to the control and supervision of the mayor in this model wields sufficient power and authority to lead the city's administration and guide the political leadership. However, critical to the success of the system:

> is the granular definition of roles and the balance of power between the mayor and commissioner, in which the commissioner's role provides effective checks and balances on the mayor. In fact ... not having this appropriate balance of power was responsible for Mumbai's failed mayor-in-council experience ... Kolkata's model is far from perfect, but its structure still represents progress in local administration in India.
> (McKinsey, 2010: 92)

Even so, while an indirectly elected mayor survives in office as long as he enjoys the support of the majority in the council, it is argued that such a system is prone to 'horse-trading', which weakens the authority and credibility of the mayor. It is also contended that the system only works successfully as long as the same party rules both the city corporation and the state. Even so, there should be few illusions about the standing of any Indian mayor:

> Inspired by the Mumbai slum rehabilitation model (intended to decongest the central areas of the city), the Mayor of KMC announced PPPs for slum development in the city. The Confederation of Real Estate Developers Association of India (CREDAI) approached the Mayor with a proposal to decongest slums in prime localities and build integrated low-cost housing complexes ... The CREDAI proposal was being considered along with a joint venture housing formula under which low, medium and high-income group apartments would be developed on a cross-subsidy basis. However, the Mayor faced a severe political backlash not only from the opposition but also from his own party colleagues in the Corporation, as a result of which the plan has been shelved.
> (Ghosh *et al.*, 2009: 50)

Tensions arise between the mayor, who is a political appointment, and the municipal commissioner, who is looked on as holding an 'apolitical' post and is normally a senior bureaucrat of the Government of India. The mayor is the *public face* of the corporation and accountable to the citizens, while the commissioner, directly accountable to the mayor, remains responsible for expenditures and the delivery of policies and programmes.

Acknowledging the various strengths and weaknesses of the various systems, the report of the High Powered Expert Committee (HPEC) in 2011 recommended a unified system under a mayor for each city, stating that local conditions should determine the choice of any particular model. It suggested that the spirit of a 'single point accountability' of the mayor as executive head of the city should prevail, in which the elected representatives are given the power and autonomy to run the city for a sufficient length of time. From the point of view of leadership development, SARC highlighted the further advantage of a strong directly elected mayoral system in that it would provide the training ground for future leaders. The system of a directly elected mayor, which promotes strong visible leadership in cities, is indeed an important source of recruitment of talent into public life and leadership development.

The Kasturirangan report on the analysis of governance in the Bangalore metropolitan region similarly concluded that the challenge of governance in a complex metropolis like Bangalore required a new leadership paradigm able to provide political and administrative dynamism and stability. The reporting committee took the view that the best way to fulfil this requirement would be a directly elected mayor assisted by a committee, chosen by the mayor, from among elected and nominated councillors. The report recommended that Bangalore metropolitan region should have a directly elected executive mayor, who would serve for a fixed term of five years, be politically accountable at local government level, and have a democratic mandate comparable to political leaders at other levels of government. It further stated that the mayoral committee should be given delegated functions such as finance, projects, municipal and social services, administration and planning, and that decisions taken by the mayor should have to be ratified by the committee:

> The Corporation Council must retain a strong deliberative and scrutiny function but should no longer be vested with the executive powers of the municipal government as these should be vested with the Mayor. The number of wards and Councillors must be increased, in keeping with the increased jurisdiction as determined by the delimitation process and this should be provided for in a new legislation. The number of nominees may be fixed at 10 per cent of the total number of elected members and the nominations may be from persons having special knowledge and experience in municipal administration or matters relating to health, town planning or education.
> (Kasturirangan Committee, 2008: 7–8)

Among other recommendations were the need to separate the role of chairperson and mayor, in keeping with the broad notion of separation of powers. This is not dissimilar to the way the national and state legislatures have their own presiding officers, while the executive government is headed by the prime minister/the chief minister. The commission took the view that such separation of the functions at the local level would be unnecessary and cumbersome, as the mayor acting as chairperson would in fact facilitate harmonious functioning between the council and the executive. A unified and clearly defined role would better inform the public, while establishing clear links between voting and service provision. In relation to the issue of whether the chief executive should be the elected mayor or the appointed commissioner, SARC was firmly of the view that the elected mayor must exercise executive power and should be the chief executive of the city or urban government with the power to appoint all officials, including the commissioner, and to hold them to account.

The final issue related to the way in which the mayor's executive authority might be exercised, given the growing scale and importance of urban governments. SARC concluded that some form of cabinet system would be desirable, with functionaries appointed by the mayor exercising authority on his behalf in various departments of the executive branch. In systems where the chief executive is directly elected, and separation of powers is practised, the cabinet is often drawn from outside the legislature. But in a city government, the imperatives of separation of powers should be tempered by the need for greater harmony between the elected council and the mayor. The commission recommended that a mayor's 'cabinet', chosen by the elected mayor from among the councillors, should be constituted in all municipal corporations, with the size of the cabinet not exceeding 10 per cent of the strength of the council, or 15 per cent, whichever is higher. Such a cabinet would function directly under the control and supervision of the mayor, and the final authority on any executive matter vested in the mayor.

The role of municipal commissioner in urban management

The municipal commissioner is the chief executive officer and head of the executive arm of the municipal corporation. All executive powers are vested in the municipal commissioner. Although the corporation is the legislative body that lays down policies for the governance of the city, it is the commissioner who is responsible for the execution of the policies. The commissioner is appointed for a fixed term as defined by state statute, although the term in office can be extended or reduced. He or she can be removed if found to be under-performing or guilty of misconduct or neglect. The powers of the commissioner are a combination of those provided by statute and those delegated by the corporation or standing committee. This is the closest that India has come to the council-manager system, with the critical differences of accountability of the manager to the elected arm of government and the fact that the power of the unelected executive arm of government is thus weighted in its favour.

Although appointed by the state, the commissioner is answerable to both the corporation and the public at large, assisted by additional municipal commissioners and deputy municipal commissioners. In Mumbai and Hyderabad, which do not operate an elected mayor system, the municipal commissioner holds the key position. Though, in principle, the corporation formulates policy and the commissioner implements it, the initiative in policy making as dictated by practice and convention is most often taken by the commissioner, who also uses his technical knowledge and expertise to assess policies and functions of various departments. It is the commissioner who prioritises and finalises the budget, in consultation with heads of directorates, ward officers, chief engineers and chief accountants, and also has the authority to finalise contracts on behalf of the corporation within financial limits specified in the municipal regulations. Though the commissioner has immense powers, there are a number of checks and balances prescribing the way in which those powers are exercised. The corporation controls and directs the administration through the committees and has a share in the appointment and promotion of staff. In a commissioner driven model, his position is typically described as:

> one of a loner who does not have the protective mantle of a minister, and with pulls and pressures brought to bear on him all the time, he runs the risk of being politicized. Much depends on his personality and calibre and how he functions as the link between the deliberative and administrative wings and the link between the corporation and the state government.
>
> (Pinto, 2008: 49)

As with the role of the mayor, there is considerable debate surrounding the appointment of the commissioner. Some take the view that unless the role is filled by an 'outsider' appointed by the state government, the municipal commissioner may not be able to resist pressures from within, a situation that is not always in the public interest. For others, unless the mayor/chairperson, as the chief executive of the local government, has entire control over staff, including the commissioner, it would not be possible fully to discharge his duties towards the electorate. On this view, the suggestion is for the mayor/chairperson to appoint the commissioner/chief officer. SARC's position is unequivocal. As the elected mayor/chairperson is accountable to the electorate, this accountability requires that person to have authority over local government staff. The mayor/chairperson should, accordingly, have a final say in the matter of the appointment of the commissioner or chief officer. However, in order to ensure that the right person is selected, the state must lay down, by law, the procedure and qualifications for selection and appointment to this post. The Kasturirangan Committee, however, recommended that the commissioner should be selected by a high-powered search committee, set up by the state government in consultation with the mayor. The mayor, it suggested, might appoint any of the candidates short-listed by the search committee, while the commissioner's role should be redefined in legislation so has to make him responsible and accountable to the mayor and the corporation. On other matters, the power of the state to direct the commissioner to provide records or take particular actions was deemed unnecessary, although it was important for the state government to have the power to give directions or dissolve the corporation in times of emergency.

Whatever the nature of debates, India's cities are experiencing a period of growth and change, and proliferation of urban partnerships. It is important that any assessment of a model should take account of the influence that mayors, as leaders or chairpersons, can exercise within the networks and partnerships that characterise the changing nature of governance, as well as their formal powers in relation to the council.

Engaging the public in policy making

Interest in strengthening public participation in policy making is underpinned by several considerations, including the need to accommodate public demand for a larger say in managing public affairs and the increasing role of governments in setting frameworks within which individuals and groups may organise their own activities. Yet, policy making based on the principle of partnership between governments, individuals and civil society organisations varies considerably between the different cities under study.

The establishment of area sabhas and ward committees has been a landmark development in urban municipal administration. The CAA enabled the constitution of such committees, with membership comprising the elected representatives and nominated members, with a view to bringing decision making closer to the public. No more than ten states have constituted ward committees, with those such as Kerala, Karnataka and Maharashtra showing higher levels of participation and representation from a range of professions, non-governmental organisations, neighbourhood groups and other civic agencies. Under the present arrangements, the ward committees are authorised to identify the problems of the locality, supervise municipal works, plan development priorities, convene annual general meetings and submit administrative reports to the municipality. They do not enjoy the right to initiate development plans, raise resources or take independent decisions. As participatory organisations, the area sabhas and ward committees have yet to receive proper autonomy to work as grassroot organisations. As the report for the MoUD concluded:

> Not all States have the enabling state legislation for the constitution of ward committees, not all the cities in States having the legislation, have ward committees, and wherever the ward committees are functioning, they are not delegated proper functions and finances ... the proximity between citizens and government is neglected even in those states where ward committees are established.
>
> (TERI, 2010: 6)

In examining the various structures, statutes and practice, the second administrative reform commission also came to the conclusion that the average citizen plays little role in governance and that this, together with a lack of accountability of elected representatives and officials, often undermines efficiency and transparency in decision making. The commission made a number of recommendations to modify the structures of urban governance with a view to promoting greater participation, including achieving a good representative ratio between citizens and their elected representatives, which is currently almost ten times higher in urban compared with rural areas. It also recommended establishing and extending ward committees where they do not exist.

Ward committees

The present constitutional position requires state governments to constitute ward committees consisting of one or more wards within the territorial area of any municipality having a population of 300,000 or more. They have not been constituted in many states, but even where they do exist, the population served by a single ward committee is often well in excess of 300,000. In most cases ward committees are advisory bodies with either limited or no financial powers. In Mumbai, the provision for ward committees was incorporated in the Mumbai Metropolitan Corporation Act of 1994, although it was not until 2000 that they were first constituted. In accordance with the rules framed by the state government and the resolution passed by the MMC, 16 ward committees were formally constituted, with all the councillors within the ward committee jurisdiction as members of the committee. The corporation now comprises 24 wards, with 17 ward committees, and the 227 elected councillors serve a population of 18.3 million. Each committee corresponds to the jurisdiction of an existing ward officer, who is viewed as merely fulfilling the constitutional obligation of creating a ward committee. Each such committee has nine or ten corporators' divisions in its jurisdiction, covering a population ranging from 700,000 to 1.1 million. On average, there are 14 to 15 members in each of the ward committees. The chairperson of the ward committee, who is elected from among the councillors on the particular committee, has a term of office that is coterminus with the duration of the corporation. The Municipal Acts and government guidelines in Maharashtra provide for the nomination of three representatives of NGOs that have implemented municipal projects in the ward.

Decisions regarding the membership of wards committees are left to the discretion of state governments. As noted in the previous chapter, in the case of Kerala, there are as many ward committees as the number of councillors. In Hyderabad the convention is for municipal commissioners and officers to attend ward committee meetings, while a much higher level of participation from civil society and non-governmental organisations is expected in the city of Mumbai.

180 *Urban leadership and civic engagement*

West Bengal was the first state to establish ward committees, following the West Bengal Act of 1993, which was amended the following year. The number of nominated members depends on the size of the ward. A ward committee has four nominated members for a population of up to 2,500 and another one member is added for every 500, with the total number not exceeding 17 and being no less than seven, as set by the West Bengal Municipal (Amended) Rules of 2003. The councillors and local body have the right to appoint members, and at least two members must be from the community development society. The functions of the ward committee range from supervisory, financial, planning and execution of development projects. Although the State of West Bengal took the lead in establishing ward committees, great scepticism has been expressed about public engagement in Kolkata. A recent study found that a large gap exists between the rhetoric surrounding the constitutional provisions and their actual implementation.

> Political nature of the ward committee and thin attendance of the citizens in the meetings put a question mark on the efficacy of the ward committee as a true participative forum at the municipal level. The numerical representation has not transformed into effective representation with respect to participation of elected representatives and their accountability in municipal governments.
>
> (Chattopadhyay, 2012: 185)

In the State of Andhra Pradesh there is provision for the constitution of ward committees in all ULBs with populations of more than 100,000 people, and ward sabhas in ULBs with populations smaller than that. The ward committees consist of the councillor representing the ward, who also serves as the chairperson of the ward committee, along with not more than ten persons representing civil society in the ward, who are nominated by the municipality based on prescribed criteria. The functions of the ward committees include supervision over sanitation and drainage, water supply, street lights, road repairs, maintenance of parks, playgrounds and implementation of poverty programmes. Among other tasks are those relating to facilitation of collection of taxes and non-taxes, the preparation of annual ward development plans, and preparation of an inventory of municipal assets. In Hyderabad, there are ten ward committees for 100 corporators' divisions, each committee serving about 400,000 people. The practice of amalgamating or grouping wards, as has happened in Hyderabad and elsewhere, to create committees that represent populations the size of a normal city, is criticised for its size and remoteness, as neither citizen participation nor local decision making is feasible in such large committees. A large ward committee also reinforces the tendency to resort to a 'spoils' system by rotation of membership or chairmanship and reduces accountability and transparency.

More specifically, SARC argued that the present system of having a ward committee acting for more than one ward is illogical and recommended a committee for every ward, each effectively representing a local political boundary. A directly elected ward councillor or corporator, as the chairperson of the ward committee, would represent the ward in the municipal council, thus giving him essentially two roles – that of a representative on the city council, and an executive on the ward committee. The commission was of the view that in smaller towns, with populations of less than 300,000, it is necessary to have formal mechanisms for citizen participation and local decision making through ward committees. It recommended that members of the ward committee have regular meetings with elected members from area sabhas and the citizens they represent in order to review programmes, their planning and implementation.

A study of the effectiveness of ward committees shows that these committees do not have any power or authority to generate resources and are not entrusted with responsibility for implementation, and hence no funds are allocated to them (Sivaramakrishnan, 2008). The author argues that ward committees need to have legitimate functions and appropriate financial devolution covering all the relevant activities that may be delegated by the legislature or the municipal council. A proposed functional and financial devolution to the ward committees lists such activities as street lighting, sanitation, water supply, drainage, road maintenance, maintenance of school buildings, maintenance of local hospitals and dispensaries, local markets, parks and playgrounds. The proposal is for funds to ward committees to be transferred en-bloc and the committee be given a share of the property taxes collected from the ward, depending on the economic profile of the locality. Amongst other powers, ward committees should be empowered to raise funds through other sources, and meetings should be widely publicised to ensure maximum presence and participation of the residents of the ward (National Advisory Council, 2005). There is growing recognition that in urban areas, it is not just the individual voter whose involvement is critical, but also that of commercial organisations, businesses and enterprises that contribute to the local economy. As urban areas have pockets that are predominantly commercial, they would need representation at ward level. The limit for such positions may be restricted to a proportion of the seats in the ward committee.

Area sabhas

At the lowest level in the hierarchy of governance, beneath the municipal council or corporation, and the ward committees are the area sabhas. The Community Participation Law (CPL), also known as the Nagar Raj Bill, prescribes the structure, powers and functions of these sabhas. Area sabhas are constituted for the entire geographical territory in which all persons mentioned in the electoral roll of any polling booth in such a territory are ordinary residents. 'This creates an urban equivalent of the gram sabha, retains a reasonable level of intimacy, and recognises the unique features of urban dwellings', and the benefits of such a structure are that it inherently

182 *Urban leadership and civic engagement*

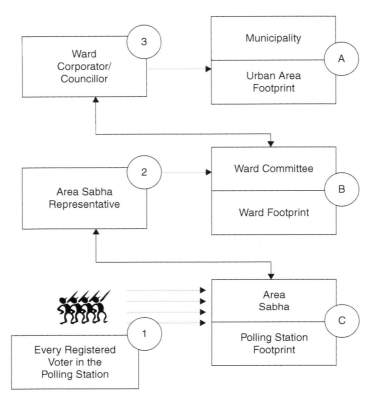

Figure 7.2 Ward committees and area sabhas
Source: Sinha (2011).

adjusts for the size of a municipality or ward and gives formal voice to every voter to participate in issues of local governance and a reasonable sense of belonging and inclusion (Sinha, 2011). Large municipalities may have wards with greater population, more polling booths, and therefore a greater number of area sabhas, resulting in larger ward committees. Conversely, smaller municipalities may have a smaller population in each ward, hence fewer area sabhas with fewer members in each ward committee. Each area is governed by an area representative, and the election to the office is conducted by the state election commission. The area sabha representatives must constitute no less than two-thirds of the total membership of the ward committees.

Still in their infancy, area sabhas are not as commonplace and established as ward committees. The functions of the area sabhas are broadly in line with those of the ward committees, and cover such responsibilities as proposing development programmes and determining priorities for inclusion in the ward's development plan. They are also responsible for preparing the list of beneficiaries under different schemes, verifying the eligibility of persons receiving welfare assistance, identifying deficiencies in the systems of water supply, street lighting and recommending appropriate remedial measures. The area sabha has a right of access to information about decisions taken by the ward committee concerning the area as well as the implementation of those decisions. It is expected to work in collaboration with the ward committee on the provision of sanitation, undertake awareness programmes on cleanliness, preservation of the environment and the prevention of pollution. According to a report for the MoUD, of the 12 states that have so far enacted the CPL several are not in conformity with the Nagar Raj Bill. The study found that some states such as Andhra Pradesh defeat the basic spirit of the CPL by empowering community based organisations and resident welfare associations to choose area sabha representatives who do not necessarily represent popular opinion or interests. Several others do not provide for two-thirds majority representation from ward committees, as required by the law (TERI, 2010: 16).

New accountabilities

Opponents of decentralisation have argued in terms of the risks of increased corruption that devolution entails. The response has been to empower and enable local governments by putting in place rigorous accountabilities. Direct forms of accountability through institutionalised mechanisms have involved participatory budgeting and public disclosures. The Public Disclosure Law (PDL) requires ULBs to release quarterly audited financial statements of performance to the public and information on key service level benchmarks for such services as water supply, drainage and solid waste management. It is deemed as an extension of the Right to Information Act, in that it moves away from an expectation that the citizen has to ask for information to one in which the local body has a duty to disclose information in a *suo moto* manner. There are many examples of direct accountability, but the essential thrust here is the need to ensure that the accountability of local government moves away from upward accountability to other levels of government and towards outward accountability directly to the citizens and voters who elect their local governments (Kasturirangan Committee, 2009: 7).

The CPL serves as an important tool in driving transparency and accountability in governance. According to the Ministry of Urban Development, while only 12 states have enacted the CPL, just 19 states have enacted the PDL.[3] Hyderabad stands out as a lone champion of full citizen participation among Indian cities, having both pioneered the enactment of the CPL and introduced the PDL. Accountability is also secured through social audit reports, independently verified by third parties and published on a regular basis. Other proposals to promote accountability include the creation of a local ombudsman to address corruption among officers and members, as put forward by HPEC, while the Kasturirangan Committee recommended state governments to set up appellate tribunals to resolve municipal taxation and

184 *Urban leadership and civic engagement*

service disputes. The latter also recommended a municipal services commission to recruit employees for all ULBs. Citizen surveys, such as the World Bank's CRCs, have been adopted by Bangalore's Public Affairs Centre, and recommended for wider adoption by other cities. These measures not only ensure accountability, but are means by which ULBs may respond actively to citizen's concerns. The use of ICT and continuous monitoring based on mobile phones is also being encouraged, and is currently in use in GHMC, as noted in the previous chapters. Citizen forums are another popular means by which citizens can directly influence local affairs, as are town hall meetings in which local government officials meet with the public to review performance, monitor progress, and prioritise future developments for the city.

Integrating information and communication technologies

Many countries regard ICTs as promising tools for strengthening government–citizen connections. They offer powerful mechanisms for searching, selecting and integrating vast amounts of information held by public administration as well as presenting the results in a form that can be used by individual citizens. While the extent of their use varies, the potential of ICTs to provide better public services, enhance transparency and accountability and promote greater public engagement in democratic processes is in little dispute. Some cities place great emphasis on their use for online service delivery, while others focus on their potential application in strengthening public deliberation and participation in policy making.

The extent to which ICTs can strengthen government–citizen relationships depends to a considerable extent on the levels of access to these new technologies. Websites are commonly used, as are portals, which provide single entry points to help citizens gain access to information and services. Kiosks in public offices or other public places also enable consultation with residents and facilitate participation. ICTs also provide new opportunities for government to receive feedback from, and consult with, individual citizens directly during policy making. Yet, despite significant investments in technology and efforts in bringing governments and public online, practice varies considerably and few expect new ICTs to completely replace traditional methods for consultation, participation and the sharing of information.

Cities that have either implemented or are experimenting with smart technologies have done so mainly in the areas of intelligent transport management systems, energy efficiency in service delivery, public safety, online procurement, the monitoring of physical assets, and making information available in real time. The MoUD is taking the lead in promoting the use of smart technologies in Indian cities by bringing together the full range of stakeholders from within and outside government to share knowledge on city-specific technologies. It has initiated a nationwide e-District project under the national e-Governance Plan to scale up the best practices at national level. The project aims to enable the delivery of high-volume public services by creating a robust and scalable infrastructure so that ULBs can tap into this e-infrastructure, together with State Data Centres and State-wide Area Networks for service delivery.

By including e-governance as part of its agenda for mandatory reform, the JNNURM has contributed to the use of ICTs in some local bodies. However, an area that did not receive adequate attention under the JNNURM was the development of standardized e-tools that can be adopted by ULBs across the country, such as online birth and death registration systems, GIS-based property tax information systems, and municipal accrual-based accounting systems. Currently, no city in India has an open data policy or framework whereby all financial and operational records of the ULB are made easily accessible to the public through *suo motu* disclosures, including in electronic formats on their websites.

Accountability through financial reporting, disclosure and audits

Nationally, it is recommended that ULBs should consider adopting transparent budgeting practices based on double-entry bookkeeping, performance reporting, cost accounting, and auditing. This would make them more accountable to their citizens and attractive for potential investors of capital. The accrual-based accounting system is a mandatory reform for ULBs under the JNNURM, but only about 20 per cent are implementing it (NIUA, 2010). The HPEC recommends that state governments should make accrual-based double-entry accounting mandatory and also encourage urban bodies to draw upon the model accounting system prepared by the MoUD. Standardisation of financial statements and accounting practices would lower the costs of evaluating ULBs and facilitate comparison of city finances. Regular, timely and standardised financial disclosures would help create a city information ecosystem that could be independently reviewed and analysed by all stakeholders. This was demonstrated in the case of Bangalore, where a new method of fund-based accounting system was taken up by Bangalore Forward, a not-for-profit agency supported financially by private corporates, as an instrument for achieving reforms in municipal accounting. It replaced the cash-based single-entry accounting system, which had several limitations in financial planning and made it vulnerable to un-accounting or under-accounting of its assets. The new system uses double-entry methods of accounting and is coupled with appropriate IT and management systems that have led to better management of municipal finances together with enhanced transparency and accountability of its operations

To meet the requirements of accessing capital markets and achieve greater transparency and public participation in decision making, the HPEC proposed a Market Worthiness Disclosure Standard, which would require cities to report data in a regular and timely manner in a Market Worthiness Disclosure Statement. The statement would report on cash flow statements, key financial ratios and city management capacity, covering aspects such as staff, the institutional framework and information flow. It would be prepared by each ULB and made available on its website in a standardised format. All this would be in accordance with the provisions of the disclosure laws that either have been or will be enacted by states under the JNNURM. It is advocated that this should be initially enforced on all municipal corporations and extended over a period of time to the ULBs of bigger towns. The current status of ULB audits shows them to be in a chronic state of arrears. HPEC recommended that state governments should ensure that all ULBs conduct annual audits of their financial statements, and set up Local Fund Audit Commissions that can provide for the engagement of qualified chartered accountants. In addition to external audits, it recommended that systems of internal audit and performance audit must be put in place.

Inclusive urban management

The role of civic agencies, including non-governmental organisations, in enhancing public involvement has been gaining prominence, although public participation is highly context sensitive and varies from city to city based on political commitments, social networks, local capacity and the objectives of city governments themselves. Legislative frameworks in some countries have mandated inclusive practices requiring equal representation in urban development projects, such as the National Reconstruction Development Programmes in South Africa, or the City Statutes in Brazil that have shaped urban reforms in Brasilia and Sao Paulo. In Britain and Europe, the Local Agenda 21 Programmes of the 1990s, a United Nations non-binding agreement, gave a much-needed impetus to participatory initiatives. These called for each local authority to consult with its community and develop a vision and plan of action for the future of the locality. Public participation and consultation were central to Local Agenda 21, which offered an opportunity radically to re-appraise and redevise local authority participative structures, and to develop fresh and innovative methods of working with and for the community (Norma and Darlow, 1997).

Yet, most people find themselves in tokenistic relationships with decision makers; they feel that they are informed and consulted but not engaged. In large metropolitan areas, people are less likely to attend public meetings, be active in community organisations, sign petitions, volunteer or work on community projects. A recent study found that levels of trust and community participation – two dimensions of social capital – tend to be significantly higher in rural areas than in urban areas. Although the poor in some cities exhibit high levels of community participation, their levels of trust are generally low. In urban areas, high residential mobility makes it difficult to develop a sense of common identity, which, together with other factors such as apathy and distrust in the establishment, inhibits the development of effective participatory programmes. The views and actions of citizens are often simplistic and sometimes contradictory:

Urban leadership and civic engagement 187

Most are not interested in engaging and participating in the political process, locally or nationally, and when they are motivated to do so they prefer options which demand very little by way of sustained time and commitment. They want a voice in the process in order to exercise influence but do not necessarily expect or want a greater level of involvement. And yet, they feel they lack influence in decision making if politicians do not listen to what they say and they most value those methods of engagement and participation that deliver their preferred policy outcome. Altruistic views of politics and the policy process have a role but self-interest may be a more powerful motivating factor for many. They have a well developed sense of what it takes to be a good citizen.

(Fox, 2009: 683–684)

A variety of populist measures to enhance engagement through more direct and participatory decision making have been used in recent years to overcome barriers to participation and engagement. Citizens' juries, panels and forums, ballots, referenda initiatives, MP recall petitions and open primary contests to select parliamentary candidates are some of the measures used in the Western world, although the rationale for adopting them may vary:

Some value public participation in its own right as a form of enriched citizenship and accountability, others because of the legitimacy it confers on decision making, the improved representativeness of decisions it secures or the more efficacious policy outcomes that can result. But, whatever the rationale, it is now generally accepted in party political circles that it is necessary to provide a range of mechanisms to enable the public to have a greater voice in the political and policy making process outside the normal election cycle and that establishing new and more robust means for the public to hold politicians to account will be a vital tool in the battle to restore public trust and confidence.

(Fox, 2009: 674)

In recent years, several Indian cities have displayed an abundance of participatory programmes in which the public are involved alongside non-governmental agencies, community based organisations and municipalities to improve city infrastructure and promote economic growth. Kerala pioneered experiments in participatory budgeting involving slum representatives, middle-class volunteers, women's groups, elected representatives and government officials, and providing training to enhance their participation in public service planning and delivery. The People's Plan Campaign was designed to give a high degree of autonomy to the public in planning, budgeting and expenditure. Among other initiatives, CRCs actively seek residents' views about the state of public services and developmental programmes and can lead to the formulation of clear and actionable interventions for government, donors and civil society. This model is now increasingly being adopted across the country as a strategic tool both for enabling participation and building public awareness of civic issues and developmental matters.

Bangalore Forward has undertaken several initiatives to improve the city, including the introduction of a new fund-based accounting system to improve accountability and transparency in municipal finances. In collaboration with Bangalore Agenda Task Force (BATF), it provided strategic guidance for developments in the city and made a number of improvements to city governance in various areas, including traffic and road infrastructure, civic amenities, pedestrianisation and park renovations. The BATF consists of members of the public, CEOs and other representatives from the private sector, civic agencies including the city corporation, development authority and those involved in the provision of transport, sewerage, water supply, communication and police, and the back office staff in charge of implementing the BATF projects. The members of BATF are not elected, but bring together non-state agencies to overcome the 'stigma of corruption and ineptitude associated with government bodies and, in turn, improve their management' (Kamath, 2006). Citizen input, via opinion polls, is used to prioritise and set targets on a range of issues such as those relating to roads, waste disposal, traffic and safety issues.

Another initiative, the Bhagidari Programme, a platform for citizen–government partnerships, initiated by the Government of Delhi, aims to make governance responsive and participatory through joint ownership of multi-stakeholders. Citizen groups, non-governmental organisations, residents' welfare associations and market trade associations and the public engage with various departments of the government such as the Municipal Corporation of Delhi, Delhi Development Authority, New Delhi Municipal Council, Delhi Police and the Department of Environment and Forest. There are estimated to be more than 2,000 citizen groups engaged in such tasks such as water saving/harvesting, the payment and collection of water bills and taxes, maintenance of community parks, roads and other common areas, supervision of sanitation services, waste collection, crime prevention through neighbourhood watch schemes, traffic regulation and the prevention of encroachments (Koreth and Wadhera, 2013). In common with BATF, and marked contrast with area sabhas, the Bhagidari Programme does not involve elected representatives. Added to this restriction, it is limited to registered associations which consequently excludes a significant number of people such as those living in slums, resettlement colonies and other unauthorised areas where such associations do not exist (Saha, 2011: 12).

In recent years, social networking sites have emerged as an alternative means by which citizens can air grievances and share ideas. At least five state government agencies have opened Facebook pages in order to interact with citizens. Kolkata Traffic Police, one of the first government agencies to set up a Facebook page in 2010, receives around 60 complaints weekly through this medium. The success of the traffic police page has prompted other government agencies to adopt similar schemes using a variety of social media. It is estimated that India will be second only to China in terms of Internet users by 2015, with 330 million Indians online. Given its growing importance, a recent study by McKinsey suggests state governments, with the help of civil society organisations, should use this opportunity to work towards deepening the connection with the public, instilling a greater sense of trust and driving increased citizen participation (McKinsey, 2012).

Localism in Mumbai

Partnership institutions in Mumbai are wide-ranging, including Bombay First (BF), a non-profit initiative of private corporates, and Citizens' Action Group (CAG), an institution appointed by the state to strategise and monitor the various initiatives for Mumbai city development. More recently, other initiatives such as Action for Good Governance Network of India (AGNI) and the PRAJA Foundation have also emerged as civil society groups that partner with local and state governments. Bombay First is a private non-profit initiative that was formed by private corporates under the umbrella of the Bombay Chamber of Commerce and Industry with a view to transforming Mumbai into a globally competitive city through improvements in economic growth, infrastructure and the quality of life. It drew inspiration from London First, but with a larger mission to address the issues and problems confronting the city through partnerships with government, business and civil society. Under the guidance of Bombay City Policy Research Foundation, Bombay First undertook a comprehensive diagnosis of the city's development, its economic and social structure, the causes of decline in certain activities and infrastructure, possible solutions and pilot scale projects. It commissioned relevant studies and carried out surveys, which led to a renewed understanding of the structure and nature of employment, sectoral growth patterns and infrastructural issues. Bombay First was instrumental in providing development perspective in the form of a vision plan.

The Advanced Locality Management (ALM), initiated by the MCGM, is illustrative of a successful scheme that mobilises citizens' participation in sustainable, environment friendly waste management through the principles of reducing, recycling and segregating at source biodegradable waste from recyclable waste. Rag-pickers are engaged for door-to-door waste collection and speedy removal of the segregated dry waste. The adoption of the scheme, however, is unevenly spread across the city of Mumbai and concentrated mostly in wards with higher income levels (Baud and Nainan, 2008). The key participants in the scheme include the residents and the executive wing of the municipal corporation. ALMs vary in membership, size and composition and are registered with the local municipal ward office, which conducts monthly meetings with the residents to identify and address the problems. The corporation appoints a nodal officer to assist ALMs in presenting their problems to the various departments of the corporation. The residents, on the other hand, organise meetings to spread awareness and contribute towards a maintenance fund that is used to finance all expenditures. In addition to the residents and the administrators of the municipal corporation, civil society organisations and the corporate sector are also involved in the scheme. NGOs assist with organising and mobilising local communities and lend expertise. AGNI, an advocacy group on local governance issues, is one such agency which plays a key role in facilitating the formation, networking and capacity building of ALMs, as do others such as Street Mukti Sangathana (SMS) and Force and Akkar Mumbai. The corporate sector also supports ALMs by taking responsibility for managing roads, sanitation and solid waste (Shivdasani, 2005). More recently, success with solid waste management initiatives has led to other activities by the ALMs such as beautification of the localities, maintenance of gardens, parks and roads, tree plantation, prevention of encroachment on pavements, maintenance of open spaces and improvements in water supply.

Another initiative taken by the Municipal Corporation of Greater Mumbai is the Slum Adoption Programme (Dattak Vasti Yojna). Unlike the ALM programme, this scheme focuses specifically on slums and works through community based organisations (CBOs). These CBOs comprise members of the community who undertake activities such as door-to-door garbage collection, and the cleaning of drains, internal roads, public places and public toilets, and also create awareness among slum dwellers and encourage them to help keep their areas clean. Appointed on behalf of the municipal corporation, the CBOs are registered with the charity commissioner's office and provided with training, equipment and financial assistance. Currently, 419 CBOs are involved in providing services to a slum population of around 700,000.

In slums, the process is institutionalised and for the most part concerns solid-waste management and sanitation. The World Bank's role in slums and sanitation programme was instrumental in the delegation of responsibilities to the slum communities, generating an unparalleled 'capacity to aspire'. As Appadurai observed:

> important segments of Mumbai's slum dwellers are exercising collectively the sinews of the capacity to aspire, while testing their capacities to convince skeptics from the funding world, the banking world, the construction industry and the municipality of Mumbai that they can deliver what they promise, while building their capacities to plan, coordinate, manage and mobilise their energies in a difficult and large-scale technical endeavor.
>
> (Appadurai, 2004: 73)

Engaging communities in Kolkata and Hyderabad

Unlike in Mumbai, where civil society is represented by active groups of non-governmental and other voluntary organisations functioning without political links, such activism has been historically limited in Kolkata. The unchallenged dominance of partisan political actors in public decision making and the hierarchical structure of the state government was partly responsible for obstructing bottom-up pressures in metropolitan decision making (Pal, 2006). This is despite the fact that Kolkata has had a longer, richer tradition of civic participation and activism than either Mumbai or Hyderabad. In his study, exploring the scope for bottom-up planning, Pal concluded that non-partisan civic activism was possible in Kolkata only when power structures permitted and initiatives from the bottom were given the required political space. Therefore:

> even though one political party dominated Kolkata's decision making in high investment planning for economic growth, infrastructure, education etc., there are other areas of urban health – such as HIV/AIDS prevention among the prostitutes of Kolkata's red light district of Sonagachhi – which no political parties saw as having the potential to mobilise popular support. The social stigma attached to prostitution in Kolkata's conservative society allowed NGOs and civic activists the space to work with the sex workers in a way that was hugely successful, not just nationally but internationally.
>
> (Pal, 2006: 519–520)

The economic and political crisis of the 1970s gave rise to a new politics of assertiveness, in which civil right groups and voluntary organisations challenged national and state impositions and focused on empowering the poor and under-privileged. The role of NGOs in education, health and slum rehabilitation took on a different character:

> challenging the state's or city government's decisions in courts of law through public interest litigations, for instance, against the violation of environmental norms and regulations, or to represent the poor and slum dwellers displaced in the name of development projects.
>
> (Ghosh *et al.*, 2009: 37)

One such non-governmental organisation was Unnayan ('development'), consisting of a community-based organisation, Chhinnamul Sramajibi Adhikari Samity, and the National Campaign for Housing Rights, which for several years engaged in advocacy and lobbying within the government's policy-making process.

On the other hand, Hyderabad benefited from targeted urban development programmes initiated by the state government. The Andhra Pradesh Urban Services for the Poor project, funded by DfID and implemented by the Andhra Pradesh Department of Municipal Administration and Urban Development (DMAUD) through 32 municipal authorities and corporations, aims to improve municipal performance, fund environmental infrastructure and services for the poor and strengthen civil society organisations. Public participation in the project has been through the development of the basic Municipal Action Plan for the Poor (MAPP). The MAPP was a transparent, participatory planning tool developed in the early stages of the project to identify and prioritise municipal reforms and urban services for the poor. The stakeholders involved in the development of the MAPP include representatives from political parties, municipal administration, local civil society organisations, the private sector, slum residents and neighbourhood group committees of the poor. A recent assessment of the project revealed the extent to which consultation with local communities has resulted in improved relationships between politicians and the public, increased transparency and raised awareness about the roles and accountabilities of ULBs. Interestingly, only women were chosen as representatives of slums and neighbourhood committees, as the project acknowledged them to be:

> economically responsible and efficient while men are incapable and irresponsible, characterised *inter alia* by the irresponsible use of alcohol and the avoidance of work ... Such democratisation of decision making helped in identification and prioritization of problems and solutions and empowered the non-traditional decision makers to communicate their concerns.
> (Dove, 2004)

There are several non-governmental organisations in Hyderabad involved in development-related activities such as Lok Satta (People's Power) and People's Union for Civic Action and Rights (PUCAAR) that focus specifically on political reforms and governance. Lok Satta's main objective is to address corruption and promote good governance. It enjoys an extensive grassroots network and has recently established its presence in other cities of Mumbai and Bangalore. The empowerment of local governments is a major theme for Lok Satta. PUCAAR – meaning 'a call' or 'a cry' – is closely linked with the Confederation of Voluntary Associations (COVA), an important and well-known confederation of NGOs, whose emphasis is on communal harmony and the empowerment of the marginalised and poor. Identifying themselves as 'the residents of the old city of Hyderabad', they hold the ruling parties accountable on all matters relating to the development and governance of their city (Kennedy, 2006: 16).

An interesting study that analysed ways in which different users improve access to services – water supply and sanitation – in Hyderabad revealed how user expectations, and the means deployed to channel their expectations and grievances, shape the pattern of democratic interaction between the public and the authorities. These have led to the opening up of new avenues to facilitate speedier, more efficient, direct public contact via computerised complaints centres, single window cells for simplifying licensing and applications, metro water board citizens' charters, and developing socially relevant policies (Huchon and Tricot, 2008). The city of Hyderabad in recent years has shown encouraging signs of increasing community participation, with active women's groups, resident associations and non-governmental organisations working together with corporate actors taking an interest in governance and developmental issues.

*****

If municipal democracy is to be taken seriously in India it must be redesigned, not in terms of executive deliberative separation, but in terms of a suitable political executive. Whereas mayoral systems abroad are both long-standing and widespread, the Indian system of metropolitan governance has been a commissioner-driven model in which elected mayors, where they exist, are generally little more than figureheads. The significant limitations in the mayor's actual power are defined by statute and this, in conjunction with the mayor's *de facto* subservience to the corporation and the commissioner, produces a relationship between the mayor and council that is quite different from that which exists in the stronger mayoral models of the United States, Europe and elsewhere. A cabinet system should be explored, as is employed at the higher levels of government, or perhaps a presidential system under which the mayor can be the real executive. Whichever model is found suitable, the use of an appointed chief officer, like the present-day commissioner, will still be necessary, but in a position that is subordinate to the political executive.

Alongside strong political leadership it is important to have a people-centred governance process that enhances participation and the legitimacy of any political system. Although decentralisation initiatives in India have greatly increased the scope of local engagement, participation in formal structures of decision making is still quite limited. The changing urban politics in recent years, however, has given rise to new social groups that are organising themselves to achieve greater local autonomy and ensure effectiveness and accountability in service delivery. An important consequence of the rise of this civil society has been a proliferation of voluntary or non-governmental organisations, some that endeavour to raise the political consciousness of other social groups, encouraging them to demand their rights and challenge social inequities, while others serve as watchdogs to uphold the spirit of the laws and implement policies in accordance with the stated objectives. Yet others serve as innovators, experimenting with new approaches to solving social problems, and working with their state governments in a manner that augments their capacity to implement public policy – such as slum development and poverty alleviation programmes – in a decentralised manner.

Notes

1 Pherozeshah Mehta drafted the Bombay Municipal Act of 1872 and is considered the father of Bombay Municipality. He became the municipal commissioner of Bombay Municipality in 1873 and served as its president four times, in 1884, 1885, 1905 and 1911.

2 This was the case in Jaipur elections held in November 2009. It took six months before the standing committee (a committee of councillors which acts as a cabinet) could be formed and for the administration to function.
3 In both cases, these include Andhra Pradesh, Maharashtra and West Bengal.

8 The future of India's urban governance

Urban growth poses the most profound challenge to India's large and complex cities. The nature of urbanisation, the challenges it entails and the policy responses it triggers are highly varied. While giving due consideration to the specific structures through which cities are governed and managed, the preceding chapters have highlighted some common themes of urban change and governability that all cities, in their different ways, must confront. The cities of Mumbai, Hyderabad and Kolkata, examined in this book, are at the forefront of change and innovation. Their emerging 'new' condition has been extensively examined, described and analysed by scholars, policy makers and independent commentators. While drawing on the work of these experts and the experiences of those directly involved in managing and governing these cities, this book has opted to deal with the key topics of devolution, metropolitan consolidation, structures and processes for service delivery, leadership and community participation.

There have been many concrete proposals for the reform of India's urban governance. Some find easy acceptance as they build on the experience of particular cities, which serve to establish good precedence and require little more than a transfer of experience between cities. A second order of change involves transposing the experience of cities in countries other than India, introducing some organisational novelty that can reasonably be expected to take root. Beyond these are proposals that could be expected to encounter difficulties in their implementation and require legislation and strong commitment at the state level. Finally, some proposed changes are so radical they can be expected to encounter formidable roadblocks and incite political conflicts. Such changes are further reaching, may require a longer time span for their realisation and are predicated on political alignments that have yet to come into being. Debates on these issues are yet to mature and the analysis presented in this book takes, as its starting point, the experience of London in thinking about the future of city government in India.

London has much to tell us by the way it has approached the seemingly intractable problems of urban government. The creation of the mayor and assembly for the capital city was based on the assumption that London can 'learn' from other cities and, indeed, the current form of urban government is recognisably derived from the experience of several other countries and from the United States in particular. The validity of the assumption was subject to extensive discussion as the differences between patterns of urban leadership in the United States, France and Germany on the one hand, and Britain, with its council based structure, on the other, was thought to vitiate any comparison. It was soon acknowledged that cities, wherever they are in the world, face analogous problems, suggesting that some solutions, be they specific policies or governmental arrangements, might indeed be transferable.

Even if the organisational outcomes of the new London government are not fully successful, nor wholly satisfactory, its experience can help illuminate some difficult problems of metropolitan governance. The theoretical and pragmatic contributions of the capital's development can help guide India's cities through their progressive transformations. It therefore seems appropriate that such an analysis of metropolitan governance presented in this book should begin by exploring how London, a great world city, reorganised itself through the struggles of post-war urbanisation and the subsequent challenges of establishing a democratically elected city government.

Chapter 2 explored the nature of governance and five particular conditions for effectiveness, and concluded that any solutions taken from elsewhere must be introduced with sufficient regard to local circumstances and with intrinsic flexibility. Local history, culture and ecology are among the most important considerations shaping governance and these specificities are forceful reminders that the replication of formulas may not be a sustainable solution. Therefore, while it is tempting to look directly for lessons to be learned, it is important to bear in mind that models are usually never directly transferable, and that the peculiarities of each case must be attended to and their limits recognised.

How distinctive is London?

London has a long and complex history. Its dominant influence within the UK and its functional roles makes it a unique metropolis. What happens in London, how it deploys its resources and ways in which it interacts with local, national and international players are of key importance, not just to Londoners, but to the rest of Britain and beyond. Its particular distinctiveness lies in, amongst other things, its role as a strategic authority, the strong leadership it displays in the form of a directly elected mayor, and in its ability to manage a complex network of relationships – local, regional and national.

The dominant role of central government in Britain is critical and any reforms to local governments take place only through parliamentary action and upon the initiative of central government. Local authorities in Britain have only those powers as are accorded to them by the central government; they are decentralised administrative units that carry out the mandate of parliament and follow the regulations of central government departments. In some respects this makes the acceptance of hierarchy in Britain more acceptable and, in turn, makes for easier implementation of policies at the lower levels. It is virtually impossible to stress enough this feature of British system: central government can and does act on major reforms and, once legislated, they are generally accepted and implemented.

London, in particular, is too important for Whitehall to give it complete autonomy. The GLA's ability to act is heavily qualified by the balancing power of the Secretary of State for Communities and Local Government, who can issue guidance and can impose limits on the expenditure incurred by the authority in pursuit of its general powers. More specifically, with regard to the spatial development strategy for London, the reserve powers of the secretary of state are extensive. Government ministers have powers of discretion with regard to achieving consistency and the secretary of state is empowered to intervene if the mayor is in default. Yet, in absolute terms, the powers of the mayor are wide ranging in the areas of transport, policing and economic development. The mayor is responsible for developing safe and efficient transport facilities within Greater London, for developing a coherent strategy for the prevention of crime in the capital city, and facilitating economic growth. The mayor and assembly enjoy the level of autonomy identified by Greasley and Stoker (see Chapter 2) as being so important for metropolitan governance.

While it is difficult to give a definitive verdict on the success of London's relatively new metropolitan government, a number of aspects of its functioning make it distinctive. The extent to which the new authority has helped sustain the prosperity of the capital in the face of growing international competition, while at the same time meeting the needs and aspirations of Londoners, is widely acknowledged. Mayors Ken Livingstone and Boris Johnson made London's status as a world city the central plank of their policies, supporting the notion of the capital as a command post of the global economy, and infusing it with a distinctive vision – each in his own way – to make it a global magnet for business and talent. Despite the impact of the global financial crisis, London's status as a dynamic world city and as the country's leading centre of high value, export-oriented employment showed no signs of decline. The city's financial and business services sector, at the heart of a globally connected economic world, grew by nearly 6 per cent a year during the decade before the global financial crisis, noticeably faster than growth in the same sector in other mature economies. At the same time, its share of the market for financial services across Europe, the United States and Japan grew from 2 per cent in the late 1990s to 3.7 per cent by 2008 (City of London, 2011: 3).

A significant feature of the new London government is the quality of partnerships and the relationships that it has established with local, regional and national bodies. Policing, transport and the regeneration of the London economy highlight the ways in which these relations have worked out so far. Although early debates over each of these issues were marred with frictions and tensions, significant strides have been made in all three areas. Increases in rail and underground capacities, investments in infrastructure developments and long-term funding streams, and the provision of an integrated transport network for the capital have been among the major achievements of Transport for London, while the capital's Metropolitan Police Service has demonstrated its ability to deliver strategically on public priorities. Crime in the capital has been at its lowest level for ten years, and public safety and confidence among Londoners has shown improvements (MPA, 2010). Likewise, the LDA played a vital role in shaping London's economic achievements for over a decade until its abolition in 2012, facilitating planning, managing London's economic and physical growth, and supporting Londoners and businesses through the recession. It was instrumental in implementing the mayors' economic development strategy, while the London Plan, which presents an original approach to spatial development for Greater London, provides for an integrated economic, environmental, transport and social framework for the development of the capital city.

London's plan is novel and unique, and provides a framework with distinct clarity. London boroughs' local plans need to be in general conformity with the plan, and its policies guide decisions on planning applications by councils and the mayor. While acknowledging the complexities of delivering new developments in London, it expresses a commitment to working with a range of bodies including the government, other public bodies and agencies, private businesses and voluntary groups. The monitoring regime, based on key performance indicators, enables a periodic assessment of the effectiveness of the plan.

Planning in India, on the other hand, due to its un-coordinated nature, poses considerable challenges for India's cities. As McKinsey's study observed:

> On paper, India does have urban plans – but they are esoteric rather than practical, rarely followed, and riddled with exemptions ... India needs to make urban planning a core ... plans need to be detailed, comprehensive, and enforceable and exemptions should be rare rather than the norm.
> (McKinsey, 2010: 26)

Although DPCs and MPCs were set up to have an oversight of planning, they are not fully operational in most states. The evidence from the three cities examined confirms that even though DPCs have been constituted they are generally not empowered to function. As was discussed in Chapter 5, although all three cities initially set up MPCs they have not been stable and rarely effective; MPCs have yet to take root.

> Confusion about the purpose and role of the MPC, lack of political interest and most importantly, the fear of the development authorities losing power once MPCs are set up appear to be the main reasons for the failure to set them up ... The failure to recognise the MPC as a high level, democratically set up body, which will provide the constitutional mandate to

the whole exercise of metropolitan development planning, has resulted in an impoverished statutory frame work for this body.
(Cited in Kasturirangan Committee, 2008: 34)

The lack of functioning metropolitan planning committees is to a large extent responsible for the growth of slums, unauthorised and haphazard development and, above all, environmental and transportation problems within and around urban areas. The absence of an effective area-wide agency to ensure integrated land-use planning with key services such as transport, health, water and energy has resulted in uncoordinated urban growth, while the limited forecasting capabilities of the plans themselves has hindered planning from keeping pace with policy changes. While identifying the need for a more energetic and democratic administration, which would envisage the problems of the whole region rather than its particular parts, HPEC called for greater integration of regional plans with state governments' spatial plans. In the context of metropolitan governance for Bangalore, the Kasturirangan Committee concluded that:

To enable the MPC to carry out a coordinating and integrating role, we need to put in place a clear hierarchy of planning institutions and plans where the Metropolitan Development Plan (MDP) under the MPC should override all other plans developed by other state functionaries and local bodies in the metropolitan region. This institutional hierarchy whereby the MPC is conferred with the overall decision making power must be established in the statutes to be drafted for creation of the MPC in Karnataka.
(Kasturirangan Committee, 2008: 4)

The committee called for an amendment of the related statutes including the Karnataka Town and Country Planning Act, 1961 and the Bangalore Metropolitan Regional Development Authority Act, 1985 (BMRDA Act) so as to give primacy to the MPC.

The patterns of growth and development had posed similar problems for London during the mid-twentieth century when its reach had extended beyond its boundaries, raising concerns about the relationship between London's core and its metropolitan hinterland. Questions were raised about how London and its surrounding regions should work together, and the need was felt for an overall metropolitan authority to address the problems of growth, fragmentation and complexity. The South East Regional Planning Conference (SERPLAN), which brought together county councils, representatives of district councils and London boroughs, undertook this task and did a creditable job for over 20 years in planning for London and the south-east, and in later years, between 1986 and 2000, the London Planning Advisory Committee (LPAC), an ad hoc London wide joint committee, provided strategic planning for the metropolis. LPAC's principal task, as was seen in Chapter 3, and statutory *raison d'être* was to make representations to the secretary of state on behalf of the London boroughs over the periodic strategic guidance, which provided a framework of general policy within which boroughs prepared their own unitary development plans.

In place of the essential directness and relative straightforwardness of the central–local government system that exists in Britain, India has a vastly more complex system involving partnerships between federal government and the various states. There are also highly varied relationships between state governments and their local governments, as well as emerging relationships between federal government and local units. Although the role of the state government is paramount in India's federal system, preceding discussions have revealed the non-prescriptive nature of central government reforms, which leaves considerable discretion to state governments to decide on the functions that may be devolved to the Urban Local Bodies. The limited degree to which many of the reforms enshrined in CAA and further federal initiatives have been implemented is testimony to the fact that states governments, largely for reasons of power, often impede reform.

Strategic authorities for India's cities

As was seen in Chapter 2, the intellectual case for a city-wide authority for London was ardently made by William Robson, whose impatience with fragmentation and chaotic governance arrangements – reflected in his writings – led to proposals for a single local authority for the metropolis. His seminal work *The Government and Misgovernment of London* (1939) called for an energetic pan-London authority, combining efficiency with accountability. A tenacious proponent of metropolitan government, Robson's vision for the capital city was for an overall strategic authority, one that people from all over the world recognised as London, a vision that was to be espoused half a century later by the capital's directly elected mayors. Robson's view was that such a machinery would involve:

> the administrative integration of the whole metropolitan area for the large-scale services which require unified planning, coordination or administration. It also involves smaller, more compact units of local government to perform the functions which can best be administered by smaller municipal organs. The reform of metropolitan government demands both more centralisation and more decentralisation; in other words, both larger and smaller areas and authorities.
>
> (Robson, 1954: 99)

Robson's proposals did not command universal support at the time. In line with other debates that did not emphasise the need for an area-wide government there were some who held the view that London did not require a metropolitan authority. Opponents of consolidation such as Tiebout, whose views were referred to in Chapter 2, saw fragmentation as an asset. Others argued that the outer boundaries of the city were indeterminate and that physical built-upness was an inappropriate basis for metropolitan definition. For them, the management of this wider metropolitan region could best be provided through a special agency of central government. In subsequent years, however, the wider benefits that consolidation would bring in terms of promoting regionalism and providing an avenue for the emergence of political leadership were strongly emphasised. After 14 years of London's new system of governance, the case for strong political leadership across a consolidated metropolitan region is almost unassailable. Region-wide development of policies for such services as mass transportation, airports, housing, parks and open spaces are shown to have generated significant benefits, together with facilitating inter-governmental dialogue on a wide range of issues. More importantly, such wider governance has been credited with limiting urban sprawl as it enables the establishment of a metropolitan growth boundary that encourages intense use of land (Harrigan and Johnson, 1978).

India's urban areas are beset with serious problems of poor delivery of services, a weak policy environment and limited institutional and financial capacities. There is an acknowledged need for the widespread reform of service delivery to achieve better service outcomes, and for governance to assume a role commensurate with emerging metropolitan needs. As the committee charged with examining metropolitan governance in Bangalore observed, 'a paradigm policy shift from the previous focus on city level urban local government to a metropolitan level institution is a necessary first step for enabling better strategic planning and coordination' (Kasturirangan Committee, 2008: 20). In considering the appropriateness of metropolitan governance, the committee warned of the diversity of factors that need consideration, including the need for governance structures to stay ahead of the expansion of built up areas and an effective decentralisation of governance functions. While acknowledging that 'metropolitan systems are much more networked with the outside world than smaller cities', the committee concluded that there was no single model of government that would be appropriate for all urban settings: 'even within the same country or the same State, metropolitan cities may require a distinct institutional mechanism and governance processes which may be at great variance with other existing models' (Kasturirangan Committee, 2008: 33).

McKinsey's study on *India's urban awakening* recommended the need for a fully formed metropolitan authority with clearly defined roles for the 'successful management of large cities in India' (McKinsey, 2010: 25). While many urban functions are more suited for delivery at the local level, such as parks, schools or local shopping areas, there are a number of functions that are better undertaken at the metropolitan level; individual municipalities are not adequately placed to raise the resources required for such developments nor have the capacity to manage delivery. The case is often made for services such as waste management and pollution control, water resources, economic development and large-scale transit and transport systems to be undertaken at the metropolitan level, with strategic level coordination.

The analyses of traffic and transport issues examined in this book highlight many opportunities for developing a strategic transport infrastructure for India's cities as well as the need to improve planning, financing of infrastructure projects, and the development of national policy frameworks that are better adapted to the needs of transport infrastructure. Crucially, there is a need for strategic, multimodal core networks capable of handling the rapidly growing transport needs of India's metropolises. Strategic metropolitan authorities can provide access to such a network of area-wide affordable transportation services. Traffic and roads in all the three cities examined are currently distributed uneasily between state government, parastatal agencies and municipalities, and there is no single point of responsibility within the complex array of agencies. As a senior planning official remarked, 'the absence of a single agency responsible for developing transport and highway network makes it difficult and cumbersome to transcend municipality boundaries when responsibility resides with municipalities'. The HPEC acknowledged the importance of rationalising the reality of multi-level government in large metropolitan regions such as Mumbai, Hyderabad and Kolkata, arguing 'that central, state and local governments carry out activity in the same sector – such as building roads and public transport systems ... and it is critical to delineate the nature and structure of inter-governmental relations in these sectors' (HPEC, 2011: 96).

Indeed, transit and metropolitan highway development, planning of greenfield areas and transit expansion are some of the functions identified by the Mumbai metropolitan region business plan as requiring consideration at the strategic level. The provision of electricity and transport services by BEST, which operates as an autonomous agency under the MCGM, serves as an example of a well coordinated and strategic approach to service delivery. Working in partnership with the Bus Rapid Transit system, the municipal corporation and the state government, BEST is managed by a 17-member committee comprising the chairman of the standing committee and other members appointed by the corporation. A general manager, appointed by the state government as CEO, heads the agency and has autonomous powers over day-to-day decisions. The agency operates a clear accounting system of revenue and expenses, and the 17-member committee presents the budget to the corporation, takes decisions on salary revisions and fare changes within limits prescribed by state government notification. BEST manages the red double-decker buses – one of the defining characteristics of the city – modelled on the Routemaster buses of London. This strategic approach to traffic management has addressed many of the problems facing the city, while making the transport network a more attractive prospect for private investment.

The example of Mumbai's integrated approach supports those who argue that a single governance entity is both more effective in terms of the power to raise resources and enhances the administrative capacity that such an authority brings. However, expansions of municipal boundaries and the amalgamation of surrounding areas into larger consolidated entities in cities such as Hyderabad and Mumbai have not always been accompanied by improvements in the resource-raising powers of local bodies. As a result, smaller municipalities on the fringes compete for those developments that are perceived to provide tax revenues and other financial benefits, circumstances that exacerbate the problems of metropolitan fragmentation and contribute to chaotic and unsystematic developments.

The multiplicity of agencies involved in urban development across all the three study cities was highlighted in Chapter 6. The different agencies work independently, without any practical coordination and sometimes in open conflict with each other. As HPEC noted, 'the need for convergence at the level of the city government must be recognised in order to provide a single platform for coordinating the activities of local planning, building urban infrastructure, and delivering urban services' (HPEC, 2011: 95). Coordination is fundamental not just for administering basic urban services, but also for addressing issues of poverty and social exclusion. This is particularly true of cities such as Kolkata and Mumbai, which manifest striking social and economic imbalances. Indeed, the high incidence of poverty and inherent spatial inequality poses considerable challenges to overcoming the lack of coordination across the various agencies concerned with the provision of housing and services in the metropolitan areas of these metropolises.

It would be a mistake to underestimate the difficulty of securing area-wide action, which is subject to the vagaries and whims of each governmental unit, and although sometimes advocated in the Indian context, has seldom been debated thoroughly. Several reasons have been cited, including the unwillingness among higher-level governments to cede significant powers to lower levels of government, even to the point of what Pethe and Gandhi clearly saw as a damaging level of state control in metropolitan governance, or perceiving them as politically unpopular. Opponents have argued that metropolitan governments often lack legitimacy, tend to be top-down impositions and undemocratic and, more importantly, considered too weak fiscally or jurisdictionally to carry out their assigned functions effectively. These perceptions are not confined to the Indian context. Experiments in metropolitan governments elsewhere attracted similar concerns, as was the case with the GLC before its abolition; the authority was considered too weak to be effective and too strong to be politically acceptable.

Significantly, it is only from the standpoint of federalism that metropolitan and regional solutions are seen to have advantages. On this perspective, the larger governmental units have the virtues of rationalising fragmented and overlapping governmental jurisdictions, creating more equitable spending mechanisms and reaping economies of scale. While it would be premature to suggest what particular form of consolidation should be best pursued for India's large metropolises, any new governmental structure, if adopted, should be given the necessary powers to solve the problems it is designed to address.

Greater devolution: lessons from London

When the new GLA was originally established, it was prohibited from spending on education, health, social services or housing, though it had some influence over the way national programmes directed spending in London. Its powers changed when the subsequent GLA Act of 2007 increased the number of statutory strategies in new policy areas and introduced further supervisory roles for the mayor. The Localism Act 2011 further conferred additional expenditure powers on the GLA in relation to housing and regeneration, although spending restrictions remained on education (with the exception of academies), health and social services. Against the backdrop of an ongoing debate about greater financial autonomy, the London Finance Commission was established in 2012 to examine the potential for greater devolution of both taxation and the control of resources for the capital city. Its report, published in 2013, called for greater financial freedoms to enable local authorities to direct growth more effectively. The report, *Raising the Capital*, recommended a comprehensive package of measures to give Londoners a direct say over a greater proportion of the taxes raised in their city, outlining the benefits for London of a more devolved financial and fiscal system. The report argued that, in terms of fiscal autonomy, London is an outlier compared with other cities, with a heavy reliance on transfers from central government: 73.9 per cent of its income is received through grant, compared with 37 per cent in Madrid, 30.9 per cent in New York, 25.5 per cent in Berlin, 17.5 per cent in Paris and only 7.7 per cent in Tokyo. London also lacks comparable access to the diverse tax bases enjoyed in other cities:

> The council tax in London does not meet all of the criteria for local fiscal autonomy because the GLA and boroughs do not determine the base of the tax and tax rate setting is restricted by national government. Non-domestic rates are not included as a local tax because these rates are a national tax in which the central government determines the tax base, sets the tax rate, collects the revenues, and distributes the funds to local government.
> (London Finance Commission, 2013: 35)

Following the recommendations of the report, the mayor and London councils (representing the boroughs and the City of London), are jointly working with the core cities group to develop proposals for fiscal reforms. The aim is for greater devolution of property tax revenues streams, which would enable a move away from ad hoc financing for specific projects and allow cities to raise sustained investment for vital infrastructure such as transport, schools, housing and technology. Property taxes are suitable for local control by virtue of their immobile bases, the ease with which they can be collected and enforced, and are economically efficient. While observing that property taxes are largely devolved to sub-national government in other international cities, the commission proposed that:

> The full suite of property taxes (council tax, business rates, stamp duty, annual tax on enveloped dwellings and capital gains property development tax) should be devolved to London government which should have devolved responsibility for setting the tax rates and authority over all matters including revaluation, banding and discounts. The yields of these newly devolved taxes should be offset through corresponding reductions in grant to ensure a fiscally neutral position for the Exchequer, at the outset. If all property taxes were transferred to London government in this way, their yield would represent at least 50 per cent of the income required to fund all existing GLA and borough services apart from schools, which are now almost entirely financed by central grants.
> (London Finance Commission, 2013: 62)

The underlying assumption of the 'city centred' campaign is that empowered and incentivised cities can grow faster and be more competitive. Further:

> There is also a powerful democratic argument for allowing sub-national governments a reasonable degree of autonomy. Unless sub-national governments have both an electoral mandate and the power to raise resources, there is a risk that over-centralised national government will operate in a way that precludes pluralism and innovation. London and other cities in England fall well short of respectable international standards in terms of their freedom to direct their own finances. We therefore believe there is an unanswerable case for additional fiscal autonomy in London.
> (London Finance Commission, 2013: 57)

There is a similar case to be made for India's cities if the goal is to achieve effective governance. The lack of adequate financing at the local level has hampered city governance, and the redistribution of responsibilities among different levels of government has not been sustained by a corresponding allocation of resources, empowerment or financing tools that would make it possible to raise the necessary funds. As the previous chapters have demonstrated, in almost all states, with the exception of West Bengal and Kerala, political decentralisation has not been matched by adequate financial and technical devolution, leaving urban bodies dependent on their state governments to access funds and expertise. The HPEC called for greater sharing of resources between central government, state governments and ULBs and recommended that the former should finance 'agency' functions that are executed by Urban Local Bodies, on grounds of efficiency and proximity to clients (HPEC, 2011: 88–89).

206 *The future of India's urban governance*

Similarly the study by McKinsey concluded that 'India should allow its cities a stake in their own growth by sharing a portion of the taxes that they generate', arguing that:

> such a share would allow local governments to take advantage of their own growth, become financially stronger, and create a virtuous cycle of internal revenue generation, public investment in infrastructure, and economic growth.
>
> (McKinsey, 2010: 78)

At its root, the study observed, the country lacks the right enabling infrastructure to facilitate revenue sources; municipalities do not have the right to raise debts and they lack basic accounting infrastructure, which makes it difficult to forecast revenue and expenditure. Most spending programmes, therefore, remain focused on addressing short-term problems rather than taking a long-term strategic view.

The argument that cities are engines of economic growth, and that city leaders are the best custodians of their future, applies to India's major cities just as well as to London. The previous chapters have identified the infrastructure needs and the scale of investment required for sustaining India's capital cities. Mumbai, Hyderabad and Kolkata are becoming some of the world's pre-eminent city economies, and the strong demographic and economic growth they are experiencing is forecast to continue. It is estimated that, over the next 20 years, India needs to invest almost eight times the current level of spending in per capita terms, representing an increase in urban infrastructure spending from an average of 0.5 per cent of GDP today to 2 per cent annually. It is further estimated that more than half of the capital investment is necessary to erase the country's infrastructure backlog and the rest to fund cities' future needs. The McKinsey report estimated the increase in spending over the next decades:

> The challenge for India will be to ramp up investment in line with economic growth. One trajectory would involve annual spending of around $30 billion through 2015, ratcheting up to $60 billion a year by 2020, and $90 billion annually by 2030.
>
> (McKinsey, 2010: 20)

The large metropolises of Mumbai, Kolkata and Hyderabad will require capital spending of more than $200 per capita per annum.

Financial devolution apart, the devolution of key functions from state government to Urban Local Bodies has been equally weak. Although the intention clearly was for a devolved model of governance, there remains a gap between intent and implementation. There has been insufficient action to define and implement the national strategy for shifting relevant functions from state to metropolitan-level governments. Few states have used the opportunity

The future of India's urban governance 207

presented by the CAA to clarify municipal functions listed as 'obligatory' and 'discretionary' and such evidence as there is suggests that only marginal changes have been carried out, even in those areas that were regarded as mandatory. According to McKinsey, 'India has defined governance quite well for the first two tiers of administration – the central and state level ... But no clear definition of governance and accountability yet exists for the third tier comprising India's 5,400 cities and metropolitan areas' (McKinsey, 2010: 85). The intention of the CAA was to enable devolution, but in reality power is retained by state governments over and above local bodies.

The position is different in London, where, although the higher government retains significant powers, including the right to overrule certain decisions, it is principally the locally elected representatives who develop and deliver the strategy for the city. Even Kolkata's system, with a directly elected mayor, does not match London's level of autonomy, for the state retains significant local control through a wide range of agencies. Indian cities need to push for an improved process by which prescribed functions and finance are devolved from state to metropolitan governments, with priority accorded to determining those services and infrastructure developments that can take advantage of economies of scale. As each city has different governance requirements and varying capacities to manage devolved functions actions to devolve constitutional functions must be adapted and prioritised based on these circumstances.

Enhancing accountabilities in India's governance

Foremost among the arguments for change to London's governance was the need to provide clear mechanisms of accountability: a strategic authority and a mayor, each directly elected. 'Both will speak up for the needs of the city and plan its future. They will not duplicate the works of the boroughs, but take responsibility for London-wide issues – economic regeneration, planning, policing, transport and environmental protection' (Labour Party, 1997). While the GLA replaced the plethora of other bodies and joint arrangements that had characterised the interregnum that followed the abolition of the GLC in 1986, concerns remain as to how effectively the new system has dealt with jurisdictional accountabilities. The chapter on London showed how, despite creating clear structures for service delivery such as TfL for transport, MPA for policing and the LDA dealing with regeneration, the new system retained some of the problems of overlap and duplication.

Such problems are acute in India's rapidly growing cities, where functional overlaps, lack of coordination and clarity of responsibilities characterise much of the decision making. Here, arguably, considerations of accountability and transparency loom large. The analysis of governance presented in Chapter 2, which told a story of the new emerging forms of differentiation and networks in decision making, helps us understand better this phenomenon of India's cities. The implications of the shifting patterns of urban governance can be far-reaching, including opaqueness and blurred accountabilities. The problem of jurisdictional coordination in India's governance operates in two ways: *vertical*, multi-level jurisdictional coordination of services across different tiers of government in which multiple tiers of government and various levels of state agencies are involved in urban governance; and *horizontal*, inter-jurisdictional coordination of services across the metropolitan region characterised by ad hoc governing institutions that operate in a piecemeal and fragmented manner, arising from multiple jurisdictional and electoral boundaries that span the territories of vast metropolitan areas. Both forms often function at the expense of municipal agencies and lead to ineffective and uncoordinated decision making:

> In light of the multiple agencies involved, most urban infrastructure projects are conceived as standalone projects without due planning or impact assessment on how to best derive or gain efficiencies from such projects. The simplest example of this is the perennial digging of city roads by various agencies to lay utility infrastructure. The same road could, at different times within a short span of time, be excavated upon by telephone utility providers, city gas distribution providers, sewerage utility, water supply utility, public transport corporation and electricity utility as a result of which stretches of city roads may not be available for large section of time continuously.
> (FICCI, 2011: 12)

Such lack of coordination obscures accountabilities, allowing each agency or service provider to abrogate responsibility for problems or planning and leaving the recipients of urban services in the dark. Should a business or an individual citizen wish to complain about road closures or repair works, for example, it is extremely hard to know who to approach or whom to hold accountable.

Parastatal agencies and their role in urban service delivery compound the problems of accountabilities. They were set up to provide technical competence for the provision of various services and utilities with greater capacity and professionalism. However:

> This structure directs the accountability of officials upward rather than towards local governments. Citizens as well as their representatives have no ability to hold parastatal officials accountable for their performance, which in turn limits citizens' ability to hold local officials, and elected representatives, accountable.
> (Second Administrative Reform Commission, 2007: 244)

While Urban Local Bodies clearly need to demarcate their jurisdictions, parastatal agencies need to be made more accountable and constituted on the basis of broad local representation.

Although the new government of London retains some of the diffused responsibilities, on the whole it has produced more streamlined structures for service delivery with greater accountabilities. In metropolitan London, there is clear articulation of what the city has to deliver. TfL maintains overall responsibility for roads, buses, trains, the underground, traffic lights and regulating taxis, and has delegated authority to prepare the transport strategy for London. It is controlled by a board whose members are appointed by the mayor, who also chairs the board, while the commissioner of TfL reports to the board and leads a management team with individual functional responsibilities. Likewise, the MPA, now the Mayor's Office for Policing and Crime (MOPC), was set up to supervise the Metropolitan Police Service, the police force for Greater London. Accountable to the GLA, it has broad representation of 23 members, including assembly members appointed by the mayor in accordance with the political balance on the assembly, magistrates and independents. Together, the new governance has undoubtedly induced greater accountability for transport, the police and planning than when such services were embedded within Whitehall.

Focused leadership for urban management

Perhaps the most significant lesson offered by the new government of London is in the conception of an executive mayor and an elected assembly. Such a model empowers the mayor to provide the vision and direction, but with built-in checks and balances and an elaborate system of constraints to prevent an undue concentration of power in the mayor's office. From 1999, the GLAA gave authority to the mayor to do anything considered to further any one or more of its principal purposes – these in turn are defined as promoting social development, wealth creation, promoting economic development, and promoting improvement in the environment of Greater London. However, in determining how to exercise these general powers, the GLA would need to have regard to its effects on the health of the people of Greater London and the achievement of sustainable development in the UK as a whole. These are ambiguous, but potentially severe, constraints. A powerful mayor can drive the development of the city and pull together the partnerships needed to make things happen. The mayor can build consensus and coordinate actions among municipalities to facilitate the type of investments in infrastructure and amenities that make cities internationally more productive and competitive. This form of focused leadership in the affairs of metropolitan governance can bring together fragmented interests in a way that builds legitimacy and accountability to stakeholders in the process.

The challenge of governance in complex metropolises like Mumbai, Kolkata and Hyderabad requires a new style leadership that would guarantee much needed dynamism and stability in the political and administrative structures. A directly elected mayor with a council would provide the solution, concluded the report of the Kasturirangan Committee, with longer tenures that would allow for politically accountable leadership with a strong democratic mandate:

> The Mayor should be vested with executive powers of the Municipal Government ... should be assisted by a Mayoral Committee not exceeding 8 members (excluding the Mayor), chosen by the Mayor, from among elected and nominated councillors. These members may be given delegated subjects such as Finance, Projects, Municipal and Social Services, Administration, Planning etc., by the Mayor ... The Corporation Council must retain a strong deliberative and scrutiny function and ... the Commissioner's role should be redefined so as to make him responsible and accountable to the Mayor and the Corporation.
> (Kasturirangan Committee, 2008: 9)

There is a strong case for achieving a better balance between accountability and empowerment in India's urban governance, and further for executive and regulatory functions to be separated. City governments in India need powerful leadership in order to establish an impact. Limited and short tenures make for poor planning and implementation of policies. The lack of dedicated and empowered representatives is seen as a serious impediment to solving metropolitan problems, not dissimilar to the circumstances in London when the case was first made for a directly elected mayor. There is no single body responsible for managing and governing India's cities and, where there are accountable representatives, they are not empowered to deliver. In Mumbai and Hyderabad the executive power of the corporations is vested in the commissioner, leaving the mayor as a figurehead, but a figurehead without power. In order for metropolitan leadership to be effective, as Chapter 2 explained, not least through the story of Bogota's remarkable turn-around, it must be accompanied by political responsibility and accountability. In Kolkata, where the system of mayor-in-council is recognised as a municipal authority, the commissioner, as the chief administrative head functioning under the supervision of the mayor-in-council, is still quite powerful. But, as the findings presented in Chapter 7 suggest, perhaps Kolkata's model provides a good starting point for rethinking municipal structures, with its combination of a vested political executive and official support.

Supporting the case for directly elected mayors, McKinsey's report warned of the dangers to India's governance of bureaucratic control by civil servants, who can be transferred out of office at short notice. This represents a striking contrast to large cities elsewhere that have empowered mayors with long tenures and clear accountability for city's performance. As we have seen, the powers of London's mayor are wide-ranging, covering transport, policing, economic development and planning. Such powers enable effective planning and governance and particularly relevant to Indian cities, where responsibilities are diffused among parastatal organisations, state departments and

The future of India's urban governance 211

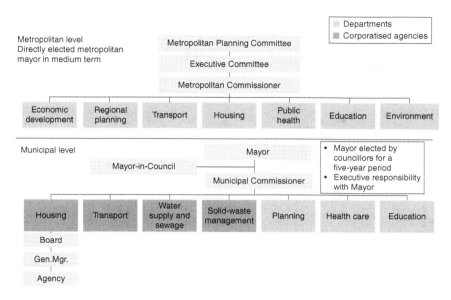

Figure 8.1 A mixed model of governance at the metropolitan and local level
Source: McKinsey Global Institute analysis.

central agencies. A directly elected mayor would have oversight, provide focused leadership and represent broad interests.

McKinsey's in-depth study recommended mixed governance at the metropolitan and local level along the lines of Figure 8.1. The findings echo some of the recommendations of the Kasturirangan Committee: a directly elected mayoral system at the metropolitan level, in which there is clear devolution of functions and decision-making powers from state government to metropolitan body, and commissioner and department heads appointed by the mayor. The MPC, as legislative authority, would approve budgets and portfolio committees formed out of members of the MPC and would monitor the delivery of departments. While this solution was proposed for the medium term, functional municipal authorities were proposed as a possible solution for the short term, in which services such as transport, housing, planning, economic development, health, education and environment would be overseen by the municipal commissioner accountable to the executive committee and the mayor. Irrespective of which model is considered best suited, India's cities need focused and empowered leadership and agencies with clear structures and budgets.

Improving the competitiveness of cities places considerable demands on urban governance and management. As well as strong and visible leadership, it requires effective participation and broad civic representation in order to generate a sense of belonging and enhance the prospects of policies being widely accepted and effectively implemented. The dynamics are highly interdependent and require cooperation from all key players in the metropolis, including, state, central and local governments, private businesses, non-governmental organisations, local citizens and community groups. While city governance in India has witnessed a considerable shift in recent years towards greater participation by individuals and communities, the processes as well as structures to facilitate participation are yet to mature. Studies of community participation presented in the previous chapter show engagement at operational level, whilst strategic level decisions involving setting targets, allocating priorities or determining policies do not connect adequately with the public. The focus of citizens demands need to shift from minor operative issues to calls for more radical institutional change.

London boroughs exhibit a stronger track record, with their longer history of supporting the development of local plans, in building local capacity for participation, and encouraging a positive approach to development. Across the city, a number of institutional structures for facilitating productive participation came into being with the centrally driven Localism Act, 2011, bringing about a step-change in consultation and engagement. But, ultimately the public's views about engagement are complex and contradictory and rarely consistent. City planners in India complain about poor public participation, but the reality is that residents are rarely interested in political engagement and when motivated to do so prefer options that demand little by way of sustained time and commitment. In both India and Britain there is widespread scepticism about whether public consultation and involvement genuinely affects what the politicians and administrators eventually do. It is true that not every aspect of public participation is necessarily to everyone's advantage; there are those such as Mosse and Olson who suggest that it is mostly powerful minority interests that are heard. These negative aspects, however, do not invalidate calls for constituting formal mechanisms for participation. In London, for instance, even though few citizens take an active part and it may be that weaker interests are marginalised, the mechanisms nevertheless appreciably widen the range of views considered in policy debates. It is clear that there is scope to define a clearer role for citizen participation in India's urban governance. A greater commitment to reforming and tackling the knowledge and awareness deficit that bedevils public participation would afford at least the possibility of enhanced participation as well as enabling the public to respond positively and imaginatively to policy dialogues and discourses.

Despite the many divergences from London's experience, certain lessons come through with irresistible force. Both nations recognise that the emerging urban forms require new and more viable versions of local governance. While London's multi-purpose, directly elected, metropolitan government has a longer history and is more highly evolved, the debates are yet to mature among India's cities. Despite legislative efforts at promoting greater devolution and giving greater autonomy to India's Urban Local Bodies, its slow progress appears to be reflected in a general acceptance of the blurring of responsibilities and a sharing of functions in strict hierarchical terms. As the

McKinsey's report observed, 'despite the perilous state of many Indian cities, there seems to be comfort with the status quo, resistance to change, and a lack of recognition of the urgent need for change' (McKinsey, 2010: 30).

A fundamental self-imposed obstacle to reform in India is a belief that state governments are all too powerful, that they are unwilling to initiate change and unprepared to assent to it. One of the lessons from London's experience is the need for a determined insistence on having focused leadership to take strong, independent policy initiatives, with a greater public voice in decision making through both formal and informal structures of referendums, juries, panels and other channels of participation. Urban management in India can be said to be intractable because the main players have so little control over its governance; the mayors do not control their administrators and bureaucracies, while citizens and citizen groups have little say in policy making, however strong their demands. London's localism, while providing a useful reference in showing who is instrumental in making decisions, does not, however, tell us how they are made and how effective they are in dealing with different urban problems. On balance what this does shed light on is how cities in different institutional settings and with different political cultures combine urban leadership and community involvement to produce more or less effective and legitimate outcomes.

Prospects for the future

While the creation of functional responsibilities at the metropolitan level – either by way of transfer from local government or as part of new government activity – has occurred most markedly in London, it can be argued that Indian cities have experienced the process of 'metropolitisation' in a different form, resulting from state governments stepping in to fulfil gaps left by the inability of local bodies to perform the needed functions. This has occurred mostly via the formation of parastatal authorities. The problem, however, has been a lack of coordination among these different agencies, leading to greater diffusion and compartmentalisation. This has, in turn, necessitated a greater need for institutional arrangements to forge coordination and integration for effective functioning at all levels. While state governments have the capacity to provide area-wide integration and coordinated policies and programmes, they have generally fallen behind in their ability to bring about such arrangements. Reshaping city governance in India, then, is crucially dependent on the reform of institutions and would require a fundamental shift in culture, attitudes, skills and mechanisms:

> Residents of Indian cities have over decades accepted the poor and deteriorating quality of urban services without much protest. There is evidence to suggest that this is beginning to change especially over the past few years with rapid economic growth, rising aspirations, and increased demand for accountability ... Indian cities today are larger, with more

diverse population, and are growing rapidly. They require technical skills to manage the delivery of urban services as well as provide a socio-economic environment in which the industry and services sectors can become globally competitive. Larger expenditures have to be combined with better governance structures, strong political and administrative will to collect taxes and user charges, and improved capacity to deliver. Cities must be empowered, financially strengthened, and efficiently governed to respond to the needs of their citizens.

(HPEC, 2011: 87)

Accountability and responsiveness to changing needs are the keys that will unlock India's ability to build the cities of tomorrow. Although the immediate prospect is one of doubt and uncertainty, as cities struggle to find ways of working around governance structures that are ambiguous, it will be for scholars, practitioners and policy makers to turn their attention to the problem of how to construct dynamic systems of metropolitan governance that are less fractured and fragmented, accepting that a perfect metropolitan system is almost impossible to construct.

References

Acuto, M. (2013) 'City Leadership in Global Governance', *Global Governance*, 19, pp. 481–498.
Aijaz, R. (2010) 'Water for Indian Cities: Government Practices and Policy Concerns', *Observer Research Brief*, Issue brief 25, September.
Allen, A. and J.D. Dávila (2002) 'Mind the Gap: Bridging the Rural-Urban Divide', *Insights*, Issue 41, Institute of Development Studies, Brighton, United Kingdom.
Allen, A., J.D. Dávila and P. Hofmann (2006) *Governance of Water and Sanitation Services for the Peri-urban Poor: A Framework for Understanding and Action in Metropolitan Regions*. London: The Development Planning Unit, UCL.
ALG (1996) *London's New Government*. London: Association of London Governments.
Appadurai, A. (2004) 'The Capacity to Aspire: Culture and the Terms of Recognition', in V. Rao and M. Walton (eds), *Culture and Public Action*. Stanford: Stanford University Press, pp. 59–84.
Arnstein, S.R. (1969) 'A Ladder of Citizen Participation', *Journal of the American Planning Association*, 35(4), pp. 216–224.
ASICS (2013) *Annual Survey of India's City Systems*. Bengaluru: Janaagraha.
Azfar, O., S. Kähkönen, A. Lanyi, P. Meagher and D. Rutherford (1999) *Decentralization, Governance and Public Services: The Impact of Institutional Arrangements – A Review of the Literature*. IRIS Center, University of Maryland, College Park.
Aziz, A. (1998) 'Utilisation of Ford Foundation Untied Grant by the Selected Gram Panchayats: A Concurrent Evaluation', mimeo, Institute for Social and Economic Change, Bangalore.
Bagchi, S. (2001) 'Financing Capital Investments in Urban Infrastructure: Constraints in Accessing Capital Market by Urban Local Bodies', *Economic and Political Weekly*, pp. 385–398.
Banerji, S., K. Gangopadhyay, A. Thampy and Z. Wong (2013) *Constraints and Prospects of Financing via Municipal Bonds in India: An Analysis with Case Studies*. International Growth Centre.
Barclay, C. (2011) *Neighbourhood Planning in Localism Act*. House of Commons Library.
Bardhan, P. and D. Mookherjee (1999) 'Relative Capture of Local and National Governments: An Essay in the Political Economy of Decentralization', Working Paper, Institute for Economic Development, Boston University.
Barlow, I.M. (1991) *Metropolitan Government*. London and New York: Routledge.

References

Baud, I. and N. Nainan (2008) '"Negotiated Spaces" for Representation in Mumbai: Ward Committees, Advanced Locality Management and the Politics of Middle-Class Activism', *Environment and Urbanization*, 20(2), pp. 483–499.

Bentinck, J.V. (1996) 'Brick Quarries in Delhi's Rural-Urban Fringe: A Model of Land Degradation in Socioeconomic Terms', paper presented at the 28th International Geographical Congress, The Hague.

Berry, B.J.L. (1976) 'Urbanization and Counter Urbanization', *Urban Affairs Annual Reviews*, 11, pp. 17–30.

Bhagat, R.B. (2011) 'Emerging Pattern of Urbanisation in India', *Economic and Political Weekly*, 46(34), pp. 10–12.

Bhattacharya, M. (1978) 'Machinery for Metropolitan Planning and Development', in *Urban Planning and Development Authorities*. New Delhi: Indian Institute of Planning and Administration.

Bhide, A. and Waingankar, S. (2011) *Maharashtra State Level Background Paper*. Urban India Reforms Facility (UIRF), School of Habitat Studies, Tata Institute of Social Sciences, Mumbai.

Bird, M.R and Bahl, R.W. (2008) *Tax Policy in Developing Countries: Looking Back and Forward, Working Papers Series 13*. Rotman Institute for International Business. Rotman School of Management, University of Toronto.

Bowyer-Bower, T.A.S. (2006) 'The Inevitable Illusiveness of "Sustainability" in The Peri-Urban Interface: The Case of Harare', in D. Mcgregor, D. Simon and D. Thompson (eds), *The Peri-Urban Interface: Approaches to Sustainable Natural and Human Resource Use*. London: Earthscan, pp. 151–161.

Brenner, N. (2004) 'Urban Governance and the Production of New State Spaces in Western Europe, 1960–2000', *Review of International Political Economy*, 11(3), pp. 447–488.

Brihanmumbai Electric Supply Transport Undertaking (2011) *Petition for Annual Revenue Requirement and Tariff Proposal for FY 2011–12*. Available at: www.bestundertaking.com/pdf/20feb/BEST%20ARR%20&%20Tariff%20Petition%20for%20FY%202011-12.pdf [accessed on 20 December 2013].

Brook, R.M., S. Purushothaman and C.S. Hunshal (eds) (2003) *Changing Frontiers: The Peri Urban Interface Hubli-Dharwad*. India: Books for Change.

Burris, S., T. Hancock, V. Lin and A. Herzog (2007) 'Emerging Strategies for Healthy Urban Governance', *Journal of Urban Health: Bulletin of the New York Academy of Medicine*, 84(1), pp. 154–163.

Centre for Cities (2010) *Press Release: Centre for Cities Sets Out an Ambitious New Approach to Regeneration in Cities and Neighbourhoods Facing Decline*. Centre for Cities.

Centre for Economics and Business Research (CEBR) (2013) CEBR World Economic League Table. CEBR.

Centre for Policy Research, New Delhi (2013) 'How to Govern India's Megacities: Towards Needed Transformation', unpublished report for the Ministry of Urban Development, Government of India.

CGG (2003) *A Guide to Developing and Implementing a Citizens' Charter, Hyderabad*. Centre for Good Governance.

Chandrashekar, C.P. (2010) 'How Significant is IT in India', *The Hindu*, 31 May.

Chattopadhyay, S. (2012) 'Decentralized Urban Governance: Participation and Accountability in West Bengal's Municipalities', *Environment and Urbanization Asia*, 3(1), pp. 185–202.

References 217

Christensen, M. (2004) 'Calcutta', in D. Levinson (ed.), *Encyclopaedia of Homelessness*, Vol. 1. Thousand Oaks: Sage Publications, pp. 39–41.

City of London (2011) *London's Competitive Place in the UK and Global Economies*. City of London Corporation Economic Development Office, Oxford Economics Ltd, Oxford.

CLG (2011) *Localism Bill: Creating Executive Mayors in the 12 Largest English Cities, Impact Assessment*. Department for Communities and Local Government, London, January.

Commission on London Governance (2006) *A New Settlement for London: Report by the Commission on London Governance*. London: Greater London Authority.

Conservative Party (2010) *Open Source Planning Green Paper*, Policy Green Paper 14. London.

Dalton, R.J. (1996) *Citizen Politics: Public Opinion and Political Parties in Advanced Industrial Democracies*. Chatham: Chatham House.

Datta, A. (1999) 'Institutional Aspects of Urban Governance', in O.P. Mathur (ed.), *India: The Challenge of Urban Governance*. New Delhi: National Institute of Public Finance & Policy, pp. 85–107.

Datta, R.N. (2007) 'Financing and Management of Infrastructure in Peri-Urban Areas of Indian Cities', *Planning and Development of Peri-Urban Areas, 56th National Town and Country Planners Congress*, Kolkata, 20–22 December, Institute of Town Planners, New Delhi.

Datta Dey, P., U.P. Raghupati, S. Thakur and S. Gupta (2006) *Looking Back to Look Ahead: Background Paper on CDP Appraisals*. National Institute of Urban Affairs.

Desfeux, A. and de Bercegol, R. (2011) *An Alternative to Conventional Public Water Service: 'User Group Networks' in a Mumbai Slum*. CNRS, CSH occasional paper, No.30.

Dove, L. (2004) 'Providing Environmental Urban Services to the Poor in Andhra Pradesh: Developing Strategic Decision-Making', *Environment and Urbanization*, 16(1), pp. 95–106.

Dreier, P., J. Mollenkopf and T. Swanstrom (2001) *Place Matters: Metropolitics for the Twenty-first Century*. Lawrence: University Press of Kansas.

Dwyer, J.F. and G.M. Childs (2004) 'Movement of People across the Landscape: A Blurring of Distinctions between Areas, Interests, and Issues Affecting Natural Resource Management', *Landscape and Urban Planning*, 69, pp. 153–164.

Fenwick, J. and H. Elcock (2005) 'The Elected Mayor and Local Leadership', *Public Money and Management*, 25(1), pp. 61–66.

FICCI (2011) *Urban Infrastructure in India*. New Delhi: Federation of Indian Chambers of Commerce and Industry.

Foster, C. (2006) 'The Challenge of Change: Australian Cities and Urban Planning in the New Millennium', *Geographical Research*, 44(2), pp. 173–182.

Fox, R. (2009) 'Engagement and Participation: What the Public Want and How Our Politicians Need to Respond', *Parliamentary Affairs*, 62(4), pp. 673–685.

Frey, H.W. (2000) 'Not Green Belts but Green Wedges: The Precarious Relationship between City and Country', *Urban Design International*, 5, pp. 13–25.

Geissel, B. (2012) 'Impact of Democratic Innovations in Europe: Findings and Desiderata', in B. Geissel and K. Newton (eds), *Evaluating Democratic Innovations: Curing the Democratic Malaise?* London: Routledge, pp. 163–183.

Ghosh, A., L. Kennedy, J. Ruet, S.T. Lama-Rewal and M. Zerah (2009) 'A Comparative Overview of Urban Governance in Delhi, Hyderabad, Kolkata, and

Mumbai', in J. Ruet and S.T. Lama-Rewal (eds) *Governing India's Metropolises: Four Case Studies*. Delhi: Routledge, pp. 24–54.

Gilbert, A. (2006) 'Good Urban Governance: Evidence from a Model City?' *Bulletin of Latin American Research*, 25(3), pp. 392–419.

Gilbert, A. and J.D. Dávila (2002) 'Bogotá: Progress within a Hostile Environment', in D.J. Myers and H.A. Dietz (eds), *Capital City Politics in Latin America: Democratization and Empowerment*. Colorado: Lynne Rienner, pp. 29–63.

Gleeson, B., J. Dodson and M. Spiller (2010) 'Metropolitan Governance for the Australian City: The Case for Reform', Urban Research Program, Issues Paper 12, March.

Goswami, T. (2001) 'Joka Lacks Basic Infrastructure', *The Statesman*, Kolkata, 13 September.

Government of India (2003) *Model Municipal Law*. New Delhi: Ministry of Urban Development and Poverty Alleviation.

Government of India (2007) *Second Administrative Reforms Commission: Local Governance*. Sixth Report, New Delhi.

Government of India (2009) *Report of the Thirteenth Finance Commission: 2010–2015*, Vol. I. Report, New Delhi.

Government of India (2012) *High Level Committee on Financing Infrastructure: Report of the Sub-Committee on Financing Urban Infrastructure in the 12th Plan*. New Delhi: Ministry of Urban Development.

Greasley, S. and G. Stoker (2009) 'Urban Political Leadership', in J.S. Davies and D.L. Imbroscio (eds) *Theories of Urban Politics*, 2nd edn. London: Sage Publications Ltd, pp. 125–136.

Greater London Authority (2002) *Replacement London Plan: Draft Spatial Development Strategy for Greater London*. London: Greater London Authority.

Greater London Authority (2009) *The Mayor's Transport Strategy: A Consultation on the Key Policies and Proposals*. London: Greater London Authority.

Greater London Authority (2010) *Mayor's Transport Strategy*. London: Greater London Authority.

Greater London Authority (2013) *Homes for London: The London Housing Strategy*. London: Greater London Authority.

Hall, P. (1989) *London 2001*. London: Unwin and Hyman.

Hall, P., H. Dracey, R. Drewett and R. Thomas (1973) *The Containment of Urban England*. London: George Allen and Unwin.

Halsworth, M. and J. Rutter (2011) *Making Policy Better*. London: Institute for Government.

Harrigan, J.H. and W.C. Johnson (1978) *Governing the Twin Cities Region: The Metropolitan Council in Comparative Perspective*. Minneapolis: University of Minnesota Press.

Heinelt, H., D. Sweeting and P. Getimis (eds) (2006) *Legitimacy and Urban Governance: Studies in Governance and Public Policy*. London and New York: Routledge.

HMDA (2010) *Making Hyderabad the Most Liveable City: Revised Master Plan for Core Area*. Hyderabad: Hyderabad Metropolitan Development Authority.

HM Government (2011) *Open Public Services*. White Paper, CM 8145.

Howell, S. (2012) *Growing Your Own Way: Taking a Localist Approach to Regeneration*. London: Local Government Association.

HPEC (2011) *Report on Indian Urban Infrastructure and Services*. New Delhi: High-Powered Expert Committee, Ministry of Urban Development.

Huchon, A. and G. Tricot (2008) *Between Citizens and Institutions: The Dynamics of the Integration of Water Supply and Sanitation Services in Hyderabad*. CSH Occasional Paper No. 22, Centre de Sciences Humaines, New Delhi.
HUDA (Hyderabad Urban Development Authority) (2003) *Hyderabad 2020, Master Plan for Hyderabad Metropolitan Area*. Hyderabad: HUDA.
IDFC (2008) *Comprehensive Mobility Plan: Back to Basics Kolkata Metropolitan Area*. Kolkata: Infrastructure Development Finance Company Ltd.
Indu, R. (2012) *The Challenges of Implementing Urban Decentralisation Reforms in India: Developing a Conceptual Framework to Understand the Functioning of Multiple Urban Agencies*. Working paper. Available at: patnet2012.files.wordpress.com/.../indu-rayadurgam_patnet-paper-draft.
Innes, J.E. and D.E. Booher (2004) 'Reframing Public Participation: Strategies for the 21st Century', *Planning Theory and Practice*, 5(4), pp. 419–436.
Institute of Town Planners (2013) *National Symposium on Managing Lands in Urban Fringes: Controlling Urban Sprawl*. West Bengal Regional Chapter, Kolkata, 7 December.
Irwin, E.G. and N.E. Bockstael (2004) 'Land Use Externalities, Open Space Preservation, and Urban Sprawl', *Regional Science and Urban Economics*, 34(6), pp. 705–725.
Janaagraha (2013) *ASICS: Annual Survey of India's City Systems*. Bangalore: Janaagraha Centre for Citizenship and Democracy.
John, P. and A. Cole (2000) 'Policy Networks and Local Political Leadership in Britain and France', in G. Stoker (ed.), *The New Politics of British Local Governance*. Basingstoke: Macmillan, pp. 72–90.
JNNURM (2009) *Modified Guidelines For Integrated Housing And Slum Development Programme*. Government of India, Ministry of Housing and Urban Poverty Alleviation, February, New Delhi.
Kamath, L. (2006) *Achieving Global Competitiveness And Local Poverty Reduction? Examining the Public-Private Partnering Model of Governance in Bangalore, India*. PhD thesis, Rutgers, the State University of New Jersey.
Kasturirangan Committee (2008) *Report of the Expert Committee on Governance in the Bangalore Metropolitan Region and Bruhat Bangalore Mahanagara Palika*. Bangalore.
Kasturirangan Committee (2009) *An Analysis of the Report of the Expert Committee on Governance in the Bangalore Metropolitan Region and Bruhat Bangalore Mahanagara Palika*. Bangalore: Janaagraha Centre for Citizenship and Democracy.
Keating, M. (1995) 'Size, Efficiency and Democracy: Consolidation, Fragmentation and Public Choice', in D. Judge, G. Stoker and H. Wolman (eds), *Theories of Urban Politics*. London and Thousand Oaks: Sage, pp. 117–134.
Kennedy, L. (2006) 'Decentralisation and Urban Governance in Hyderabad: Assessing the Role of Different Actors in the City', *GAPS Series Working Paper 8*, Governance and Policy Spaces (GAPS) Project, Centre for Economic and Social Studies, Nizamiah Observatory Campus, Hyderabad.
Kennedy, L. (2007) 'Regional Industrial Policies Driving Peri-Urban Dynamics in Hyderabad, India', *Cities*, 24(2), pp. 95–109.
KMDA (2007) *City Development Plan*. Kolkata Metropolitan Development Authority, Kolkata, Bengal Integrated Infrastructure Development Ltd.
Kooiman, J. and M. Van Vliet (1993) 'Governance and Public Management' in K. Eliassen and J. Kooiman (eds), *Managing Public Organisations*, 2nd edn. London: Sage.

Koreth, G. and K. Wadhera (2013) *Building a Citizens' Participation in Democratic Governance: The Delhi Bhagidhari Process through Large Group Dynamics.* New Delhi: Sage.

Kraus, N. (2000) *Race, Neighborhoods, and Community Power: Buffalo Politics, 1934–1997.* Albany: SUNY Press.

Kundu, A. and N. Sarangi (2009) 'Inclusive Growth and Income Inequality in India under Globalisation: Causes, Consequences and Policy Responses', Country Policy Dialogues on Inequality, UNDP Regional Office, Colombo.

Labour Party (1997) *New Labour: Because Britain Deserves Better.*

Laquian, A. (2005) *Beyond Metropolis.* Baltimore: The Johns Hopkins University Press.

Lee, C.M and K.H. Ahn (2003) 'Is Kentlands Better than Radburn? The American Garden City and New Urbanist Paradigms', *Journal of the American Planning Association*, 69(1), pp. 50–71.

Lemanski, C. and S. Tawa Lama-Rewal (2012) 'The "Missing Middle": Class and Urban Governance in Delhi's Unauthorized Colonies' in the *Transactions of the Institute of British Geographers.* London: Royal Geographical Society (with the Institute of British Geographers), pp. 91–105.

Lewis, P.G (1996) *Shaping Suburbia: How Political Institutions Organize Urban Development.* Pittsburgh: University of Pittsburgh Press.

London Assembly (2011) *Beyond Consultation: The Role of Neighbourhood Plans in Supporting Local Involvement in Planning.* London: Greater London Authority.

London Councils (2009) *London City Charter.* Mayor of London, 29 April.

London Finance Commission (2013) *Raising the Capital: Report of the London Finance Commission.* May, London.

Marshall, A., D. Finch and C. Urwin (2006) *City Leadership: Giving City-Regions the Power to Grow.* London: Institute for Public Policy Research.

Mathur, M.P. (2007) *Impact of the Constitution (74th) Amendment Act on the Urban Local Bodies: A Review.* April, National Institute of Urban Affairs

Mathur, O.P., R. Bahl, D. Thakur and N. Rajadhyasksha (2009) *Urban Property Tax Potential in India.* New Delhi: National Institute of Public Finance and Policy.

McGee, T.G. (1991) 'The Emergence of Desakota Regions in Asia', in N. Ginsburg, B. Koppel and T.G. McGee (eds), *The Extended Metropolis: Settlement Transition in Asia.* Honolulu: University of Hawai Press, pp. 71–86.

McKinsey (2010) *India's Urban Awakening: Building Inclusive Cities, Sustaining Economic Growth.* McKinsey & Company.

McKinsey (2012) *Online and Upcoming: The Internet's Impact on India.* McKinsey & Company.

Milne, R. (2010) *Cautious Welcome for Localism Bill but Questions on Detail.* Planning Portal. Available at: www.planningportal.gov.uk/general/news/stories/2010/dec2010/16dec2010/161210_2 [accessed on 27 November 2012].

Ministry of Environment and Forests (2000) *Municipal Solid Wastes (Management and Handling) Rules.* Government of India, Available at: www.moef.nic.in/legis/hsm/mswmhr.html [accessed on 4 February 2014].

Ministry of Housing and Urban Poverty Alleviation (2012) *Minutes of the Second Meeting of the Central Sanctioning and Monitoring Committee.* Government of India. Available at: http://mhupa.gov.in/ray/csmc_2nd_mom.pdf [accessed on 26 January 2014].

Ministry of Urban Development (2012) *Report of the Sub-Committee on Financing Urban Infrastructure in the 12th Plan*. Government of India.

Mitra, T.K. (2007) 'Financing and Management of Infrastructures in Peri-Urban Areas', *Planning and Development of Peri-Urban Areas*, 56th National Town and Country Planners Congress, Kolkata, 20–22 December, Institute of Town Planners, New Delhi.

MMR (1996) *Mumbai Metropolitan Region, Regional Plan: 1996–2011*. Mumbai.

Mohan, R. (2005) 'Asia's Urban Century – Emerging Trends', Keynote address to the Conference on Land Policies and Urban Development, organised by the Lincoln Institute of Land Policy, Cambridge, Massachusetts, 5 June.

Mohan, R. and S. Dasgupta (2004) *Urban Development in India in the 21st Century: Policies for Accelerating Urban Growth*. Stanford: Stanford University Press.

Mohanty, P.K., B.M. Mishra, R. Goyal and P.D. Jeromi (2007) 'Municipal Finance in India: An Assessment', Development Research Group (DRG) Study, No.26, Reserve Bank of India, Mumbai.

Mosse, D. (1994) 'Authority, Gender and Knowledge: Theoretical Reflections on the Practice of Participatory Rural Appraisal', *Development and Change*, 25(3), pp. 497–526.

Mouritzen, P.E. and J.H. Svara (2002) *Leadership at the Apex*. Pittsburgh: University of Pittsburgh Press.

MPA (2010) *Policing London Business Plan: 2010–13*, V0.6.1. London: Metropolitan Police Authority/Metropolitan Police Service.

MTSU (2006) 'Concept Note on Governance Issues', Document of Sub-group on Governance, Mumbai Transformation Project Support Unit, Mumbai, January.

Mukherjee, M. (2006) 'Waste-Fed Fisheries in Peri-Urban Kolkata', in D. Mcgregor, D. Simon and D. Thompson (eds), *The Peri-Urban Interface: Approaches to Sustainable Natural and Human Resource Use*. London: Earthscan, pp. 104–113.

Mukhopadhyay, A. (1999) 'Politics and Bureaucracy in Urban Governance: The Indian Experience', in O.P. Mathur (ed.), *India: The Challenge of Urban Governance*. New Delhi: National Institute of Public Finance & Policy New Delhi, pp. 107–128.

Mukhopadhyay, P., M.H. Zerah and E. Denis (2010) 'Subaltern Urbanisation in India', *Economic and Political Weekly*, 47(30), pp. 52–62.

Nallathiga, R. (2005) 'Institutional Innovations of Urban Governance: Some Examples of Indian Cities', *Urban India*, 15(2), pp. 1–28.

Nangia, S. (1976) *Delhi Metropolitan Region: A Study in Settlement Geography*. New Delhi: K B Publications.

National Advisory Council (2005) *Empowerment of Local Governments, Stakeholders and Citizens*. Discussion paper, New Delhi, March.

National Institute of Urban Affairs (NIUA) (1998) India's Urban Sector Profile, Research Study series number 61, New Delhi, January.

National Institute of Urban Affairs (NIUA) (2010) *Status of Municipal Accounting Systems in Selected Urban Local Bodies of India: Report and Annexure*, Indo-USAID Financial Institutions Reform and Expansion Project (FIRE-D), India, Habitat Centre, New Delhi, August.

Neelakanthan, K., S. Kulkarni and V. Raghavaswamy (2007) 'Economy, Population and Urban Sprawl: A Comparative Study of Urban Agglomerations of Bangalore and Hyderabad, India, Using Remote Sensing and Gis Techniques', paper to workshop on *Urban Population, Development and Environment Dynamics in Developing Countries*, Nairobi, Kenya.

References

Nijman, J. (2010) 'A Study of Space in Mumbai's Slums', *Tijdschrift voor Economische en Sociale Geografie*, 101(1), pp. 4–17.

Norma, C. and A. Darlow (1997) 'Local Agenda 21 and Developers: Are We Better Equipped to Build a Consensus in the 1990s?', *Planning Practice and Research*, 12(1), pp. 45–58.

ODPM (2005) *The Greater London Authority: The Government's Proposals for Additional Powers and Responsibilities for the Mayor and Assembly: Consultation Paper*. London: Office of the Deputy Prime Minister.

OECD (2010) *Tax Policy Reform and Fiscal Consolidation*. OECD.

Olson, M. (1965) *The Logic of Collective Action: Public Goods and the Theory of Groups*. Cambridge, MA: Cambridge University Press.

Ommen, M.A. (2010) 'Have the State Finance Commissions Fulfilled their Constitutional Mandates', *Economic and Political Weekly*, XLV(30), pp. 39–44.

Ostram V., C.M. Tiebout and R. Warren (1961) 'The Organization of Government in Metropolitan Areas: A Theoretical Inquiry', *American Political Science Review*, LV(4), pp. 831–852.

Pal, A. (2006) 'Scope for Bottom-up Planning in Kolkata: Rhetoric vs Reality', *Environment and Urbanisation*, 18(2), pp. 501–522.

Pethe, A.S. and V.T. Gandhi (2011) 'Assessing the Mumbai Metropolitan Region: A Governance Perspective', *Economic and Political Weekly*, 46(26 and 27), pp. 187–195.

Phatak, V.K. and S.B. Patel (2005) 'Would Decentralisation Have Made a Difference', *Economic and Political Weekly*, 40(36), pp. 3902–3905.

Pierre, J. (1999) 'Models of Urban Governance: The Institutional Dimension of Urban Politics', *Urban Affairs Review*, 34, pp. 372–396.

Pimlott, B. and N. Rao (2002) *Governing London*. Oxford: Oxford University Press.

Pinto, M. (2008) 'Urban Governance in India', in I.D.A. Baud and J. De Wit (eds), *New Forms of Urban Governance in India: Shifts, Models, Networks & Contestations*. Delhi: Sage Publications, pp. 37–63.

Planning Commission (2000) *Population Growth: Trends, Projections, Challenges and Opportunities*. The Government of India.

Planning Commission (2011) *Approach to the 12th Plan: The Challenges of Urbanization in India*. The Government of India.

Planning Commission (2012a) *Report of the Steering Committee on Urbanisation for the 12th Five Year Plan*. Government of India.

Planning Commission (2012b) *Recommendations of Working Group on Urban Transport for 12th Five Year Plan*. Government of India.

Planning Commission (2012c) *Twelfth Five Year Plan (2012–2017): Social Sectors*, Volume 3. The Government of India.

Podder, A. (2013) 'Planning and Urban Sprawl in the Eastern Fringes of Kolkata', in *Managing Lands in Urban Fringes: Controlling Urban Sprawl*. National Symposium, Institute of Town Planners (West Bengal Regional Chapter), India, pp. 140–146.

PRIA (2008) *Democratic Decentralization of Urban Governance: A Study of Four States in India*. PRIA. December

Pucher, J., N. Korattyswaroopam and N. Ittyerah (2004) 'The Crisis of Public Transport in India', *Journal of Public Transportation*, 7(4), pp. 1–20.

Raje, A.P. (2013) *India's Urban Challenge*. Mint. Available at: www.livemint.com/Home-Page/DQwAhxYdc7BJn53pVs2OeP/Indias-urban-challenge.html [accessed on 20 January 2014].

References

Ramchandran, R. (1988) *Urbanisation and Urban Systems in India*. Delhi: Oxford University Press.
Rao, G.M. and Bird, R.M. (2010) *Urban Governance and Finance in India*. National Institute of Public Finance and Policy.
Rao, N. (2000) *Reviving Local Democracy: New Labour, New Politics?* Bristol: Policy Press.
Rao, N. (2002) 'London: Metropolis Redux', *GeoJournal* special issue on *Developments in the Government of Seven European Metropolitan Areas*, 58(1), pp. 3–9.
Rao, N. (2007) *Cities in Transition: Growth, Change and Governance in Six Metropolitan Areas*. London: Routledge.
Report of the Working Group on Capacity Building (2011) *Urban Development Management for the Formulation of the Twelfth Five Year Plan (2012–2017)*. New Delhi, India.
Rhodes, R.A.W. (1997) *Understanding Governance: Policy Networks, Governance, Reflexivity and Accountability*. Buckingham: Open University Press.
Robson, W. (1954) *Great Cities of the World: Their Government, Politics and Planning*. London: Allen and Unwin.
Robson, W. (1966) 'Metropolitan Government: Problems and Solutions', *Canadian Public Administration*, 9(1), pp. 45–54.
Roy, A. (2003) *City Requiem, Calcutta: Gender and the Politics of Poverty*. Minneapolis: University of Minnesota Press.
Roy, A. (2009) 'Why India Cannot Plan its Cities: Informality, Insurgence and the Idiom of Urbanization', *Planning Theory*, 8(1), pp. 76–87.
Roy, S. (2013) 'Urban Sprawl, Social Polarisation and Governance in Mertopolitan and Megacities', *Managing Lands in Urban Fringes: Controlling Urban Sprawl*. National Symposium, Institute of Town Planners (West Bengal Regional Chapter), India, pp. 1–8.
Ruet, J., V.S. Saravanan and M.H. Zérah (2002) *The Water & Sanitation Scenario in Indian Metropolitan Cities: Resources and Management in Delhi, Calcutta, Chennai, Mumbai*. CSH occasional paper No. 6, French Research Institutes in India.
Rydin, Y. (1998) 'The Enabling Local State and Urban Development: Resources, Rhetoric and Planning in East London', *Urban Studies*, 35(2), pp. 175–191.
Saha, S. (2011) *Local Expressions in Community Participation*. New Delhi: Centre for Policy Research.
Samanta, G. (2012) 'In Between Rural and Urban: Challenges for Governance of Non-Recognized Urban Territories in West Bengal', *West Bengal, Geo-spatial Issues*. West Bengal: Department of Geography, The University of Burdwan.
Sanhati (2010) *Canal Bank Dwellers: Displacement in the Name of Development in Kolkata*. Available at: http://sanhati.com/excerpted/2321/ [accessed on 23 January 2014].
Sarkar, B., H. Banerji and J. Sen (2013) 'Land Management Systems in India: Some Issues', in *Managing Lands in Urban Fringes: Controlling Urban Sprawl*. National Symposium, Institute of Town Planners (West Bengal Regional Chapter), India, pp. 60–64.
Savitch, H.V. and R.K. Vogel (2000) 'Introduction: Paths to New Regionalism', *State & Local Government Review*, 32(3), pp. 158–168.
Second Administrative Reform Commission (2005) *Report on Urban Governance*. New Delhi: Government of India.

Second Administrative Reform Commission (2007) *Local Governance: An Inspiring Journey into the Future: Sixth Report*. New Delhi: Government of India.
Self, P.J.O. (1971) *Metropolitan Planning: The Planning System of Greater London* (Greater London Papers No. 14). London: London School of Economics.
Sen, S. (2011) 'Effect of Urban Sprawl on Human Habitation in Urban Fringe and Peri-Urban Areas in Kolkata Metropolitan Area', *India Journal*, Institute of Town Planners, 8(4), October–December, pp. 58–66.
Sengupta, B.K. and J. Thiagarajan (2013) 'Dynamics in Metropolitan Fringes: In the Context of Urban Sprawl', in *Managing Lands in Urban Fringes: Controlling Urban Sprawl*. National Symposium, Institute of Town Planners (West Bengal Regional Chapter), India, pp. 19–30.
Shaw, A. (1996) 'Urban Policy in Post Independent India: An Appraisal', *Economic and Political Weekly*, 31(4), pp. 224–228.
Shaw, A. (1999) 'Emerging Patterns of Urban Growth in India', *Economic and Political Weekly*, 34, pp. 969–978.
Shaw, A. (2005) 'Peri-Urban Interface of Indian Cities: Growth, Governance and Local Initiatives', *Economic and Political Weekly*, 40(2), pp. 129–136.
Shaw, A. (2012) 'Metropolitan City Growth and Management in Post Liberalized India', *Eurasian Geography and Economics*, 53(1), pp. 42–46.
Shivdasani, M. (2005) 'Citizens' Initiatives Sparkle', *Hindu Business Line*, 17 June. Available at: www.thehindubusinessline.in/life/htm.
Siddiqui, A. (2003) 'Urban Sprawl – A Phenomenon', in *Managing Lands in Urban Fringes: Controlling Urban Sprawl*. National Symposium, Institute of Town Planners (West Bengal Regional Chapter), India, pp. 50–59.
Simpson, D. (2001) *Rogues, Rebels, and Rubber Stamps: The Politics of the Chicago City Council, 1863 to the Present*. Boulder: Westview Press.
Singh, S.K. (2005) 'Review of Urban Transportation in India', *Journal of Public Transportation*, 8(1), pp. 79–97.
Singh, S.K. (2012) 'Urban Transport in India: Issues, Challenges, and the Way Forward', *European Transport \ Trasporti Europei*, 52(5), pp. 1–26.
Sinha, P. (2011) *Making Citizen Participation Sustainable*. Bangalore: Janagraha Centre for Citizenship and Democracy.
Sivaramakrishnan, K.C. (2008) 'The 73rd and 74th Constitutional Amendments: A Shell without Substance', *Indian Advocate*.
Sivaramakrishnan, K.C. (2011) 'Urban Development and Metro Governance', *Economic and Political Weekly*, xlvi(31), pp. 49–55.
Sivaramakrishnan, K.C. (2013) 'Revisiting the 74th Constitutional Amendment for Better Metropolitan Governance', *Economic and Political Weekly*, XLVIII(13), pp. 86–94.
Sivaramakrishnan, K.C. and B.N. Singh (2003) *Research Project on Urbanisation*. Centre for Policy Research, pp. 4–35.
Smith, G. (2009) *Democratic Innovations: Designing Institutions for Citizen Participation*. Cambridge: Cambridge University Press.
Smith, L. (2006) *Neither Public nor Private: Unpacking the Johannesburg Water Corporatization Model*. UNRISD.
Sridharan, N. and A. Razak (2003) 'Urban Energy and Water: A Need for Rethinking on Management', paper presented at the *International Conference on Sustainable Development*, School of Planning and Architecture, New Delhi.

Sridharan, N. and V. Yadav (2001) 'Regional Dimensions of Urbanization: A Quick Analysis of Census 2001', *Spatio-Economic Development Record*, 8(6), pp. 25–29.
Stoker, G. (1998) *Governance as Theory: Five Prepositions*. UNESCO.
Stoker, G. (1999) *The New Management of British Local Governance*. London: Macmillan.
Stoker, G. (ed.) (2000) *The New Politics of British Local Governance*. Basingstoke: Macmillan.
Stone, C.N. (1989) *Regime Politics: Governing Atlanta, 1946–1988*. Lawrence: University of Kansas Press.
Talen, E. (2005) *New Urbanism & American Planning: The Conflict of Cultures*. New York and London: Routledge.
TCPA (2010) *TCPA Press Release: First Response to Localism Bill*. TCPA.
TERI (2010) *Enhancing Public Participation through Effective Functioning of Ward Committees: Final Report*. A report prepared for the Ministry of Urban Development, Government of India, The Energy and Resources Institute, India.
TERI (2011) *Mainstreaming Urban Resilience Planning in Indian Cities: A Policy Perspective*. A report prepared for the Asian Cities Climate Change Resilience Network (ACCCRN) in India.
Telegraph (2013) 'India Plans "New Mumbai" as Overcrowding Chokes City', 4 October.
Thirteenth Report: Second Administrative Reforms Commission (2009) *Organizational Structure of Government of India*. Government of India.
Tiebout, C.M. (1956) 'A Pure Theory of Local Expenditure', *Journal of Political Economy*, 64, pp. 416–424.
Times of India (2013) 'Merger of 36 Villages with GHMC', 18 November.
Travers, T. (2011) *Engaging London's Communities: The Big Society and Localism*. London Councils/City of London.
UN (1989) *Yearbook of the United Nations*. Department of Public Information, United Nations
UNDP (2011) *Governance Principles, Institutional Capacity and Quality*. UNDP.
UNESCAP (2006) *What is Good Governance?* Available at: www.unescap.org/huset/gg/governance.htm.
UN Habitat (2003) *The Habitat Agenda Goals and Principles, Commitments and the Global Plan of Action*. UN Habitat Agenda.
United Nations Population Division (2008) *United Nations Expert Group Meeting on Population Distribution, Urbanization, Internal Migration and Development*. New York: United Nations Secretariat.
United Nations Report (2005) *World Urbanization Prospects: The 2005 Revision*. New York: United Nations.
Urban India (2011) *Census of India 2011*. Government of India.
Urban Task Force (1999) *Towards an Urban Renaissance*. London: E&FN Spon.
Vaidya, C. (2009) *Urban Issues, Reforms and Way Forward in India*. Working Paper No. 4, Department of Economic Affairs, Government of India.
Vedachalam, S. (2012) 'Water Supply and Sanitation in India: Meeting Targets and Beyond', *Global Water Forum*, UNESCO, 23 September. Available at: www.globalwaterforum.org/2012/09/23/water-supply-and-sanitation-in-india-meeting-targets-and-beyond [accessed March 2014].

Veermani, C. (2012) 'Anatomy of India's Merchandise Export Growth, 1993–94 to 2010–11', *Economic and Political Weekly*, 47(1), pp. 94–104.

Walmsley, A. (2006) 'Greenways: Multiplying and Diversifying in the 21st Century', *Landscape and Urban Planning*, 76(1–4), pp. 252–290.

Warren, M.E. (2009) 'Governance-driven Democratization', *Critical Policy Studies*, 3(1), pp. 3–13.

Warwick Commission (2012) *Elected Mayors and City Leadership, Summary Report of the Third Warwick Commission*. Warwick, Warwick University.

Way to Go! Analysis of Responses (2009) Available at: http://static.london.gov.uk/mayor/publications/2009/docs/waytogo-responses.pdf [accessed on 2 January 2013).

Webster, D. (2004) 'Bangkok: Evolution and Adaptation Under Stress' in J. Gugler (ed.), *World Cities Beyond the West: Globalization, Development and Inequality*. Cambridge: Cambridge University Press, pp. 82–118.

Westergaard, J. (1961) 'The Structure of Greater London' in Centre for Urban Studies, *London: Aspects of Change*. London: MacGibbon and Kee, pp. 91–144.

World Bank (2010) *Social Accountability and Local Government*. World Bank.

World Bank (2013) *Urbanisation beyond Municipal Boundaries: Nurturing Metropolitan Economies and Connecting Peri-Urban Areas in India*. Washington, DC: World Bank.

World Bank (2014) *Corporate Score Card*. World Bank Group, April.

Yadav, V. (2013) *Metropolitan Governance: Cases of Ahmadabad and Hyderabad*. India: Copal Publishers.

Yaro, R.D. and N. Ronderos (2004) 'International Metropolitan Governance: Typology, Case Studies and Recommendations', *Metropolis Initiatives* [Electronic]. Available at: www.metropolis.org/sites/default/files/meetings/first-meeting-metropolis-initiative-metropolitan-governance/background_paper_2_-_rober_yaro.pdf [accessed on 29 December 2013].

Young, I.M. (2000) *Inclusion and Democracy*. Oxford: Oxford University Press.

Zeiderman, A. (2008) 'Cities of the Future? Megacities and the Space/Time of Urban Modernity', *Critical Planning*, 15, pp. 23–40.

Index

Abercrombie, P. 53
ABS *see* Area Based System
Accelerated Urban Water Supply Programme (AUWSP) 15
accountabilities: financial reporting, disclosure and audits 185–86; India's governance 207–9; information and communication technologies 184–85
Action for Good Governance Network of India (AGNI) 189–90
active metropolitan community 48–51
Advanced Locality Management (ALM) 189–90
agglomeration index 3
AGNI *see* Action for Good Governance Network of India
ALG *see* Association of London Government
ALM *see* Advanced Locality Management
Andhra Pradesh Industrial Infrastructure Corporation (APIIC) 126–27
Andhra Pradesh Municipalities Act 110
APIIC *see* Andhra Pradesh Industrial Infrastructure Corporation
Area Based System (ABS) 93
Asian Development Bank 15
Asoka Metha Commission of 1978 79
Association of London Government (ALG) 62
AUWSP *see* Accelerated Urban Water Supply Programme

Bangalore Agenda Task Force (BATF) 188
Bangalore Metropolitan Regional Development Authority Act 199
Bangkok Metropolitan Administration (BMA) 43, 45

Basic Services for the Urban Poor (BSUP) 9
BEST *see* Brihanmumbai Electric Supply and Transport
BMA *see* Bangkok Metropolitan Administration
BMTPC *see* Building Material Technology Promotion Council
Brihanmumbai Electric Supply and Transport (BEST) 44
BSUP *see* Basic Services for the Urban Poor
Building Material Technology Promotion Council (BMTPC) 8

CAA *see* Constitutional Amendment Act
CAG *see* Citizens' Action Group
Calcutta Metropolitan Planning Area Control Act 118
CAP *see* City Assistance Programme
CBOs *see* community based organisations
ceremonial mayor system 170
Chirac, J. 168
Citizens' Action Group (CAG) 124
City Assistance Programme (CAP) 117
city master plans 112–13
civic engagement: accountabilities 184–86; ceremonial mayor system 170; commissioner and directly elected mayor 173; communities in Kolkata and Hyderabad 190–93; directly elected mayor and council 172–73; financial reporting, disclosure and audits 185–86; inclusive urban management 186–93; indirectly elected mayor and council 173–76; information and communication technologies 184–85; localism in

civic engagement (cont.)
  Mumbai 189–90; mayor-council government 170; public in policy making 179–83; strong mayor system 170; weak mayor system 170
CLIFF see Community Led Infrastructure Finance Facility
coalition governance 33–35
Cockell, M. 70
commissioner: and directly elected mayor 173; in urban management 176–78
Commission on London Governance 61
community based organisations (CBOs) 190
Community Led Infrastructure Finance Facility (CLIFF) 15–16
community participation 48
Community Participation Law (CPL) 181, 183
comprehensive development plans 130
Confederation of Real Estate Developers Association of India (CREDAI) 174
Congress of Leaders 69–70
consolidated governance: governance conditions 41–44; responses to 35–38; structures for service delivery 44–46
Constitutional Amendment Act (CAA) 8, 11, 40, 80, 84, 134
Constitution of State Finance Commissions 89
corporatist governance 30
Council for the Prevention of Rural England 53
CPL see Community Participation Law
CREDAI see Confederation of Real Estate Developers Association of India

Das, C. 169
decentralisation 40, 78
democratic deficit 41
Department for International Development (DfID) 16
devolution: digital governance 103–5; financing urban services and infrastructure 95–98; greater London 204–7; human resource management 98–103; municipal corporations 85; municipal revenues 85–90; non-tax revenues 94–95; opportunities and challenges 79–81; parastatal agencies 81–85; tax revenues 90–94; 13th Finance Commission 84
DfID see Department for International Development
digital governance 103–5
directly elected mayor: commissioner and 173; and council 172–73
District Development Review Committee 137
District Planning Committees (DPCs) 80
DPCs see District Planning Committees

economy: pattern and growth 5; urban 4
effective devolution 39–41
elected dictatorship 173

financial burden 111
Floor Space Index (FSI) 109
focused urban leadership 46–48, 209–13
FSI see floor space index

GLC see Greater London Council
GLDP see Greater London Development Plan
global, agglomeration index 3
Global Shelter Strategy (GSS) 8
goBATF see Bangalore Agenda Task Force
Goods and Service Tax (GST) 14
governance: academic studies of 27; accountabilities in India 207–9; agglomerations and fragmented jurisdictions 17–18; blurred accountabilities 157, 166–67; characteristics 29; coalition 33–35; consolidation as response 35–38; corporatist 30; cumulative and complex 27–28; definition 28; digital 103–5; good and effective 16–17; Greater Johannesburg 43; institutional framework 136; Kasturirangan report 175; local level 211; London 57–60; managerial 30; metropolitan 211; mixed model of 211; new public management 28; participatory 30–33; planning process 111; regime theory 33–35; Stoker's analysis 28; UN definition 29; urban 16
governance conditions: active metropolitan community 48–51; consolidated governance 41–44; consolidated structures for service

delivery 44–46; effective devolution 39–41; focused urban leadership 46–48
governance deficit 19
governance-driven democratisation 31
Greater London Council (GLC) 33, 52
Greater London Development Plan (GLDP) 55
'green belt' concept 53
GSS *see* Global Shelter Strategy
GST *see* Goods and Service Tax
G.V.K. Rao Committee of 1985 79

HADA *see* Hyderabad Airport Development Authority
HDFC *see* Housing Development Finance Corporation
High Powered Expert Committee (HPEC) 13, 15, 175
HMC *see* Hyderabad Municipal Corporation
HMDA *see* Hyderabad Metropolitan Development Authority
HMWSSB *see* Hyderabad Metropolitan Water Supply and Sewerage Board
Homes and Communities Agency (HCA) 62
horse-trading system 174
Housing and Urban Development Corporation (HUDCO) 7, 79, 97
Housing Development Finance Corporation (HDFC) 142
housing sector 140–43
HPEC *see* High Powered Expert Committee
HUDA *see* Hyderabad Urban Development Authority
HUDCO *see* Housing and Urban Development Corporation
human resource management 98–103
Hyderabad: city development strategy 116–17; Floor Space Index 109; Green project 116; Inner Ring Road 115; master plan 112–13; master plan implementation 113–16; metropolitan growth and expansion 106–9; multiplicity of institutions 164–65; Municipal Corporation of Hyderabad 114; municipal corporations 85; Outer Ring Road 116; polycentricity 107; Regional Ring Road 115; tax regimes 91; World Bank study, growth and expansion 108–9

Hyderabad Airport Development Authority (HADA) 114
Hyderabad Information Technology Engineering Consultancy (HITECH) City 126–27
Hyderabad Metropolitan Development Authority (HMDA) 87
Hyderabad Metropolitan Development Authority Act 110
Hyderabad Metropolitan Water Supply and Sewerage Board (HMWSSB) 87
Hyderabad Municipal Corporation (HMC) 87
Hyderabad Urban Development Authority (HUDA) 114–15

IALAs *see* Industrial Area Local Authorities
ICTs *see* information and communication technologies
IDSMT *see* Integrated Development of Small and Medium Towns
inclusive urban management: communities in Kolkata and Hyderabad 190–93; localism in Mumbai 189–90; overview of 186–89
Independent Commission Against Corruption (ICAC) 50
India: accountabilities in governance 207–9; capacity building initiatives 101–2; 2011 census 3; financing basic amenities 13; Information Technology (IT) sector 5; patterns of urbanisation 4–5; strategic authorities 200–204; subaltern urbanisation 118; urbanisation 2–4; urban planning and development 139; urban policy development 6–10; urban reform 11–19; World Bank, urbanisation study 3
India's Urban Awakening (McKinsey's report) 5
indirectly elected mayor 173–76
Industrial Area Local Authorities (IALAs) 127
information and communication technologies (ICTs) 184–85
Information Technology (IT) sector 5
Inner Ring Road (IRR) 115
institutional frameworks: Kolkata 138–40, 158–61; metropolitan authority 133–36

Index

Integrated Development of Small and Medium Towns (IDSMT) 7, 15, 80
IRR *see* Inner Ring Road

Japan Bank for International Cooperation 15
Japanese International Cooperation Agency (JICA) 115–16
Jawaharlal Nehru Urban Renewal Mission (JNNURM) 9, 11, 15, 18, 78, 97, 142
JICA *see* Japanese International Cooperation Agency
JNNURM *see* Jawaharlal Nehru Urban Renewal Mission
Johnson, B. 60, 63, 70

Kasturirangan report, governance analysis 175
KEIP *see* Kolkata Environment Improvement Project
KIT *see* Kolkata Improvement Trust
KMC *see* Kolkata Municipal Corporation
KMD *see* Kolkata Metropolitan District
KMDA *see* Kolkata Metropolitan Development Agency
Kolkata: institutional framework 138–40, 158–61; managing peripheries 119, 121; municipal corporations 85; peri-urban area 125; planning process 117–22; public transport 151; spatial development 119; tax regimes 91; transport agencies 152–54; *Vision 2025* 119
Kolkata Environment Improvement Project (KEIP) 97
Kolkata Improvement Trust (KIT) 118
Kolkata Metropolitan Development Agency (KMDA) 138
Kolkata Metropolitan District (KMD) 117
Kolkata Municipal Corporation (KMC) 17, 134
Kolkata Urban Agglomeration (KUA) 117
KUA *see* Kolkata Urban Agglomeration
kutcha houses 141

land-use planning 53, 110
Laquian, A. 40
LCC *see* London County Council
LCCI *see* London Chamber of Commerce and Industry
Learning and Skills Council (LSC) 61
local governance, urban sector 2
localism 189–90
Localism Act 70, 72
London: abolition of GLC 56–57; blurred accountabilities, governance 66–68; Congress of Leaders 69–70; distinct from other countries 196–200; dominant role 196–200; governance 38, 57–60; greater devolution 204–7; Greater London Council 33, 52; housing developments 62–63; land-use planning 53; Localism Act 70, 72; London City Charter 68–69; National Planning Policy Framework 72–77; new planning approach 59–60; Outer Metropolitan Area 54–55; planning for sustainability 53–57; revised transport strategy 64–66; self-government towards 68–70; strategic authority 54–56; traffic and transport 63–64
London Chamber of Commerce and Industry (LCCI) 67
London Community Recycling Network 66
London County Council (LCC) 54
London Finance Commission 62
London Government Act of 1965 55
London Legacy Development Corporation 60
London Planning Advisory Committee (LPAC) 57, 199
London Thames Gateway Development Corporation (LTGDC) 62
London Tourist Board 67
LPAC *see* London Planning Advisory Committee
LSC *see* Learning and Skills Council
LTGDC *see* London Thames Gateway Development Corporation

Maharashtra Regional and Town Planning Act 110
Maharashtra State Road Development Corporation (MSRDC) 81
managerial governance 30
MAPP *see* Municipal Action Plan for the Poor
Maragall, P. 169
Market Worthiness Disclosure Statement 185
mayor-council government 170

Index 231

mayor office: ceremonial mayor system 170; commissioner and directly elected mayor 173; directly elected mayor and council 172–73; indirectly elected mayor and council 173–76; mayor-council government 170; strong mayor system 170; weak mayor system 170
MCGM *see* Municipal Corporation of Greater Mumbai
MCH *see* Municipal Corporation of Hyderabad
Megacity Programme for Infrastructure Development 98
Mehta, P. 169
Metha Commission of 1957 79
metropolitan authority: blurred accountabilities, governance 157, 166–67; delivering services 140–54; housing sector 140–43; institutional arrangements 133–36; modernising service delivery 154–57; planning for cities 136–40; traffic and transport issues 147–54; water supply and sewerage 143–47
metropolitan growth and expansion: Floor Space Index 109; polycentricity 107; World Bank study 108–9
Metropolitan Planning Committee (MPC) 80, 130
Metropolitan Rapid Transit Authority (MRTA) 45
Ministry of Urban Development (MoUD) 9
Ministry of Works and Housing 7
MMC *see* Mumbai Municipal Corporation
MML *see* Model Municipal Law
MMRDA *see* Mumbai Metropolitan Regional Development Authority
Model Municipal Law (MML) 9, 80
MoUD *see* Ministry of Urban Development
MPC *see* Metropolitan Planning Committee
MRTA *see* Metropolitan Rapid Transit Authority
MSRDC *see* Maharashtra State Road Development Corporation
MTSU *see* Mumbai Transformation Support Unit
Mumbai: localism 189–90; Maharashtra Regional and Town Planning Act 110; multi-level (central and state) agencies functioning 161–63; municipal corporations 85; prevalence of slums 12; regional planning 121–24; tax regimes 91
Mumbai Metropolitan Corporation Act 179
Mumbai Metropolitan Regional Development Authority (MMRDA) 44, 139–40
Mumbai Municipal Corporation (MMC) 17
Mumbai Transformation Support Unit (MTSU) 156
Municipal Action Plan for the Poor (MAPP) 192
municipal commissioner 176–78
Municipal Corporation of Greater Mumbai (MCGM) 81, 134
Municipal Corporation of Hyderabad (MCH) 87
Municipal Corporation Urban Development Authorities 110
municipal revenues 85–90
Municipal Service Regulator 94

Nagar Raj Bill *see* Community Participation Law (CPL)
National Building Organisation (NBO) 7
National Commission on Urbanisation report 8
National Housing Bank (NHB) 8
National Housing Policy (NHP) 8
National Planning Policy Framework (NPPF) 72–77
National Urban Information System (NUIS) 92
NBO *see* National Building Organisation
Nehru, Pandit J. 7, 169
New Public Management (NPM) tools 6
New York, property tax collections 13
NHB *see* National Housing Bank
NHP *see* National Housing Policy
non-tax revenues 94–95
NUIS *see* National Urban Information System

ORR *see* Outer Ring Road
Outer Ring Road (ORR) 116

parastatal agencies 81–85
participatory budgeting 51
participatory governance 30–33
Participatory Performance Monitoring 50

Index

Patna model 93
Patna Municipal Corporation 93
PDL *see* Public Disclosure Law
peri-urban areas: comprehensive development plans 130; developmental opportunities 124–26; HITECH city 126–27; metropolitan planning committees 130; stresses and strains 128–31; targeted development 126–27; and urban fringe 124–27
Peri-Urban Interfaces (PUIs) 43
Philippine's Local Government Code of 1991 40
Pierre, J. 29
Planning Commission of India 155
Planning for a Better London (Johnson) 60
planning process: financial burden 111; governance 111; land-use planning 110; regional plans 110; urban development authorities 111–12; urban growth and inability challenges 111
post-1991 liberalisation 6
PPPs *see* Public-Private Partnerships
property tax valuation: Area Based System 93; autonomy levels 91; international experience 92
Public Disclosure Law (PDL) 183
public in policy making: area sabhas 181–83; ward committees 179–81
Public-Private Partnerships (PPPs) 9–10
pucca houses 141
PUIs *see* Peri-Urban Interfaces

regime theory 33–35
Regional Municipality of Metropolitan Toronto 44
regional plans 110
Regional Ring Road (RRR) 115
Region and Town Planning Act 110–11
Rent Control Acts 93
robust business plan 113
RRR *see* Regional Ring Road

SDS *see* Spatial Development Strategy
SERPLAN *see* South East Regional Planning Conference
sewerage sector 143–47
SFCs *see* State Finance Commissions
SHMA *see* Strategic Housing Market Assessment
single point accountability 175

South East Regional Planning Conference (SERPLAN) 57, 199
Spatial Development Strategy (SDS) 59
Special Purpose Vehicles (SPVs) 17
SPVs *see* Special Purpose Vehicles
State Finance Commissions (SFCs) 14, 89
State Town and Country Planning Acts 110
Stoker's analysis of governance 28
Strategic Housing Market Assessment (SHMA) 62
strategic spatial plans 110
strong mayor system 170
subaltern urbanisation 118

taxation: Area Based System 93; autonomy levels 91; international experience 92
tax revenues 90–94
TCPA *see* Town and Country Planning Act
13th Finance Commission 84
TLRN *see* Transport for London Roads Network
Town and Country Planning Act (TCPA) 71
traffic issues, metropolitan authority 147–54
Transparent Accountable Governance (TAG) Program 41
Transport agencies 152–54
Transport for London Roads Network (TLRN) 66–67, 69
Twelfth Schedule of the Constitution 78

UBSP *see* Urban Basic Services for the Poor
UDAs *see* urban development authorities
UDPs *see* Unitary Development Plans
UIG *see* Urban Infrastructure and Governance
ULBs *see* Urban Local Bodies
Unitary Development Plans (UDPs) 57
Urban Basic Services for the Poor (UBSP) 8
urban containment 53
urban development authorities (UDAs) 17
urban economy 4
urban explosion 5

urban fringe and peri-urban areas 124–27
urban governance 16; accountabilities 207–9; distinct from other countries 196–200; focused leadership 209–13; greater devolution 204–7; restructuring 34; strategic authorities 200–204
Urban Infrastructure and Governance (UIG) 9
urbanisation: 2011 census 3; complexity of tracking 3; patterns of 4–5; scale of 3; subaltern 118; World Bank study 3
Urban Land Act 6–7
urban leadership: accountabilities 184–86; ceremonial mayor system 170; commissioner and directly elected mayor 173; communities in Kolkata and Hyderabad 190–93; directly elected mayor and council 172–73; financial reporting, disclosure and audits 185–86; focused 46–48, 209–13; inclusive urban management 186–93; indirectly elected mayor and council 173–76; information and communication technologies 184–85; localism in Mumbai 189–90; mayor-council government 170; public in policy making 179–83; strong mayor system 170; weak mayor system 170
Urban Local Bodies (ULBs) 6, 9, 14, 18, 79, 81; borrowings 98; municipal revenues 85–90; non-tax revenues 94–95; tax revenues 90–94
urban management: inclusive 186–93; municipal commissioner 176–78
urban policy development 6–10
urban poverty alleviation 142
urban reform: capacity 18–19; governance 16–18; infrastructure 11–16

Urban Reform Incentive Fund (URIF) 98
urban sector, local governance 2
urban services and infrastructure 95–98
URIF *see* Urban Reform Incentive Fund

Vasai-Virar Municipal Corporation 130
Vision 2020 116
Vision 2025 119

Waste and Resources Action Programme (WRAP) 66
water management 145
water supply and waste water treatment 144
water supply sector 143–47
WBHIDCO *see* West Bengal Housing Infrastructure Development Corporation
weak mayor system 170
West Bengal Act of 1993 180
West Bengal Central Valuation Board 93–94
West Bengal Housing Infrastructure Development Corporation (WBHIDCO) 121
WGCP *see* Working Group on Capacity Building
Working Group on Capacity Building (WGCP) 99–100
World Bank 3, 45, 50
WRAP *see* Waste and Resources Action Programme

ZDPs *see* Zonal Development Plans
Zonal Development Plans (ZDPs) 108

eBooks
from Taylor & Francis
Helping you to choose the right eBooks for your Library

Add to your library's digital collection today with Taylor & Francis eBooks. We have over 50,000 eBooks in the Humanities, Social Sciences, Behavioural Sciences, Built Environment and Law, from leading imprints, including Routledge, Focal Press and Psychology Press.

Free Trials Available

We offer free trials to qualifying academic, corporate and government customers.

Choose from a range of subject packages or create your own!

Benefits for you
- Free MARC records
- COUNTER-compliant usage statistics
- Flexible purchase and pricing options
- 70% approx of our eBooks are now DRM-free.

Benefits for your user
- Off-site, anytime access via Athens or referring URL
- Print or copy pages or chapters
- Full content search
- Bookmark, highlight and annotate text
- Access to thousands of pages of quality research at the click of a button.

eCollections
Choose from 20 different subject eCollections, including:

- Asian Studies
- Economics
- Health Studies
- Law
- Middle East Studies

eFocus
We have 16 cutting-edge interdisciplinary collections, including:

- Development Studies
- The Environment
- Islam
- Korea
- Urban Studies

For more information, pricing enquiries or to order a free trial, please contact your local sales team:

UK/Rest of World: **online.sales@tandf.co.uk**
USA/Canada/Latin America: **e-reference@taylorandfrancis.com**
East/Southeast Asia: **martin.jack@tandf.com.sg**
India: **journalsales@tandfindia.com**

www.tandfebooks.com